Ol' Max Evans

Ol' Max Evans

THE FIRST THOUSAND YEARS

Slim Randles

UNIVERSITY OF NEW MEXICO PRESS   ALBUQUERQUE

First paperback printing 2023 | ISBN 978-0-8263-6503-3

Library of Congress Cataloging-in-Publication Data

Randles, Slim.
  Ol' Max Evans : the first thousand years / Slim Randles.
     p. cm.
  ISBN 0-8263-3589-6 (alk. paper)
  1. Evans, Max, 1925– 2. New Mexico—Intellectual life—20th
century 3. Authors, American—20th century—Biography.
4. New Mexico—In literature. 5. New Mexico—Biography.
I. Title: Old Max Evans. II. Title.
  PS3555.V23Z86 2004
  813'.54—dc22

Design and composition: Melissa Tandysh

Frontispiece: *Max Evans in 1960. Photo by Martin Schaefer.*

This book has quite a bit of salty language in it, so if you're a kid, you should probably wait a few years before reading this.

—Slim Randles

By the time I was seventeen, life was really whippin' up, and the sonofabitch never stopped. It's been a dead run for seventy-nine damn years, and my ears laid back all the time.

—Max Evans

Dedication

This book is dedicated to Dr. Roland Sanchez and Elia
Sanchez and their entire family, of Belen, New Mexico,
whose faith and sacrifice made this book possible . . .

. . . and to Ol' Max Evans (and his cowboy
honor system) who made it necessary.

Did Ol' Max ever tell you about his honor system? About his
cowboy honor system?

Well, here's how it works. You find some young guy working there on the place, and you tell him, "Son, I sure admire the
work you're doing with those young horses. In fact, you've been
riding them so well, I'm going to let you get up at three in the
morning and go wrangle the horses. And I'm going to let you
have the honor of riding ol' Widowmaker to go get them."

Seems like there's always somebody who'll do that, too.

—Jimmy Bason, rancher and friend

Max Evans is one of these guys you can take anywhere . . .
and still be ashamed of him.

—Charles Champlin,
book and film critic for the *Los Angeles Times*

Table of Contents

Overture: Coyote and Raven

℞ **"Fun!" said Coyote, grinning.** "That's it. That's it and all of it. You need more fun, sobersides."

"That's fine for you, Coyote," said Raven. "You roam around the country with that grin, always with that grin. You eat whatever comes along, and at night . . . at night you keep everyone awake with that singing of yours."

And that Raven, he shook his head all solemn-like. "Some of us have to work hard to eat."

"Ah, work!" said Coyote, closing his left eye and hopping to the left, just as an experiment. "Work is good, Raven. Sometimes even the singing is work, you know. The singing, the rapturous singing about the world. The telling of a thousand stories. Watching the world move about you, Raven. That can be work, too."

"That's ridiculous," said Raven.

"Of course it is," said Coyote. "Ridiculous and fun. But only the best lives are ridiculous and fun. You just take my brother, for example. For him, life has been both ridiculous and fun, and that's why people can't really figure him out."

"Your brother?"

Coyote lolled his tongue out in ecstasy as he rolled over and scratched behind his ear. His eyes squinted to a close as he contemplated for just a second the parameters of sanity and the direct benefits of peak rabbit years. Then he powdered his head with dust in a coyote dance and sat spraddle-legged and grinning at the regally wise bird.

"My brother," Coyote said. "Yes, my brother has made a life of ridiculous fun an art form. He howls at the moon in the books he writes. He lives a ridiculously fun life and spits in the eye of convention."

"Your brother?"

"Has been for years now," said Coyote. "A brother in every sense. He can laugh. He can howl. He can bite and scratch. He can stare at the moon and see wondrous magic."

Then that Coyote, he laughs to see Raven shaking his head.

"Scoff if you will, Raven, but I'll tell you about my brother, anyway, because it makes a great song. A great evening song. And it's worth it.

"To start with, they call him Ol' Max . . ."

For me, the Code of the West is simple. You never let a friend down . . . ever. And you don't go after your enemies if they leave you alone.

You can live a long time on those two things.

—Max Evans

In the Bunkhouse

✂ **That was the summer** we couldn't wait to get to the bunkhouse each night. It was back in the early 1960s sometime, and we who packed the mules for Sequoia-Kings Pack Trains had stumbled on a little treasure.

Each night, in the half hour or so before we blew out the coal-oil lamp in the small bunkhouse, those of us who could read would take turns reading aloud the chapters out of a novel called *The Rounders*.

We laughed until the tears poured down our cheeks in that warmly-lit room that smelled of hand-rolled-cigarette smoke, horse sweat, the mangy cow dog under Rocky's bunk, and socks that needed burying.

This horse had me slightly boogered. You would figure that most horses would come nearer bucking downhill than up. You would be right, except for Old Fooler. I don't say he bucked uphill exactly. It amounted to the same thing, though. I learned this a very hard way.

I was watching him real close as I rode across the ripened grama-grass-covered hills. We moved down into this little draw and started up the other side. Just as we topped out, he fired. Naturally, the saddle slips back a little when a horse is pulling upgrade, but the way Old Fooler jumped it had lapped right over his rear end. He lunged way out and kicked back with both hind feet. It snapped my head back like the tip end of a bullwhip. My teeth chipped enamel at every jump.

Well, I made one mistake I would never make again with Fooler. If you can use a loaded quirt, that's fine. It will take a lot of sass out of some pretty mean horses. I raised it up high and took a hard swing, aiming to hit Old Fooler right between the ears. I didn't much care if he did fall on me. I figured this might help us both. I should have kept my right hand on that saddle horn where it belonged, though, for all I hit was air. I smacked the ground like a dead buzzard.

It was about three miles by bird travel to the gate opening into home pasture. That was where Old Fooler was headed. He was still bucking, and I could see them stirrups clanging together above his back. Then he disappeared over a rise and there wasn't a thing to keep me company but one little white cloud about a thousand miles off over the northern mountains. I saw that cloud when I looked up at the sky and asked the Lord to please not let me kill myself and to give me the wings of an angel so I could fly after that horse and break his goddam neck.

—from *The Rounders*

And each night, as the story progressed, we found more and more in this book a close look at the life we led. Someone had finally put down on paper some of this ridiculously fun life we led, those of us who were starting out in life, and those of us who were about to finish. But we all laughed, and we all nodded at the right times.

One night, after the lamp was blown out and we were still chuckling in our bedrolls over that night's chapter, we finally heard from Old Grant Dalton. Grant had known Butch Cassidy and Charlie Russell, back in his younger days, and now, in his eighties, he was the Supreme Court of the bunkhouse.

"What's the guy what wrote that there book?" Grant asked.

One of us rolled over and flicked on a flashlight briefly.

"Max Evans."

"Well, hell, goddang, I mean to say, you take in there that writer?" He paused a second before delivering a cowboy's most supreme book review. "He's been there."

In the wondrous brew that makes up life, that novel, *The Rounders*, created a bittersweet effect on Max Evans' life. It made his reputation. Despite a lifetime of writing perhaps the finest literature ever written about life in the West, it is still this one book about two cowboys who can't seem to win but refuse to lose that people tend to remember best. It brought Max his first real money, his first real fame, his first movie.

But writing about Dusty and Wrangler all those many years ago also labeled him a "cowboy writer," a "Western writer," and those labels have stung him for more than forty years. But he grins and shrugs because what else can you do?

Max Evans was once an eleven-year-old cowboy himself in the foothills of the Sangre de Cristo Mountains of New Mexico. For years he lived the life, roped the calves, rode the horses, drank the booze, fought the fights. He spent his nights reading in the bunkhouses, too.

And then he taught himself to be an artist, and later he taught himself to be a novelist.

Literature about the real West has never been the same, but many people still think of Max Evans as "that Western writer" because of *The Rounders*.

Ol' Max hasn't owned a horse for many years, and none of his fictional characters has ever had a shoot out on Main Street, but the label still sticks. Maybe it's because there aren't too many literate cowboys around and there is a certain novelty about it.

But there's one . . . one former cowboy who became a soldier and a miner and a gold smuggler and a movie producer and a screenwriter and a calf roper and an artist and a hustler and a bar brawler and a teller of great stories.

And a writer.

A writer of novellas—little books, as he calls them—and novels and screenplays and short stories that look at the warts and bumps and beauties and passions of living in the West.

Each life is a succession of stories, a series of stories stacked up behind us as we travel through. Very few people have more stories behind them than Max Evans. Some of them can't be told. Most can.

These stories paint the picture, just as Max did back in the old days in Taos. His life can be told not only in his own stories, but in the stories of his friends—and, sometimes, in stories passed down from father to son. One evening when I was teaching a journalism class, we were discussing Max's work, and one of the students said his father was a Santa Fe cop who had arrested Max one drunken night for what he called "cutting down all the stop signs in Santa Fe."

Max later admitted going on a midnight revenge mission against stop signs as a way of avoiding getting more traffic tickets, but he denied cutting down all of them.

As he put it, "Hell, I didn't get more than half of them cut down before they caught me."

Max at home in 1984. Photo by Cynthia Farah.

But the prelude to long and hilarious retellings of great juicy segments of Max Evans' life often begin simply: "There was this one time when me and Ol' Max were . . . "

To a newcomer, Max comes across as a stocky-built man with a forelock that looks like it should have a surfer on it, a nose that's been broken twice by horses and twice by men, and a face that appears to have been dragged behind a freight train. He soon reveals himself as a seanachie, an old-fashioned Irish storyteller. To a newcomer, along about the third beer, it also occurs that this man with the still-thick Texas accent and the coarse language is a man of dreams and poetry and beauty and passion and love and mysticism and has an absolute lifelong loyalty to his friends.

"Let's face it," Max said before this book was begun, "I've lived many, many lives and none of them half-assed."

Which just goes to prove that a half-blind old cowboy named Grant Dalton was right when he summed it up nicely with, "He's been there."

So let's take a little ride together and have some fun . . .

The Fight

Unfortunately, the best stories about Ol' Max can't be told until about fifty years after the last cockroach dies.
—Jimmy Bason, rancher and friend

Writing about Dusty and Wrangler wasn't enough to brand Max Evans as a cowboy writer, though. According to Max, it was The Fight that did it.

In a career of legendary bar brawls ("I've been in jail twenty-two times in New Mexico alone for being drunk and disorderly, mostly when I was a very young and foolish man"), there was one fight in Taos in the early 1960s that swerved Max's canoe on the river of life, a donnybrook that took a man who wrote about the soul of the American West and relegated him to the literary purgatory of "regional writer." And for that reason, Max has always considered it The Fight.

But at least it was one helluva fight.

"This woman—meanest female that ever was—jerked her high heel off and hit me in the temple. It caught the top of my cheekbone and broke the blow, or she'd killed me. As it was, it knocked the fatal shit outa me." Morning after The Fight that Changed Literary History at Ramon Hernandez's cantina in Taos. Photo taken in the early 1960s.

It was in Ramon Hernandez's place there on the plaza in Taos, a tiny, narrow bar right next to the well-known watering hole, La Cocina. Ramon was not only a lifelong friend of Max's, but played the Spanish guitar and sang beautifully. One of his songs, "You Can Be A Louse To Your Spouse In Taos," became a local favorite.

"We were running bars in Taos, me and Chuck Miller and this guy named Tex," Max said. "We were having a helluva lot of fun, you know? Ramon had this little, tiny space for his bar. You had to go past a bunch of storage to get in there, and there was about three or four tables and some benches in the place, but he pulled all the late business. He contributed to the welfare and dignity of so many people, I thought he was one of the most beautiful people I ever knew. I plugged his place in my books every chance I got.

"It was full—absolutely jammed—and Ramon was playing. But his bartender made a mistake. I think about it later and I know he wasn't a bad guy, he just made a mistake. As soon as Ramon finished playing, (the bartender) yelled to Chuck to pay his bar bill. Everybody in the place heard it. Chuck Miller always paid his bills. He just charged it because it was convenient, but it sounded like he was running out on his bills, you know? He was as kind and tough a man as I've ever known. And deep. He had a deep metaphysical side to him. We had a wonderful goddam friendship.

"Now I'm drinking, and I just went up there and said, 'You goddam sonofabitch. That man is my friend and he has never run out on a bill in his life, nor will he. And you had to yell out in front of this crowd.' Well, some guy resented this . . . big old tall guy . . . he came up and grabbed me so . . . WHAP! And he went down. I thought when he went down, that'd end it, but it didn't. He didn't stay down, either.

"This woman—meanest female that ever was—jerked her high heel off and hit me in the temple. It caught the top of my cheekbone and broke the blow, or she'd've killed me. But as it was, it knocked the fatal shit outa me. Just about that time, the whole cockeyed thing exploded. A real . . . strange (fight) . . . people were kicking and butting heads. Turned out there was seventeen people involved in this thing.

"I said to my guys, let's get out of here, and somebody knocked me down again. Well, here came this same woman again, trying to hit me in the temple with that shoe. And Tex just knocked the wadding out of her. Nobody knew Tex, so I got the blame for that, and I was absolutely, totally innocent. Even Tex tried to tell them the truth the next day in court, but they wouldn't hear.

"So I got my two guys and headed for the door. It was narrow, just one at a time in there. And when I got to the door, there was a little downhill slope. Some guys were coming in as I was trying to get out, and it turned out they were just looking for a drink. I thought they must've been some of the (other crowd) so I just whacked the first one.

"Of all of the mistakes I've made in my life, that was the worst one. This was a guy who had trained Darby's Rangers who took those big guns that were killing us on D-Day. He'd trained them in hand-to-hand fighting. He could've killed me easy, but he just started playing with me up and down the street. He got me in front of the pharmacy and then he frappéd the shit out of me and put me backwards right through that window. I went through that so fast it didn't even cut me. I was spread-eagled in the display window like poor Jesus on the cross.

"And then he reached through there to get me—I guess he was going to fix me—and when he reached in there, a piece of that glass cut the main artery in the bend of his arm. I didn't even have a shirt by this time, so I had to tear his shirt off to make a tourniquet for that arm. After I took him to the hospital, I went back to get Tex and Chuck. They weren't doing too well. They were kinda draped over pickup truck hoods, bleeding a bit from where the fists of the Ranger's friends had worked on them.

"The cops came and took us to jail, which was downstairs, under the pharmacy . . . kind of a dungeon, you might say. . . .

"The next day we went to court and paid a fine to cover the damages, as much as it was legal to fine us for as many charges as they could legitimately nail us with. The Taos coffers were mostly empty in those days, so who could blame them?

"Now this wouldn't have been a big deal, really, except that there was a guy from UPI in court that day and the story went out all over the wire. We had *The Rounders* out then, and *The Hi Lo Country* was at Macmillan. This editor-in-chief at Macmillan was over in England putting a publishing package together for me. I didn't know any of this until years later. Hell, what'd I know? I was just an ex-cowboy in this little bitty town. I didn't know anything about these kinds of deals. I knew lots of worlds, but I didn't know that world, or what they were setting up for me.

"It was years later I read the letters going back and forth about me between my agent, Henry Volkening and various editors, then I knew what they were doing and how really gentlemanly they were, and the dedication they had to a writer. It was a marvelous thing to see. But these stories about a fight over my friend's bar bill went out over the wire and got in papers all over the country. At that moment, because of that one thing in the story about the woman—who I did not touch, but they put it in there to sell papers—that started turning academics and influential people like that against me. I was branded right there."

The story appeared in the Times of London about Max's brawl in far-off Taos, New Mexico, and when the Macmillan editor read it, Max's world changed.

"I got a letter from (the editor) telling me how disappointed he was and how he was afraid I'd turn out like Christopher

Marlowe. Now I'd read Shakespeare and Balzac, Tolstoy, Colette, Joyce Cary, and de Maupassant as well as Jack London and Zane Grey. I wasn't a goddam illiterate, you know, and had read more than most people read in their entire lives, but I didn't know who Christopher Marlowe was. I went down to the plaza and started asking people who Christopher Marlowe was, because I was afraid this editor was going to desert me. Finally I asked ol' Ruthie Swain, who had a compound she rented out to writers and artists south of town at Talpa.

"She said Marlowe was the guy some people think wrote Shakespeare's stuff. And he died in a bar brawl when he was twenty-nine!"

But five words in that wire story marked Max for life.

"'Noted Western author Max Evans.' Those words branded me forever, even though three out of four of my books don't have a cowboy in them. I was branded, just like you'd brand a damned ol' calf. That made it much harder in one way, but it also made it an awful lot of fun for me. Who knows how it balanced out? Who ever really knows? Huh?

"From a literary viewpoint, it really did knock hell out of my get-up-and-go."

Max discovered through a friend in the publishing house that the word had come down from New York to just send out a few copies for review, and only fifteen review copies went out on *The Hi Lo Country*.

"What happened was, that story in the paper just cut out what was going to be a fast-track literary career. The gossip that went out about (the fight) at that time around Santa Fe, Albuquerque, and Taos got things mixed up. I got blamed for hitting that woman, you know. I never did."

"That dumb fight . . . hurt me more than I ever knew at the time, even though it pushed me towards Sam Peckinpah and Hollywood."

Max is a cowboy, through and through. He can tell you stories that will keep you humming and laughing for the rest of your life."

—Billy Marchiondo,
family attorney and friend

Max's uncle, Elbert Evans, as he leaves the ranch in Lynn County, Texas, for France in 1916. He was killed just before the war ended.

Some Call It Ropes . . .

Those who believe in predestination, however, could make a good case for Max Evans being branded a noted Western author. After all, when you're born in a house on the corner of Roundup and Timmons in Ropes, Texas. . . .

When calling and searching the house didn't produce her three-year-old son that day, Hazel Evans, Max's mother, began searching the rest of Denver, Colorado.

The last time young Max had taken off had been about a month earlier, back in their hometown of Ropes, Texas. That day, she found him walking north on the railroad tracks. He was heading, he told her, for Lubbock, twenty miles down the track, which he pronounced "Yubbock."

But now they were in Denver, and having a preschool pirate loose in a strange big city was a more serious proposition. As she went frantically down the street, she noticed a group of people gathered on a street corner, laughing and jostling each other with elbows.

She just knew, she told Max and Pat some half-century later, that he was involved in this congregation of Denverites.

And it was a congregation, of sorts, as three-year-old Max was preaching, to the delight of the adults gathered there. As she elbowed her way through the crowd to end the sermon, she was just in time to hear him tell the group, "And we'll take the sinners . . . and stick their heads in a bucket of MUD!"

Since that time, it has never been a real problem discovering what Max's views are on sinners, mud, or just about anything else.

Max Allen Evans comes from a background of Welsh, Irish, Scottish, German, and American Indian stock; in other words, he's an American. He calls himself a true mongrel.

One grandfather, J. R. Evans, was one of the pioneers in Ropes, and served as both the local judge and storekeeper. The other grandfather, Bob Swafford, Max said, traded for just about anything, "had trail hounds and drank for fun." Max's earliest childhood recollection, in fact, is of this large bear of a man looking into his crib and laughing.

The old train station in Max's birthplace of Ropes, Texas, is now a restaurant owned by Buddy Bevers. Woody Crumbo the Younger caught this photo as he was driving through the tiny town on the Texas plains.

J.R. Evans, Max's grandfather, lived from 1875 to 1947, and during those years founded Ropes, Texas, raised cattle, and was a country judge and merchant.

The Swaffords, Max's mother's family, were German Quakers, Swabians, who went first to England and then to America to avoid persecution. They went from Tennessee to Georgia and then to Texas. Max's maternal grandmother, Bertha Swafford, had been a Ferguson and was part Indian. She was also sometimes called "Birdy" and "Little Bird."

"The Fergusons married into the Cherokee," Max says. "And, for what reason I'll never know, she was a medicine woman. She even smoked a medicine pipe. Not around everybody, they had to be special. And even down there in West Texas where, at that time, they were prejudiced against anybody but white Protestants, she didn't give a damn and she would do both physical and spiritual medicine for people."

Bob Swafford, her husband, was also part Indian, carrying both Osage and Choctaw blood, but denied it all his life. Max discovered this years after his grandfather had died. If those people had known of his Indian heritage, Max said, no one would've traded with him. And he was a trader. It was his life's blood.

The Swaffords divorced after moving to Ropes, and Birdy Swafford's Cherokee ancestry and uncanny skills as a healer would play a large part in Max's later childhood.

Despite having a hefty claim to Indian blood, and living in a literary time when being Indian or part Indian brings with it some ethereal Brownie points, Max has never mentioned this part of his heritage in print. He has also used many tactics to sell paintings and to sell books, but he has never played the Indian card.

"I don't want to be tempted to become a goddam professional Indian," he says. "I'm so mad and so sick at all these so-called Native Americans now. They go to bed white people and wake up Indians. That's how they are. And they're taking away from the real Indian people, the real Indian artists, the true spiritual world, and I don't like it."

The Evans family is mainly Celtic stock from Ireland, England, and Wales. But there almost wasn't an Evans side to Max Evans. In one of those quirks of fate, the line nearly ended during the American Civil War.

Max's great grandfather Evans (unfortunately, no one left can now remember his first name) enlisted in the Confederate Army with others from his home in Grande Prairie, Texas. He was fourteen years old at the time.

Just before Max shipped out for World War II, his father visited him in *The Hi Lo Country* and showed him a picture of his ancestor. That's how he knows how close he came to not being here at all.

"He'd been shot in the forehead by a spent (musket) ball," Max says. "All the rest of his life you could see the dent in his forehead the ball made. One more micrometer . . . maybe even less . . . and that would have ended him for sure. Then my father wouldn't have existed and I wouldn't have existed. Funny, huh? It's all a little delicate in spite of our pretensions, don't you think?"

J. R. Evans, Max's grandfather, left Grande Prairie driving a herd of cattle west, followed by the family covered wagon. They first settled on a ranch in Lynn County, Texas, but were wiped out (as were many ranchers) by the catastrophic blizzard of 1918. Max's Uncle Bernard remembers seeing so many dead cattle that the hides covered the fences for miles.

In 1916, Max's father and his uncle went to France to fight the Germans. Max's father, W. B., came home. Max's uncle was killed there by a machine-gun only a few months before the war ended in 1918.

While the two Evans boys were off to war, J. R. moved from the ranch and headed as far west as the railroad tracks went in those days. There was nothing but horizon and grass there, so he started a town. He built a store there and was elected the town's first judge.

Huge herds of cattle from ranches in West Texas and eastern New Mexico found this the closest shipping point and drove the big herds there. The story goes that, since there are no trees in that part of the world which weren't intentionally planted, there was no wood, and therefore no readily available shipping pens. Improvising, the ranchers used their catch ropes (lariats) to confine the cattle, there on the western side of the tracks. So the place was called Ropes.

"My father and mother," says Max, "got the final signatures to form Hockley County with a wagon and team. They wanted Ropes to be the county seat, but the voters decided on Levelland. My grandfather (J. R. Evans) was elected the first county judge of Hockley County and then was reelected. Later, when he moved back to Ropes, he was elected city judge and held that office for many years, until his death."

Later, when the town required a post office, the federal government thought Ropes sounded too much like the name of another Texas town and changed the name to Ropesville.

Since those days, the town has changed in many ways. In the Dust Bowl days, it became a target for the government relocation of hard-luck farmers. The Roosevelt Administration, at Eleanor Roosevelt's insistence, moved them there and gave them land. This worked well for a number of them, as some struck irrigation wells afterward. Then some of those who had been lucky or wise enough to keep mineral rights later found oil.

Ropesville, Texas had two tin cotton gins standing huge and sightless like blind elephants. The cotton lint from the ginning last fall still hung in dirty brown wads from the phone and light wires and in the weeds and grass around the town. It was a small place, maybe a thousand or twelve hundred people in and around the town. But it was a big town to me this night.

—from *My Pardner*

Today, the 489 souls who sleep there among the wind-blown old houses and the rusting pipes either work on nearby cotton and milo farms or drive the twenty-two miles northeast each day to jobs in more prosperous Lubbock.

But even though it's existed for more than eighty years now, this little town huddled tight on the Staked Plains still can't decide what its name is.

Newcomers call it Ropesville. The volunteer fire department says it protects Ropes. People who don't live there call it Ropesville. The schools say they are in Ropes. The post office says Ropesville. The cotton gin says it is in Ropes. The map says Ropesville. The old railroad depot (now a small store) says it's Ropes.

"I always use Ropes as an address," says local businessman, Buddy Bevers, "and it drives the post office nuts."

Today, Ropes, or Ropesville, looks tired and discouraged, as though it never quite found the job it was looking for. But there's something else there, too. The streets. The streets are huge. Each is wide enough to host a football game. From its junction with the Brownfield highway, Main Street is twice the width it needs to be. Judge Evans and the others had hopes for Ropes. Ol' Max's mother was the first postmistress there.

On the corner of Main and Timmons, a huge red-brick bulk is all that is left of Judge Evans' mercantile. Its solid concrete sidewalks are thick as sea ice and the windows and doors are nailed shut. High on the building the faint white of old paint tells the sharp-eyed visitor this was once the Evans store.

Back when this was end-of-tracks, the ranchers drove the big herds in, then took their money to the Evans store and bought a year's supply of goods, filling the freight wagons that followed the cattle east. Then they drove back west to the vast ranges, leaving Ropes, and the Evans family, better off.

Ropes, Texas, back in those days, stood at the crossroads of wind and grass, cattle and storms, hard work and dreams. Its 350 citizens (when Max was born) survived on homegrown beef, credit and hope. Its currency was imagination.

"The Evanses and Swaffords," Max says, "were half of Ropes. Granddad (Evans) had the feed store, so I used to listen to the old-time cowboys sit around and tell stories. I have no complaints about my childhood. I thought it was great."

Max's father, W. B. Evans, worked for a time in the family store in Ropes, but his dreams lay elsewhere. He was forever, Max says, an adventurer.

> My dad was a survivor, like me, and I admired him so much for that. He just loved the game. He didn't give a shit about the money. He was like me in a lot of ways, but he never got down in the gutter, like I did on special occasions.
>
> —Max Evans

When Max was three years old, W. B., along with his brother, Lloyd, went to Denver to try to market a peanut dispenser that delivered peanuts by voice command.

"What you did," Max says, laughing, "is you put in your nickel and said 'Peanuts!' and it gave you peanuts. Problem was, kids learned that if you just said 'Peanuts!' in a certain tone of voice, it would give you the peanuts without you having to put in the nickel first."

This was not how W. B. and Lloyd had planned to expand the family fortunes, so they returned to Ropes. Lloyd opened his own store in Ropes (next to where the Eagle Mart gas pumps are today) and was successful. W. B. and Hazel moved to Roswell, New Mexico, where W. B. built several houses, and pint-sized Max hustled money by selling used copies of the Denver Post to people for a penny.

Then it was back to Ropes again.

W. B. went through a number of ventures, including founding the town of Humble City, New Mexico (between Lovington and Hobbs), and was successful as an owner of gas companies in several West Texas towns. But between adventures, the family always returned to little Ropes, the home place. Ropes "was kinda like a headquarters my family used to wander the world," Max says. "Well . . . our part of the world."

By the time Max was born, on August 29, 1924, the cattle were being shipped from towns closer to the ranches and times weren't as easy as they had been just seven years earlier. But Ropes was still a magic place to a child.

The Spade Ranch, outside Ropes, wove young Max into its spell. On this immense stretch of Texas plains (which began just two blocks from his home and on the west side of the railroad tracks), life was much as it had been for hundreds of years. Cattle now replaced the buffalo, of course, but it was still a land of mesquite and grama grass and cat's claw and the scrubby yucca of the area. The deep black earth was as yet undisturbed by a plow. The white spots on the prairie were the delicate wildflowers called cowboy's fried eggs and the thorny beauty of cliff rose. Cotton in stately rows came much later. Oilfields were in their infancy yet, and so were the automobiles which used the oil.

It was a glimpse of a Texas that had been, of almost breathtaking grandeur punctuated by horrifying storms. It was the last look at a time when a man could carve about as wide a swath as he could for himself in Texas, and no one had ever heard of welfare or unemployment. Social security, in those days, meant people in your family loved you enough to look after you in your old age.

It was also still a time when handshakes took precedence over signed contracts, when a man's word was everything, and when credit simply meant that others knew you were good for a debt. Says Max, "When you're making a horse trade or a land trade, there wasn't always a lawyer you could get to for weeks, to get all those papers signed and that legal crap taken care of. So you had to shake hands. If you broke that loyalty, every sonofabitch knew about it. You were out of there. You were through in that part of the country."

It was a shaky time, too, in our history, when fortunes were being piled up Back East, and a few were being made in the West as well, but it wasn't that way for everyone. The common folk who worked for a living still had to set egg money aside, still had to watch spending, still had to budget carefully for their tithes at church and the occasional picture show. Many children in those days ran barefooted all summer, and not just from exuberance. Shoes cost money and, with the rate of foot growth being what it is, waiting to buy shoes until the weather turned chilly in the fall made more sense.

Humble City

✂ **W. B. was an adventurer** and a conjurer. He was a dreamer and caused the dreams to happen, at least to some extent. For that reason, Max grew up in a whole succession of tiny places on the broad, flat back of America. One of those places was Humble City, New Mexico, founded by W. B.

Max was just a kid in the days just prior to The Great Depression, but he shot rabbits and quail on the wild areas near home to help feed his family. And he rode his horse, Cricket, and drove cattle, when he could, to help. He also trapped skunks for their hides and, on at least one occasion, was sent home from school because he was still carrying with him the unmistakable aroma that marked him as an unwashed skunk-catcher.

He once drove a milk cow nine miles, from Humble City to Lovington, so his baby sister, Glenda, could have milk. "Driving one cow with one horse across open country," Max laughs, "is like pushing a rope straight in the air. It was just nine miles, but it seemed like a million."

In everyone's life there are watershed moments, and one of the first big ones for Max came when he was eight, living in Humble City. He went to his first motion picture.

"Just before I was nine and had to go leave for a year, our neighbor, Hobbs Simpson, took me to Hobbs (New Mexico) and paid my way to the picture show.

"It was my first time in a motion picture house and it was the goddamdest adventure I'd ever seen. They had the ceiling painted blue, and they had taken tin foil from the used-up candy bars and made stars out of them for up there in the indoor sky. I was so thrilled, it was just terrible! I don't even remember what the movie was, but forever and ever I knew I was going to love movies. I thought how could this exist in this huge, lonely damn country . . . this beautiful paradise of adventures on that silvery screen?

"I didn't know movie houses existed before that. I fell in love with movies and never got over it. And never will. I knew it was madness. It was a universe to me. I was seeing the whole damn universe for the first time, a wondrous magical ride through the universe.

"After that, I spent all the money I could get on movies. Mostly Westerns."

That love of movies followed him across West Texas. When the family lived in Ropes, the tiny movie theater next to his Uncle Lloyd's store had a show maybe twice a week. When the family lived down the road in Meadow, Texas, the "movie man" came to town once a week and showed a movie in a large tent he pitched there. Max would wait until his parents were asleep on movie night, then slip out of the house, crawl under the tent, and watch the film. He was unashamedly addicted to movies.

He couldn't comprehend, then, that people on the screen would one day say words he'd written, or that he, too, would get to appear on that giant screen, but he knew that movies would be a part of his life.

Max grins. "It was magic, pure magic. Pure wonderment. Without wonderment, we have nothing. We lose the gift to dream in daylight with wide-open eyes."

The Depression stepped on many dreams in West Texas, but W. B. Evans didn't let a little thing like that bother him. He bought a ranch in the middle of nowhere, on totally flat and desperately lonely land between Hobbs and Lovington, New Mexico, and founded a town, as his father had done years before in Ropes. He called the place Humble City. It was that. He was sure the cattle and oil towns of Lovington and Hobbs would grow to touch the borders of his town.

Between the Great Depression and the mid-thirties drought, Humble City's existence was a miracle of the highest order. All that kept it there, squatting scared, scattered, and lonely was the fact his dad had accidentally struck an irrigation well while hand digging a cellar. Hope. Folks believed there would come a day when the bounty from the watered land would bless them all. It did. A couple of decades after most of them were gone, the land was covered with irrigation and oil pumps, and finally the oil-rich ranching town of Hobbs grew around Humble City, and left its actuality only on road maps.

—from "The World's Strangest Creature,"
Southern Horseman, January 1984

"Why he ended up making a town is a mystery to this day," Max says. "It didn't make any sense. He sold lots and built some houses. There was a one-room schoolhouse and a post

In the early 1900s, Max's grandfather, Robert Romulus (Bob) Swafford drives a team of mules through an unidentified town in Oklahoma Territory. Swafford kept his Indian blood a secret his entire life, believing it would hurt his business as a trader.

office and a general store. My mother was the first postmistress there. The houses were scattered far apart. My dad built the schoolhouse."

Somehow, Hazel Evans managed to scrape some money together, penny by penny, and buy books for young Max to read.

"I don't know how the hell she could afford these books," Max says. "I guess she just saved a bit from what little money she got from being the postmistress there. Then she'd order these books. Without me knowing, this was to set me up for reading Balzac."

W. B., says Max, had counted on Hobbs growing like a weed and eventually taking Humble City under its wing. That still hasn't happened.

"Hobbs grew on, as did the flanking town of Lovington, but Humble City, as my father dreamed of it, is long gone in the dust clouds."

Hobbs, New Mexico, fared better than most of the towns in the nation. In 1927 oil had been struck, filling the prairies with steel, leafless, man-made trees. The population jumped from zero to thirty thousand in one year. They came from everywhere and were every kind—the dreamers, the adventurers, the greedy, the hungry, the clever and the stupid. As always, just like the coyotes, there were those who came to pick the bones. They came in old cars, trucks, wagons and teams. Some hitched rides in on anything that moved, and some came walking in, sore-footed, but with souls full of hope.

Everything was greasy. The streets were oiled down twice a week to settle the dust from all the wheels and feet that moved and churned back and forth searching for destinies, for dreams, jobs and money, for something, anything. The noise of groaning motors hauling loads of steel pipe never stopped. The babble of people, the clinking of glasses, bottles, doors opening and shutting, curses and laughter were ceaseless as well. . . .

Then, with the great depression and the terrible drought, oil dropped to ten cents a barrel, and with that price the population of Hobbs fell to three thousand. There it solidified, holding precariously together amidst the many empty buildings. What really kept it from turning back to a sandhill was government intervention again. The oil was prorated and the law said no one could sell a barrel for less than a dollar. This began to help, but it didn't bring a single extra cloud into the parched sky.

—from "The Third Grade Reunion"
in *Hi Lo to Hollywood: A Max Evans Reader*

"My dad and Pete Manning hand dug the first irrigation well in that country," Max says. "I don't know why they thought they could do that, but they did. Since then, of course, billions of dollars worth of crops have come out of that country through irrigation wells, but this was the first one. They struck some slow artesian water and my dad came up with an old Cadillac motor he'd traded for in Lubbock, Texas, and that thing kept a ten-inch pipe full of water."

And, as with other important events in Max's life, it showed up later in his fiction.

Now the year is 1933, the month is March, and things are about to start happening again in Hobbs. Most ranchers who didn't have the black liquid sold out for a pittance, but a few dry-land farmers stayed and fought it out. One of these was R. G. Warren.

On this particular day, R. G. and two of his sons stood by a hand-dug water well working on a rattling Cadillac motor they had traded from a Texas mortician. Finally it sputtered and started. They stood back and stared at the empty pipe shoving out across the land like a cannon barrel. The motor choked and stopped. They went right back to work on it. This time it ran, and so did the water—a full ten inches of rounded liquid gushed out and fell upon their dying land. The earth gulped it up blindly, feeling the life return like a lost heartbeat.

—from "The Third Grade Reunion"

"The first year, they planted a field to strawberries and watermelons. Dad would take me to Hobbs and have me peddle the melons and berries on the street."

"The people from Hobbs had the only money around in that country," Max recalls, "and there was a double windmill and rock tank just outside Humble City and the folks from Hobbs would drive out and pay a dime to go swimming in it."

The biggest mistake anyone made in Humble City, Max says, was jumping him from first grade to fourth at the one-room school.

"I hated school. The only things I liked were reading and drawing. I loved those two subjects. Couldn't stand the rest of it. I wanted to be out in the prairies with my dogs and my horse, Cricket."

Yes, there were the huge pastures, the monstrous, flat pastures that went on to the horizon, and Max and his gelding, Cricket, and his mare, Dolly, explored them thoroughly. But a shortage of grass, in those Dust Bowl and drought days, was a constant problem.

"The only grass," Max says, "was on the highway right of way. My father had promoted that highway between Lovington

Max's closest companion on the lonely plains of eastern New Mexico was his gelding, Cricket. Together with a fine four-dollar saddle, nine-year-old Max and Cricket made a dynamite duo in that open country around Humble City in 1933. This photo was taken shortly before the horse drive immortalized in "My Pardner" was made.

and Hobbs, and the right of way was fenced. I'd drive (my aunt's) cattle along the highway on one side, and then drive them back down the other side on the way home."

He had other chores to do, too, such as helping milk the cow and endless other chores for his widowed aunt and her five daughters.

"There was this other family there, too," Max says. "Some real poor people. They were on this corner in an old homestead house that my dad moved them into. Those kids were so hungry, they were starving to death. I pulled a terrible thing. I'd let them sneak out there and get a quart of milk (from the cows). Take a little out of each (teat), you know. I couldn't help it. I got to feeling so sorry for those skinny wretches. I was doing a terrible thing, but it didn't make a damn to me, because I had to do it.

"I finally told my aunt about it. She forgave me, but she said, 'Well, we both can't make it. Which one of us do you want to choose?' That was the truth. (The other family) moved, that was it. I was keeping 'em alive on just that little bit of milk."

In the spring, his dogs would catch jackrabbits and cottontails, and Max would chase them on the horse and take the rabbits away before his dogs could tear them apart. If a rabbit escaped down its hole, he'd take some barbed wire and twist it until it caught the rabbit's fur, and pull it out. He began riding through those huge pastures when he was six years old, and he clearly remembers his mother wrapping up a razor blade in cloth, and tied shut with twine (to use as a tourniquet) for him to take along in case of snakebite, "even though we know now that was the wrong way to treat them."

"All that was a wonderful goddam adventure. I'd take a slingshot with me, and later on a rifle. I was a natural born dead shot. My eyesight was really good, too. It was 20/10 until I was forty-six years old. Then it weakened within a year and a half."

I wrote a story called "The Brand New Hat" based on an incident with a blue norther. She (aunt Pearl Nettles) had an old bull so dangerous you had to ring his nose.

I saw this blue norther coming. I knew I wouldn't have any trouble getting these cattle back. They saw it coming, too.

Humble City, New Mexico, was just that, especially in the hungry years of the Great Depression, but to Max (with the hat), it was an unlimited adventure in 1929.

I turned them back toward that pasture and spurred that little horse the best I could. I got them to within 400 or 500 yards of that pasture gate when that thing hit. We just made a run for it.

The cows went into the pasture, but that old bull turned off and left. I turned the pony back after the bull and then I was going straight into that blue norther. First thing that happened is my hat blew off. It was an old hat someone gave me, but it was the only hat I had.

Well, should I go after the hat or go get that bull?

I went after the bull. I didn't have a gun, so I decided I'd run him off a bluff and kill him. Only problem was, that country's all flat.

Finally that bull made a charge at me. My little pony, Cricket, stepped out of the way and that bull hit the fence. He broke that big old cedar post into matchsticks and took out somewhere between fifty and a hundred yards of barbed wire fence with him.

Then he went into the pasture with the cows, went up to the corral and just stood there.

That was the first time I can remember getting really mad at an animal. I mean, if I'd had a gun, I'd have killed him. I knew I would've. I would've been like an Apache after a buffalo and shot that sonofabitch in the head.

I guess my hat went to Alabama. I looked for it for days. In the story, I found it on the fence, but I didn't, actually. It was gone.

—Max Evans

The funnel came down out of the seething blackness and stayed. It ripped at the earth, tore the grass from its roots and gathered up the soil, the twigs, the insects, the life of the land, and hurled it up, up. All Tatum had, all he would ever have, was down there on the flats. The whirling beast meant to suck his own from him as he rode, helpless. . . .

The wind, the rain, the thunder and lightning, the horse and his rider, all were one. The sky and the earth welded themselves together and ripped off into the great spaces above. Tatum grabbed his hat from his head and stuffed it inside the Levi jacket. A good hat cost a lot of money. He could feel the horse under him, somehow harder to ride against the force of the wind than a bucking bronc. The wind pulled at his arms where he held the reins and gripped the saddle horn. Now and then he felt the horse wrenched sideways as if he were a dry weed.

The man's eyes were so full of dirt he just clamped the burning lids tight and held on. Hard objects driven by the wind struck him in the head and all over the body. A mighty vacuum sucked and pulled at the rider and his horse, sucking the very air from their lungs and nostrils.

—from "The Far Cry" in *Hi Lo to Hollywood*

Hobbs Simpson had a place in Humble City not far from Max's childhood home there, and Hobbs's son, Wayne, was Max's best friend at that time.

Max recalls many times riding his horse to the Simpson place to arrive there right at noon, because Mrs. Simpson cooked wonderful fried chicken, and he learned that if he lingered long enough while watering his horse, he could usually wangle an invitation to dinner.

He was about seven or eight years old then.

"The Simpsons had this ol' milk cow," Max recalls, "and she had her tail chewed by a dog so there was just a knot left there on the end. Then she'd swat ol' Hobbs in the head with it while he milked.

"So me 'n Wayne got this great idea. We'd weight the tail down so she couldn't hit him with it any more."

Max laughs. "Well, you know how dumb kids can get, so we got some bailing twine and some wire and wired a sizable rock to that cow's tail.

"You know what happened. When Hobbs milked her, she hit him in the head with that rock and knocked him off that stool. He got up very calmly, went to a little shed, got an ax and just hit that cow right between the eyes and killed her.

"Killed her right in front of me and ol' Wayne. Didn't say a word. Then he went over and got a block and tackle and asked us to help him hoist her up. We strung her right up to the rafters and butchered her.

"I thought," he says, laughing, "we are truly ridiculous. This is a good guy, and he's ridiculous. If he's ridiculous, we all are. So I got to watching the human race after that and had a lot of fun. None of it made me sad for very long."

Seems like the times I'd been in bad trouble in my life it was over somebody abusing my dog. That old dog, Depression, never bothered anything but what I wanted him to bother . . . well, he did chase rabbits on his own, and he'd nip at the milk cows' heels when I was driving them home. He was just helping, and I loved him.

There was a neighbor kid in Humble City, New Mexico where I was a boy, who had been throwing rocks at Depression for a spell. So far he'd missed. I'd warned him twice. He didn't listen. Then he whacked Depression on the side of the head with a big rock, and then stood there on his front porch laughing. Old Depression headed home just like Old Rag Dog had today. He was slinging his head and one ear was bleeding. I examined him to be

The two-room schoolhouse in Humble City, N.M. was so humble
no one could afford to replace the broken windowpanes, but
time and education marched on. This 1933 photo of the school
built by W.B. Evans, Max's father, was taken about a month before
Max (standing on the right in the white shirt) stabbed another
student in the hand for throwing a rock at Max's dog, and was
banished to his grandmother's home in Texas for a year.

sure he'd live, and I took off through the mesquite making out like I was going in the opposite direction. I
didn't. I circled around and came up on the other side of
the kid's house. He was pulling a rusty toy wagon with
a wheel missing.

My granddad had given me a ten-cent pocket knife. It
wouldn't hardly sharpen up with a good whetstone and
the blade would bend when I whittled if I didn't hold it
just right. I chased that rock-throwing little sucker up
on his front porch and threw him down and got astrad-
dle him. I took that ten-cent knife out of my pocket and
opened it, spread his throwing hand out flat and stabbed.
The blade didn't have time to bend. While he was stuck

to the porch kicking and screaming, I told him never to hurt my dog again.

I really got into trouble over that one; they even sent me to West Texas to stay with my grandmother. I didn't care. I took my dog with me, and we hunted and had a good time.

—from "Don't Kill My Dog"

True. It seems there was a law in New Mexico that said if a kid was kicked out of one school, he couldn't go to school anywhere else in New Mexico that same year, so Max was sent to live with his grandmother, Birdy Swafford, in her home on the eastern outskirts of Ropes, Texas, for a year.

That year with the kindly medicine woman steered him on a course that would take him into strange places and help him accept questions for which there were no immediate answers.

Good Ol' Boggs

Even though I did knock him in the head, my admiration
for him is as deep as it is for anyone.

—Max Evans

✂ **Max met Boggs there** in Humble City. Boggs, first name long forgotten, was an old bunkhouse cowboy (thirty-five or thirty-six
years old, maybe) with one eye and the scheming brain of a
natural con man. Naturally, he was a source of wonderment
to a ten-year-old boy like Max, and he ended up playing a considerable role in two of Max's lives: that of a cowboy and that
of a writer. He was the central character in Max's autobiographical saga *My Pardner*.

Even though Boggs was "discovered" in Humble City, he
leaped from wandering cowhand to legend, in Max's eyes, over
in Ropes, Texas. The reason: The Bronc Ride.

"Boggs came to this remnant of the cowboy world, there in
Ropes," Max says, "and they had this ol' paint horse that
nobody could ride. Nobody'd ever ridden him. He'd crippled a
lot of people.

"So at the stock pens on Saturday afternoon, Boggs was
going to ride him. You know how strong those railroad stock
pens are . . . big two by sixes and all . . . and the word got out
and all these people came to see it. They were going to mug

this ol' horse and Boggs—this one-eyed guy—was going to ride him.

"People came from all over the country to watch this ride. Now that sounds kinda silly, 'cause there was just this one ride, but in those days it was just like a championship prize fight. There were cowboy remnants and business people and everybody. People were making all kinds of bets on the ride, of course, and most of them were betting on the horse. I was on the outside rail, in the corner. I had a ringside seat.

"Well, they cared this horse down and Boggs got on that sucker and the horse bucked three or four times in a circle and then he just headed for that fence. That fence is too strong for a horse to knock down, but that horse tried to jump it about four yards from me. That paint horse hung on the top rail and sorta rolled and hit the ground. Ol' Boggs side-stepped, but I could see one leg was under the horse. I thought he'd broke his leg for sure, but when that horse got up, Ol' Boggs just jumped on him as he raised up.

"Well, he didn't buck any more. The fall had knocked the hell out of him. He just took off running down the railroad tracks . . . in a dead run . . . with Boggs on him. That old horse ran about 150 yards down the track and got his foot in the cross ties and turned a flip. Ol' Boggs went down and whammed his head in the middle of the track and that horse kept going down the tracks. I guess they caught him later, or he may still be running somewhere far, far, far away.

"Well, you can see the problem. Who won? Did the horse win, or Boggs? Then the fist fights started. It was a standoff, you can see. People were screaming and yelling. My grandfather was a judge there and had the main store, and he told everybody it was a standoff and no bets were to be paid. They respected him, so that's how it was.

"I was the first one to reach Boggs. Well, when he hit the ground it ripped one of his ears nearly off. Just barely hangin' on. They sewed that ear back on, but we didn't have a fancy doctor. In fact, we just had an old guy who acted like a doctor. Owned a little drug store there. There wasn't time to get him to Lubbock. So he sewed that ear back on, but it always kinda stuck way out, that one ear."

He laughs. "Well, I didn't put this bronc ride in the book (*My Pardner*) because I already had him half-blind and so bow-legged he could hardly walk. Hell, I couldn't have him have this one ear hanging down, that would've been an insult.

"I don't know how he or the horse kept from getting killed. But after that, he was my hero."

All (Max's) books have a Western setting, but they aren't Westerns. Them old cowboys didn't have enough money to buy guns.

—David Evans, cousin and cowboy

My Pardner

My Pardner brings us back to earth with the story of a boy learning a hard lesson in life from a crusty old cowhand. It's a fictionalized account of a real life experience, and, though fictionalized, I'll bet every word is true.

—Robert J. Conley,
from his introduction to Max's collection
of novellas, *Spinning Sun, Grinning Moon*

Well, not quite *every* word. Max says *My Pardner* is about ninety percent true. This leaves a writer's tithe of ten percent for fooling around a little and making things flow better. But fact is fact.

When Max was ten years old, his father found "about two dozen horses on a little starve-to-death ranch south of Jal, New Mexico, damn near to the Mexican border."

He picked them up cheap and then hired Boggs and drafted young Max to drive them across parts of three states to be sold at a profit in Guymon, Oklahoma, in that state's panhandle.

"This meant," Max says, "driving them a day and grazing them a day, as we needed them to gain a lot of weight before we sold them. This was sometime in May, and we were to get the horses to Guymon by the middle of August."

Fans of Max Evans' work find reading *My Pardner* to be eye-opening. Many things are explained. Where does a young boy from a solid, honest, God-fearing family find the wit and drive to grow into a man who earns his living by fast-talking tourists into buying his paintings and by convincing staid editors to publish work written by someone who speaks as though English were his second or even third language? Where does a young boy learn to mix Sunday attendance at the local Baptist church with worlds of quasi-justifiable larceny?

Well . . . on this four-month horseback trip across the plains.

And how could a very long horseback ride do this? It's the company a guy keeps. And Boggs—preacher, con man, philosopher, outdoorsman and one-eyed bronc rider—was the perfect instructor.

Fiction it might be, but only for sticklers. This, out of all of Max's fictional writings, is closest to the truth. He didn't even bother to change the name of his pardner, Boggs.

No one tells it better than Max, either.

After twenty-odd years, the image of Boggs is just as clear as the day he came walking towards me with his head leading his body a few inches. His skinny legs were bowed like a bronc rider's, but he wore the bib overalls of a farmer and a dirty old brown hat that flopped all over. Both boots were run over in the same direction, so he leaned a little to the left all the time. His nose was big and flat, and his mouth so wide it turned the corners of his face.

As he moved closer, I could see that there was only one crystal in his thin-rimmed glasses. A funny thing though— he had one eye gone and the crystal was on that side, leaving a single blue eye beaming from the empty gold rim.
—from *My Pardner*

The two of them started the horse herd north across the open plains toward Oklahoma. Right off the bat, though, Max could see there was a problem. He had the only saddle. The first day on the road, Boggs rode bareback. That would change when they stopped for their first night's rest.

"Boy, get up on that horse. I want to show you something." It took me kind of by surprise, but I crawled up.

"Now look here," he said. "Look at your knees. See how they kind of bend when you put 'em in the stirrups. Now look here," he said, walking off. "See them poor old bowlegs of mine? Why you could run a grizzly through there without him even knowin' it. Now ain't that a disgrace?" he said.

"I don't see as it is," I said, having always felt bowlegs to be some sort of badge of honor.

"Well, by jingos!" he said. "You don't see, boy? You don't see? Do you realize that I'm a highly educated man—havin' traveled far and wide and knowin' all about the isns and ain'ts of the world? Young feller, I'll have you know that at one time I was made a bona fide preacher. Yessir, a man of the Lord dwellin' in his own house, spreadin' the true and shinin' light. But what happened?" And he jumped around in his runover boots waving his long arms in the air. "What happened?" he shouted, putting that sky-blue eye on me. "Here's what happened," he said as he squatted down and pulled off his boots and overalls and waded out into the dirt tank. "Look," he said, "look at them legs. By jingos and hell's fire, boy, how would you like to be baptized by a preacher with a pair of legs like that?"

I burst out laughing, even though I was half scared I'd made him mad.

"There you are," he shouted, running out of the water. "That's another thing that happened . . . peals, barrels, tubs full of laughter burstin' across the land. You see, Dan"—he suddenly lowered his voice and it was like dragging satin over satin—"a young boy like you with his bones still growin' and shapin' should never ride a saddle. Otherwise, your legs will get bent like mine. A long trip like this will doom the young sapling. Let me have that saddle, son, and save you this terrible disgrace. Grow up straight and tall like Abe Lincoln. And besides"—he leaned at me with his hand in the air signaling for silence—"besides, when our duty is done I'll buy you the fanciest present this side of the pearly gate."

—from *My Pardner*

So Max rode bareback during this leisurely trip that zigzagged all over the plains to take advantage of grass for the horses . . . and the avoidance of those who owned the grass. Max's father had assured him before he left that there would be plenty to eat on the trip, but hadn't been specific. He'd given Max three dollars, but that was to be used to buy grain for the stock.

But Max found out, early on, that he was with a master of living off the land, and of living off those who lived on the land. By the time this duo reached Guymon and the successful sale of these horses, Max had been coached in the delicate arts of netting catfish, catching rabbits, stealing watermelons and chickens, imitating coyotes, stealing grain, begging on the streets, defrauding cafes out of steak dinners and other worthwhile pursuits.

And all this time, he kept in the back of his mind that promise of Boggs' gift.

Five or six hundred miles later, the horses were sold, with his father's uncle, Pit Emery, as auctioneer, and Max says, "I don't think my father was ever really broke again, after that sale. That made a big difference. After that, no matter how hard things got, he always managed to have a little money."

Max and Boggs rode back to Ropes, from Guymon, Oklahoma, in the back of a flatbed truck.

Once back in Ropes, Max waited for the promised gift from Boggs.

He didn't show up the first day, and he didn't show up for a whole week. I was getting a trifle worried but figured maybe he'd had to go plumb up to Lubbock to find me the new pair of boots. I'd made up my mind that's what he'd give me for using my saddle.

"Well, on the eighth day I ran into him coming out of Johnson's Grocery, and said, "Hi, Boggs."

"Well, howdy yourself, Dan. How've you been?"

"Fine," I said. "Did you get me the present you promised?"

"Just a minute, boy," he said, and walked back in the store. He came out with a nickel pecan bar. I took it. He said again, "Just a minute, boy," and went back in the store.

I figured he must be getting my present wrapped up pretty for me, so I hunkered down on the porch and started eating my candy bar. It sure was thoughtful of Boggs to feed me this candy while I was waiting. I'd eaten about half of it before I noticed the funny taste. I took a close look. That candy bar was full of worms. Live ones.

I got up and went in the store. I walked on towards the back, figuring Boggs was behind the meat counter. Then I saw the table that said: ALL CANDY ON THIS TABLE PRICED ONE CENT. There were lots of those wormy pecan bars among them.

He wasn't at the meat counter, and I asked, "Mr. Johnson, do you know where Boggs went?"

He said, "No, I don't. He walked out the back door."

—from *My Pardner*

In the novella, the story ends a few paragraphs later with young Dan looking all over town for Boggs, carrying a board, ready to knock his block off.

In real life, Mr. Johnson at the store was Max's favorite uncle, Lloyd Evans. And the real ending was slightly different as well. And it's one Max regrets.

"Right next to my Uncle Lloyd's store was a pool hall where those boys'd drink that bootleg whisky and the guys would come out and piss back there, you know. Got to stinkin' that place up pretty bad.

"So my uncle put a board across (this space) and then they'd piss on the board. This went on for a long time and that ol' board got all full of moisture and salts from all that pissin' and it got real heavy. I had no idea how heavy that board really got. Finally, my uncle ran a wire across the edge of that board and hooked it up to the electric.

"Well, that did the trick. It was great fun to watch those guys when they'd piss on that wire and man, when they'd piss, it'd knock them backwards. They'd run and scream, they did everything. It was sure funny to me.

"Well, I was still mad as hell at Ol' Boggs for lyin' to me about that present, you know, so I lay in wait for him out by that pool hall. I knew he had to come out of there sooner or later, so I waited for him each night.

"Finally one night he came out of there and was walking out in the street. It was a real dark night. No streetlight. I hefted that ol' (piss) board up in the air. It was so heavy I could barely keep it in the air and I started running and sort of falling under the strain and I hit him behind the ears with all this weight. He went down hard. Well, I really loved the old guy. Didn't mean to hit him that hard. I thought I'd killed him. I ran off and hid for two days and two nights in a damned old caliche pit. They were hunting for me all over the place. I knew for sure if they found me I was gonna be hung from a tree limb for murder. I was hungry, tired, and scared.

"Finally I went home and told them some cock-and-bull story about where I'd been for two days. What I was really afraid of was hearing about Boggs' funeral. Well, it turned out I didn't kill him. He left town and none of us ever saw him again. He knew he had an enemy who wanted to kill him, but he didn't know who it was, so he just left. Smart. . . .

"Now that's a rough story, but it happened. I can't help it. I didn't mean for it to happen that way. But that's the way things turn out sometimes.

"In fact," he says, laughing, "quite often once or twice a day things will get out of control and turn out that way. And if you add it up once a month, five or six things will get out of control. Add it up for a year, there'll be twenty-five or thirty-nine that'll just get completely out of control. That's the way the world is now and was then and always will be.

"You know, Ol' Boggs taught me so much. I regret so deeply that I did that. I sure would've loved to have seen him again, but I never did. You know, he's the first one to tell me about Taos. Told me about the mountains and the Indians and everything. And that same year, my Uncle Slim came around and was telling me about that Glorieta Mesa country south of ancient Santa Fe. Dreams were being created for me by two old rank cowboys without my realization.

"Well, after that, I just flat had to go there, you know. It was just too grand. And you know . . . it *was*. In fact, it was far grander than anything they told me.

I felt confidence in that (prairie) land. I knew how to get along in it. If you shot a prairie dog in the eye or the top of his head, and he fell into the hole, you could still get him. That hole drops down about two feet and then turns off. If you drop one down in there, and you don't mind wrestling a rattlesnake, you can reach down in there and grab him. People think he's gone. They're not, and the young ones are good eating when you are hungry. If they'd been called prairie squirrels, they would now be extinct.

I got to know how hawks work out there on the prairies. I got to know the rat piles, They'd get twigs and dried manure and make a home of it, and if you're out there and need to build a fire, there's all that wonderful stuff right there for you to use. I just felt at home.

There's beautiful sunsets, even on the prairie. But it's not like in the clear air of the high country. But I'd look off at one of those prairie sunsets when I was a kid and I'd want to see a mountain there. More and more, I knew I had to leave this home, that I felt comfortable in, and that I knew I could survive in, and I had to go to the mountains.

I knew my destiny was in the mountains. And that my destiny was where the Indians and the Hispanics lived. The pull was far stronger than I was.

—Max Evans

Lamy

"You ever been up there, boy? Course you ain't. I keep forgettin' you ain't been out of West Texas. Well, Taos is one of them adobe towns full of Mexicans, Indians, gringos, and nutty artists. A feller had sold me this treasure map and told me to look up a *bruja*. You know what that is? Course you don't. Well, it's a sort of fortuneteller and witch combined."

He gave that tomato can full of money a good rattle and went on, "Well I found her. Yessir, by jingos, I found her all right, and she said the map was true and the treasure was buried there, but a lady had built a house over it. So we went to this lady, and she said she could tell by the map her bedroom was right smack over the treasure, and if we'd split we could tear up the floor and dig it up. Well, I tore up the floor. The *bruja* said, 'Dig there,' and I dug. I had dirt piled all over the place. Pretty soon the *bruja* said, 'The devils are at work, and they have caused us to dig in the wrong place.' Well, sir, she grabbed a poker hanging by the fireplace and rammed it about three inches into the dry, hard ground and said, 'There! There it is!' Hell's fire, I stood right there and pulled on that poker, trying to get it out of the way so I could dig. And the harder I pulled, the deeper in the ground it went.

Max reminisces with Glorieta Mesa resident Jerry Witte in the living room of the Rafter EY ranch house, where Max first discovered Balzac. "This room," Max says, "was once famous for the dances held there. My writing life began in this room." David Bowser photo.

When it went out of sight, I Naturally couldn't hold on any longer. Now, I ain't the kind of feller to scare easy, but I broke into a run, and I ain't been back to that insane town since. Ain't hunted much treasure either."

—from *My Pardner*

⤬ **Out on the plains** in Texas, life is mostly practical. There aren't any trees that someone hasn't planted, and the view consists mostly of fields and buildings. Mostly fields. It's a working kind of place.

But there are times. . . .

Before the sun comes up each day, and when the sky is free of clouds, you can get up and go outside. The sky to the east is turning pink, and the black of the night above is fading, but over to the west, over there on the way to New Mexico, there is still this black band . . . this terminator line that lies along the horizon. And it holds secrets and promises and unseen mountains. Sometimes you can almost see the mountains over there at that time of day.

Max was a born salesman, no question. This was a man who later earned a living peddling his own paintings from bar to bar, wet and unframed, fresh off the easel, who sold mining stock to people who didn't know a mine from a hole in the ground. This was a man who would one day convince the cream of Santa Fe society to get on all fours out in the yard during a party and pretend they were cows, even to the point of grazing on the lawn at the hotel. This was the same guy who convinced rodeo cowboy, Cotton Lee, that he could teach him to walk on water. (Lee was apparently all right for a step or two in the motel pool before he hit bottom.) This was same Max Evans who once convinced the headstrong widow of naturalist Ernest Thompson Seton to hide in her own wood box for an hour during one of her parties and who talked actor Morgan Woodward into parachuting off a second-story balcony.

Max could sell retirement plans on death row.

But getting permission from his parents to get on a bus in Lubbock, Texas (where they were living at the time) and go to Lamy, New Mexico, to seek his fortune at the age of eleven had to rank right up there.

"Finally," Max recalls, "my dad saw I was gonna go. He'd have to beat me to death to keep me from going. He bought me a bus ticket and I had saved something between three and four dollars from shining shoes. Off I went."

He was going, he said, to see his uncle, Slim Evans, who was working on a ranch in the Glorieta Mesa area. The fact that Uncle Slim hadn't invited him and wasn't expecting him was beside the point.

He had damn near four bucks and a bus ticket. His Model 62 Winchester .22 rifle was broken down so he could carry it in his war bag, so he knew he wouldn't starve, and he was already eleven years old. Seemed like the right thing. Max recalls, "I was on my own a lot, even as a small child, and no one thought anything of it at the time, not even me."

As the bus pulled away and headed across the Staked Plains of Texas and New Mexico, Max looked out the window and saw farms. Field after field of farms, where the yucca and mesquite had fallen to the plow, and (this was 1935) now the wind was taking back the land and moving it elsewhere. Many of the farmhouses were boarded up. The people gone. The towns were drying up. The land was already dry. Other people, too, were out looking for their own mountain ranges.

Although, for the rest of his life, Max would be a man of the mountains, he still recalls the plains with love and pain. The plows had done in fifteen years what hundreds of years and millions of buffalo couldn't: ruined—at least in his eyes—the land.

"This really made me ill at the time," Max says. "My grandmother, Birdy, had a section of land . . . one square mile . . . out of Ropes. In those days, they were plowing that country up as fast as they could. I really resented them not leaving some grass. In my mind, here's the way it should be: half farm, half grass. So you can run your milk cow out there and there'd be a place for the wildlife.

"As a kid, that's how I thought it should be. You know something . . . my mind hasn't changed one particle. It would also hold the dust during drought. I figured this all out by myself.

Max's cowboy uncle, Slim Evans, could put "power steering" on a cowhorse, and did so throughout the west during his long life. Here he is working "Shiner" at his small ranch in Taos about 1950.

"I'd go stay with her from time to time. Even before going back to the ranch I'd go there. And she had kept half that place in grass and mesquite, so I could carefully go and hunt quail and things for us to eat. I was having a grand time.

"My feelings on how to make the Great Drought, the Dust Bowl, OK," Max says, "was that it would ruin all the farms and the land. That the plowed-up rows would blow level and would go back to grass, and that would solve my problems. It was a good thing. That was how I worked that one out. And I meant it.

"It didn't turn out that way, of course, as they just kept plowing it.

"My Grandfather Swafford had a filling station there on the corner in Ropes. He didn't do much gas business, but he had hound dogs lying all around the station. Sold bootleg whisky out the back door. He just used the station as a headquarters for trading.

"They'd got to him and his hounds, too. Here was all this adventure in his heart—he had always planned on creating an empire in Brazil, you know—and they'd plowed up everything (around Ropes) 'til he had no place to hunt."

A long bus ride across a huge flat piece of America can be made even longer by the anticipation of an eleven-year-old boy. And a good piece of that anticipation just had to do with seeing Uncle Slim again.

Uncle Slim was a larger-than-life figure to a young boy. He was a cowboy, plain and simple. A top hand. A horse trainer without equal, at least in Max's eyes.

His real name was Robert Ion Evans, the youngest of W. B.'s brothers.

"In New Mexico, Arizona, and California," Max recalls, "he was called Slim.' In Texas, he was Ion. In Wyoming and Montana, he was known as 'Tex.'"

Max's earliest memory of Uncle Slim was back in Ropes and probably happened when Max was nine and living with his Grandmother Swafford for a year. He heard that Uncle Slim was visiting Judge Evans, and went over to see him.

"I found Uncle Slim and my grandpa sitting on the porch," Max says. "I had my big ol' black dog with me, I remember.

I had a strange habit, because even when I was a little bitty kid, I talked like I was grown up. After a while, they talked to me like I was thirty years old.

"I asked him things, like how far he was from the Indians (there in New Mexico). Slim told me about Santa Fe and Glorieta Mesa and mountains and Indians and Spanish Americans and all that stuff. I knew I had to go there someday, because I knew I would get along with them."

When Slim Evans finally died high up in the Sierra Nevada of California at the age of 83, it was as a cowboy. He fell off his horse, dead, while working the high country with a cow dog. He had been true to the code.

"Jimmy Bason (Max's friend) has the bridle bits Slim used on the horses," Max says now. "I have his chaps."

One historical note here: Slim Evans' chaps and hat were worn by James Gammon (the actor who played Hoover Young) in the movie *Hi Lo Country*, based on Max's novel.

From an historical perspective, Slim Evans belonged to the old school of cowboying and horse-breaking, where the object was to get unbroken horses fit to work cattle as quickly as possible. This method called for occasional strong-arm tactics from the cowboy—and fits of violence from the horse.

"If a horse was an outlaw, (Slim) was mean," Max says. "If they behaved, he never did anything to them. Of course, his reputation preceded him, so when he'd go to these ranches, he'd get all the outlawed horses, just like I did. They'd give him the rough stock. It's hard to understand now because it isn't done that way at all any more, but that was how it was done then.

"(The ranchers) were greedy. They wanted the horses working and the cowboys working. They didn't understand, the way the vaqueros did, that you start out slow and then things speed up for you. Now they're catching on.

"So ol' Slim, he figured to break horses the best way he could. He used all the shortcuts he could find. He was smart. He figured to use the best bits, the meanest goddam spurs he could find that wouldn't cut them. He had to. He'd knock the shit out of a horse two or three times and then never have to use them again. They knew he was up there and was boss. He made good horses pretty quick."

Max had cowboys and horses and mountains on his mind as he rode that bus across the plains.

"I kept looking for mountains too early," Max recalls, laughing. "I expected to see a big mountain and Indians and Hispanics by the time we got to Clovis."

The bus stopped in Vaughn for lunch, and Max spent some of his savings on lunch.

"We got to Santa Rosa and there was a little bitty red mesa and I thought, there's my first mountain."

The bus left Lubbock in the middle of the night. It reached Lamy just before sundown the following day.

"I was terribly disappointed as we pulled into Lamy. It was pretty barren land, and there were these hills. Not mountains. Of course, I didn't realize then that the hills just kept going up and up and became mountains. I had no experience with mountains at all."

Something for the trivia box: the Atchison, Topeka and Santa Fe Railway does not go to Santa Fe. It stops at Lamy (named for the French archbishop of Santa Fe), and people travel the last miles into Santa Fe either by a spur railway or by bus or car. As a result, Lamy has always been a kind of in-between place: more than a bus stop but less than a town.

"I got off the bus and there was this porch in front of the saloon. I got real sick of the stomach and laid down on that porch and started throwing up. It must've been that piece of bad chicken I had at Vaughn. There was this old wino guy who came out of the bar, and he heard me puking and he just lay down on the porch beside me and started puking too. The very first person I met had been as friendly as possible. Why had I waited so long to come on west?

"He stumbled off and I went in the bar to ask where my uncle was. There was two gringos in the bar and this little slight-built bartender. It was a real old time bar. The bartender looked at me and said, 'What's you doing, kid?' I told him I just got off the bus. He said, 'I saw you.' I told him I was looking for Slim Evans, and asked if he knew where he was. He said, 'Yeah, he's down there at Pete Coleman's (ranch) and he's got the south end of the San Cristobal Ranch leased. They'll be in here Saturday.'

"I believe this was Wednesday. I asked if there was any way I could get down there. He said he didn't have a car and didn't know anyone going down there. Then he asked what I wanted with Slim.

"I told him Slim was my uncle. He said, 'He is? Then you can stay here.' He showed me a pool table in the back room where I could sleep. Later he took me over to the Harvey House and fed me. I just loved this old guy.

"Next morning I asked him if it'd be all right if I go out there and climb this hill. It was my first mountain, you see. It looked like a little bitty hill. So I climbed and I climbed, and all of a sudden you find you aren't on that hill. Then I realized what mountains were. I had to get to the top of it. I didn't get back until after lunch. He gave me some peanuts to eat.

"He was just beautiful to me. No one could treat anybody any kinder. Now, unbeknownst to me, that man had come there from Back East, given up for dead, with tuberculosis, and he lived several more years. And I'm very sorry I don't remember his name. Because wherever he is, I bless him. He really gave me a wonderful welcome to that country."

On Saturday afternoon, Pete Coleman's crew pulled into Lamy and headed for the bar, Slim Evans among them.

At ten o'clock that night, Max went down to the San Cristobal Ranch in the back of a pickup with the rest of the crew. His uncle gave him an old bedroll that hadn't been washed since the Spanish-American War, but Max didn't care. He was there, with his uncle, on a cattle ranch in the mountains of New Mexico, and the world was looking like a pretty special place.

"Next morning," Max says, "he got me out of that bedroll before daylight. We were taking cattle through this rough-ass country all the way up to the top of Glorieta Mesa. They put me on a damned ol' horse just like them. We had a pack mule, and we just went up the mountain.

"My ass got so sore the very first day . . . well, I wasn't used to this. And we rode up and down and around everything. And I was choused every damn minute. 'Do this.' 'Do that.' 'Don't crowd them cattle.' 'Wait for the old cow to move before you chouse her.'

"Well, I was learning as hard as I could, but it was an awful quick study. We were up on the mesa the second day, but we had little calves, so we went real slow. It was a grand experience. We saw a little Indian ruin. My ass didn't hurt so much. There was some trees up there, cedar and piñon, and in the canyons some pine.

"We moved the cattle up there, and on the third day I saw this long rock house. It had all these rooms. Each room was separate, so you could defend it against Comanches. It was a real, true, rock hacienda. There was a little church on one end of the old-time hacienda.

"That's where we stayed. I slept out on the porch. There was another kid there my age and we became friends. We settled the cattle in. There was plenty of water up there and some wild horses. It was a beautiful time. My little butt healed up. I was learning to handle cattle real good. I was a little disheartened when Slim told me he was going to Montana.

"He said, before I go to Montana, we'll ride down south to Ed Young's ranch, the Rafter EY, and I'll introduce you to Ed.

An 11-year-old Max, right, helping with the branding on the huge San Cristobal Ranch southeast of Santa Fe in 1936. With him is his friend, Little Joe McDonald, and Mr. Gould, boss of the San Cristobal.

You can learn a lot from him if you'll stay hooked. No kid's ever been able to work for him. I thought he was kidding, but he wasn't. We rode all the way over there the next day. We stayed the night there with Ed Young and Mother Young and the next day Slim left. He was going to Montana.

"I must admit I was confused. I was really loving this adventure, but I was also sad he was going to Montana. Ed Young was really tough for about a month. I had no pay at all. But I was beginning to feel a little confident because he let me have this one ol' horse to ride, Ol' Snip.

"I've had a lot of horses since that I liked—and mostly outlaws because I couldn't afford good horses—but this was one I had a lot of good adventures on. He was a sure enough cow horse.

"(Ed) put me to doing chores right off because nobody but the richest of ranchers could afford not to have chickens and milk cows. Then there was firewood and fence posts and water. There was always something to do.

"We'd help the neighbor, Eldon Butler, brand, and he'd help us brand. We went back and forth. That's how everybody did then."

And back at the ranch there was Mother Young, and she was very special.

"I never did hear anybody call her anything but Mother Young. I never knew her real name," Max says. "She was Mother Young to everybody."

When Max first went to work for Ed and Mother Young, Ed was probably in his early fifties, and Mother Young was maybe in her late forties. Their own children, Lawrence and Eddie, were already grown and off on their own.

Despite his years, though, Max says Ed thought he was a young man.

Max was given a room in the house, and only stayed in the bunkhouse when other cowboys came to the ranch to help gather cattle.

It was in the main ranch house that Max made what he still considers the greatest discovery of his life.

Balzac.

Honoré de Balzac lived and wrote in France from 1799 to 1850 and was much heralded during his day. He was considered a literary giant even then.

"They'd inherited a few books," Max says. "and had them on this little ol' shelf there in the house.

"They'd never read these books, they just had them, you know. But I read them. They had Balzac there and that was a turning point for me."

Max pauses and speaks quietly.

"I didn't know anyone could write like Balzac. I didn't know there were translations of Balzac. This was the most wondrous discovery in all the world to me. My mother had me reading when I was three years old, and I'd already read Jack London and Zane Grey and things like that. But to read somebody like Balzac, who could take all these people and intermix them, the rich and the poor. . . . It was amazing.

"He could write about the peasantry and the aristocracy equally well, and most people don't give him credit for that. He had this wondrous, vast range that was an inspiration.

"Balzac could do tragicomedy, too. The hardest thing there is to write. Shakespeare could do it, too, but he had hell doing it. As great as Hamlet is, he got that part out of balance."

There's just so many turning points in everybody's life. You either gather onto them, or you miss. If you miss, you're going to be a miserable sonofabitch.

You're going to be miserable to a degree, anyway, until you learn to giggle and laugh at how silly it all is. Balzac helped me do that.

He became my master, just as the great pioneer Potawatomi Indian artist, Woody Crumbo, would later become my mentor and master of mostly unknown things.

—Max Evans

"I guess I must have had it in the back of my mind to write someday," Max says, "but at that time I wanted to be an archaeologist, to a degree, and an artist." In his spare time, primarily during his school months in Andrews, Max worked hard at his art. "I was always sketching and drawing," he says, "but especially during the last two years I was in high school."

"I got loaned out a lot, too," he says. "You see, everybody was so poor in those days that people just loaned cowboys out for the work. The San Cristobal Ranch, those 80,000 beautiful acres, was owned by someone Back East and they had enough money to hire cowboys and keep them, but most people couldn't.

"We'd have a roundup or branding or fences needed fixing, and here'd be these five or six cowboys show up to help. Then I'd move out to the bunkhouse and that'd piss the cowboys off because I'd take the coal oil lamp with me and read. They'd threaten me every way in the world until I'd blow out that light.

"I loved getting loaned out to the San Cristobal Ranch. It had wondrous Indian ruins, and they really fed good. Not that Mother Young didn't feed us plenty."

Ed and Mother Young died many years ago, and their children are now gone, too. Mother Young undoubtedly had a real first name, but in those five years of cowboying for them, and living in the same house, and literally being part of their family, Max never heard her called anything but Mother. And it was appropriate.

"I'm sure Mother Young had been beautiful as a young woman. You know, that's a hard life, taking care of everything. She was very beautiful to me, anyway, and I loved her deeply.

"I volunteered to stay up after a long day and after supper and every night I'd dry the dishes for her. I saw to it that when I went off to school, there was a huge pile of cedar for her cook stove and piñon for the fireplace. A huge pile. It would last the whole winter, in fact. If I had to work Sundays to do it, I did it.

"It was a beautiful time for me, and I knew it even then. I'd look around that house and see the beauty she'd made. There were paintings on all the walls that she'd painted. There were rugs on the floors that she'd made out of rags and dyed. They were lovely. There were lamps. They were just coal oil lamps, but she'd made them look like electric lamps. There wasn't any electricity there in those days, of course. No radios. No TVs. No phones. No electric lights. No water in the house. But there was beauty inside and outside that old ranch house, and we had to make our own fun. And we did. Visiting far-off neighbors was priceless. A country dance was a year's worth of fun."

Ed Young, in the meantime, was teaching Max the ways of raising cattle.

"We had all these gates on the ranch," Max says, "and they were all named. Ed would say, 'We have to gather these cattle and get them down to the Jones gate.'"

The Rafter EY was a comparatively small Ma and Pa (and Max) ranch neighboring the huge, absentee landlord San Cristobal. Max says that each year, Ed Young "borrowed" grass from his wealthy neighbor. And did the wealthy neighbor know about this loan?

"I never knew that for sure," Max says, laughing.

But this allowed Max plenty of riding time on the San Cristobal, there along the western edge of Glorieta Mesa.

"And there were a bunch of springs on the San Cristobal Ranch where the wild horses used to come, and that's where I first ran wild horses.

"We ran them ten or twelve miles to the north, where there were some springs that formed San Cristobal Creek and it runs under the road that you can see right now. It goes past a great Indian ruin that you can see from the highway between Santa Fe and Cline's Corners. You can still see part of a kiva there and an old Spanish church wall. There's great pictographs there.

"And way up there at the headwaters of the creek was where we built our trap. Only way to catch those horses in there. Country was too rough (to just rope them)."

To trap wild horses meant to built a strong corral around the spring and trip the gate shut when they went in to drink. This was done as a reliable and practical means of catching wild horses, but it didn't have the same wondrous romance or mystique of roping one off another horse. And this was something every horseman wants to do at some time in his life. Ed Young was no exception.

"Ed finally caught one up there (horseback). A yearling. Just as he caught it, it went into a gully and cut itself across the brisket. Left a big scar. Ed broke it himself. Made a helluva horse.

"Years later, I painted that horse from memory in the lobby of the Taos Inn. I painted the horse as wild, up on a mesa lookin' out across the range. Pat and I took the painting down there to show him. He saw it and said, 'Goddam, that's Raggedy Ann!'

"He made such a working horse out of it, it had such a wonderful rein on it, almost like a cutting horse, that somebody from the Kansas City stockyards bought it. It was very unusual for a wild horse to make a good cow horse.

"That painting finally sold to F. H. Chilcote, the banker in Clayton who first loaned me money for cattle. It hung there in the bank for many years, but I don't know where it is now."

It took Max pretty much all his first years on the Rafter EY before, he says, he "made a hand." However, by the time he was fourteen, he was drawing a man's wages.

"Making a hand" has only slightly to do with riding a horse and working cattle, by the way. Those things are actually a small part of a cowboy's working life. The reality is in learning to fix windmills, milk cows, gather eggs, repair broken gear, cut cedar fence posts, stretch barbed wire, cut and stack hay, patch up all the working gear—saddles, bridles, harness—and on and on.

"Dumb-ass cowboys," Max says, "could do all this and more, such as doctor any injuries or sickness the cattle, horses, dogs and the aforesaid dumb-ass cowboys may acquire."

In the strictly cowboy-skills department, he says, his lack of bronc riding ability was compensated for by a natural wizardry with a rope. He could rope anything.

> There's always imminent danger. If you're working cattle with a guy, there's gonna be wrecks and you're gonna need him to save your goddamned life. And he's gonna need you.
>
> —Max Evans

Andrews

∞ **They say a man** is never a prophet in his own land, and few things could point that out more poignantly than this "non-review" of *The Rounders* that appeared in the *Andrews County News*. The writer and exact date are unknown.

> We received a book in the mail yesterday from the McMillan (sic) Publishing Company in New York . . . and the author is a former resident of Andrews, Max Evans.
>
> As we have stated here before, Max is a painter-author now living in Taos, New Mexico but when he lived in Andrews he enjoyed the reputation as the meanest, orneriest, most trouble-making night-riding teen-ager in Andrews.
>
> In his new book, about a couple of bronc-bustin' cowhands, some of the antics of his main characters reminds us of Max.
>
> But we notice that he has none of his fictional characters climbing upon the roof of the local theatre on a bitter cold, wintry night, and placing a two-gallon lard can over the stovepipe leading up from the huge pot-bellied stove below . . . which Max did here in Andrews . . . and laid behind a sand dune near the theatre and rolled and

laughed till tears came out his eyes as the people poured from the theatre coughing, wheezing and screaming.

And we notice in Max's latest novel, that he has none of his tough cowhands doing as he did at his best girl-friend's house during her annual birthday party.

Max hid in the big closet of the house throughout the party until the group started playing post office. Max hid among the clothes in the closet until a boy and girl came in and the door was shut to total darkness . . . then Max goosed in every direction . . . and quite a few embarrassed couples poured out of that closet until someone figured out that the closet contained a third person.

Max was—and is—quite a character. The name of the book: *The Rounders* . . . and he sure was.

While eleven-year-old Max was literally learning the ropes as a cowboy on Ed Young's Rafter EY Ranch in New Mexico, his parents were moving once again. This time it was to the West Texas town of Andrews, a burgeoning oil town to the south of Ropes and Lubbock. W. B. opened a store there and, by the end of summer, when young Max came in from the range to his new home, W. B. and Hazel were already part of the community.

Now, because Max had skipped two grades in the elementary school back in Humble City, he found himself entering high school just a week after his twelfth birthday.

Right off the bat, Max had two things figured out about high school life in Andrews: football and J. Lee Smith.

J. Lee Smith was a history teacher who took a liking to this pre-teen freshman and went out of his way to help him get some extraordinary privileges over the next four years.

"We went quail hunting together," Max recalls. "I really don't know why he liked me so much unless it was just that I took him quail hunting and that I was a good shot. I almost never missed a quail in those days. But what he sensed in me, I don't know. All I know is that he had some talks with my dad . . . and I never knew what they talked about . . . and after that, I really didn't have to go to class."

Until graduation four years later, Max Evans almost never attended class or had homework. He spent his days in the school library or painting and drawing.

He drew on everything that had space to put something on.

—Wesley Roberts,
school pal, Andrews, Texas;
punting (football) star at Baylor University;
and a Texas state senator for many terms

The second thing Max figured out about life in this high school was football.

"Football," he says, "was their God."

Max weighed less than 140 pounds at this point, but he could run "like a rabbit."

In his freshman year, no one would take a twelve-year-old boy seriously for a high school football player, no matter how fast he might be. But after a second year riding for the Rafter EY, it was a different story.

"In my second year," he says, "they let me play quite a bit. They finally put me in several games and I started the final three games. I could run and I could catch a pass. The next year, I was kicking off, running, punting, catching passes, the whole thing."

In Max's sophomore year, the local oil companies discovered Andrews was sitting on entire lakes of oil. Not just lakes of oil, but several layers of lakes of oil.

"They found three layers of oil," Max says, "down to 15,000 feet. All the way down to the Devonian (layer). Now this happened in a county with only 21,000 people, and where there was a lot of land designated for schools. Every other section (640 acres) was school land."

Consequently, what had been grass and shinnery oak and sticker bushes chewed on by cattle now became land that could be sold by the square foot. Several years ago, Max received a report from the Andrews School District, telling him the school district was worth two billion, one hundred eighty million dollars.

"It became the richest school district in the country," Max says, "and they built this great library. Everybody else was busy going to class and all that, but I got to spend my time in the library. I was in there reading the classics of the world. I had no idea that I would utilize this in any way, much less writing. I just loved to read. I always have and I haven't slowed a bit in that department.

"I read everything from Will James to Zane Grey, Tolstoy, Cervantes, Shakespeare, any kind of reading you can think of. But that year (sophomore year) is the year after I'd discovered Balzac on the Rafter EY Ranch. There was a translation of Le Père Goriot and Eugénie Grandet. I went to J. Lee Smith and told him there were actually three translations of these books. A few weeks later, he told me the other two translations had arrived. It was kind of a great thing."

One might imagine that not all the students at Andrews High School—those mere mortals who were required to attend class and do homework, for example—would be thrilled and excited at having an underage student happily wandering the halls during class and holing up in the spiffy new library. One would be right about that, too.

"There were kids that were jealous," Max admits, nodding, "but I whipped all of that kind who would get in on it. Most of the students were damn fine kids and I still think of them and those days with a nostalgic fondness."

When I knew him he wanted to be strong, and he was. Several of us went to Odessa to watch Max in the Golden Gloves (competition). He lost that, you know, but Max said he hated losing to the guy who won it all. He said if it'd been a street brawl, he'd've held him with one hand and beat hell out of him with the other.
—Wesley Roberts,
school pal, Andrews, Texas;
punting (football) star at Baylor University;
and a Texas state senator for many terms

At the time, Max had no plans to be an artist or writer. He was just having fun and getting a lot of drawing and reading done. Somehow or other, year after year, teachers gave him passing grades for classes he didn't attend. He was required to write the occasional term paper, he says, but he always managed to handle that with flying colors.

What he was planning to become, during those days, was a rancher. When he came back from his first summer with Ed Young, he told his father he was going to become a rancher. His father found this amusing.

"He told me," says Max, laughing, "that most ranchers had a ranch and some cattle."

The ranch was a dream at that point. Later, it would come to fruition, only to slide into other dreams and other years and other places, as life does. But in Andrews High School, the reality was that Max was a star football player. In fact, he was the football player in a school, and in a state, where football coaches were (and still are) looked upon as prophets.

And Max, at that time and place, was considered to be the best. He played both offense and defense, of course, as all football players did at that time. He ran and caught passes and kicked the ball. On punts, he was able to boot the ball down to the very corner—inbounds—by the end zone. They called it the "coffin corner" in those days. This last ability got him scholarship offers from two mid-sized colleges.

His football pinnacle came during his junior year. He was playing every play in every game, by this point, and the team was about to play against Ropes, Max's hometown.

"It was the hometown of the school superintendent, too," Max recalls. "He spoke to the team and told them they were about to tackle the hometown of 'me and Max' and that Max would show them up. This was the most embarrassing moment I ever had there," he said.

It would have been even more embarrassing had the Andrews team not been successful against Ropes, which Max says was peopled with giant farm boys he refers to as "those huge corn-fed bastards." But the game was a smashing success for the former Ropesvillian.

"I ran six touchdowns against Ropes," Max says. "That was a record for a long time. I think some guy tied it a few years ago. But remember, I was also the place kicker, and in this game," he laughs, "I missed all six of the extra points."

Andrews won the game 36-7.

That was undoubtedly a factor in why Max was allowed free rein in high school.

"Let's face it," he admits, "I was the first subsidized athlete. But I could read better than anybody in the school. I couldn't punctuate very well but my essays were always the best."

Max attended high school (in his own unique fashion) for three months each year, during football season. Then, laden with fresh books to read from the school library, he returned to Glorieta Mesa and the Rafter EY, to the comforting presence of Mother Young and to the stern but fair leadership of Ed.

After his freshman year, Max went back to the ranch and found the Youngs with more cattle and more grass.

"That was when we got into breaking horses," he says. "I wasn't good at riding broncs, but I was a natural with a rope, and I had endurance. When it came to building fence, chopping posts, digging holes in rocks, riding forty miles, I could hang in there. But I wasn't one of these great damn cowboy bronc riders. I don't know why, I never had the rhythm and I never was any good at it."

Before his high school days ended, there was one incident that stands out in Max's memory. To this day, what might have been still frightens him.

Max's father, W. B., always looking for a good business opportunity, came up with the idea of starting a local gas company.

"He went to Guy McGill, who was one of the few rich people in Andrews," Max recalls. "He told him, 'Here's how we do it. We need this and that, and I'll get all the permits we need, and we need this much money from you to get started.'"

There was another local man, a well-to-do rancher thereabouts, who tried to stop them. He refused to give them a right of way for their pipeline, after he'd shaken hands to do so. He lived on a ranch four miles from Shafter Lake, and Max says now he can't remember the man's name, and that it's just as well, anyway.

"I saddled my horse, took my rifle, and rode out to the ranch. I rode into the ranch yard and yelled. He came out of the house.

"I was so scared I damn near turned and rode off. I was sweating like a corn-fed pig. I did the dumbest damn thing. I got down and walked around that pony, and I reached into my shirt pocket and took six shells out of it. I was shaking like crazy.

"I thought he was going to go in the house and get a gun. If he did, I was going to jump on that horse and take off and dive through the mesquites and see if the bastard would miss me. I kept thinking . . . what am I doing?

"I had him, though. If he'd have turned, I could have nailed him through his double-crossing heart.

"He said, 'What do you want?'

"I said, 'Well, I came out here to ask you if I could hunt.'

"He said, 'No, you didn't.'

"I said 'Yeah, I did. You leave my daddy alone, you sonofabitch, or I'm gonna kill you like a rabid skunk.'"

"I looked at him and he just stood there, shaking. I thought I'd better get away from here before he gets a gun. And then I thought now I am in trouble. I wondered where the cowhands were, but they were off working, and he had just been widowed six months. So then I wondered, are there any witnesses? Maybe I'd better shoot him right now. I really got scared again, and then I calmed down and rode away slowly. Turned a couple of times. He just stood there and watched me.

"I got a certain distance and I spurred that ol' roan horse into a dead run," he says, laughing. "It's a wonder I didn't run that poor old horse to death. I must've run him three miles.

"All the way back to town, that long ride, I was worried. What if he called the police? They'd throw my ass in jail. How stupid could I be?

"They were abusing my father, in a way that he couldn't fight back. He was a good and honest man, and never did anything to hurt people. Just the opposite. All his life. And this worthless sonofabitch who couldn't make a dime off his land because he's so stupid, but the big companies drilled for oil on it, and hit, and . . . well."

He pauses. "You know, I never could stand those Jim Ed Love sonsabitches. All powerful arrogant bastards. I've abhorred those

At a family reunion at Slim Evans' ranch in Taos during the winter of 1956, the elder Evans sons get together. From left is Max's father, W.B., entrepreneur and owner of several gas companies, Lloyd Evans, W.B.'s partner in many ventures and a merchant. "They worked together for 50 years," Max says, "with never a cross word." Next to Lloyd is Roland Evans, father of David Evans and a farmer and merchant, and on the right is the host, Robert Ion(cq) "Slim" Evans, a cowboy all his life.

bastards ever since. He was my first Jim Ed Love." (Jim Ed Love became—first in *The Rounders*—Max's fictional, archetypal, fat-cat rancher who rides roughshod over others.

The armed threat, however, had the desired effect. The opposition to W. B. Evans' and McGill's gas company quietly vanished.

"Five years later, after my dad sold his share, the gas company was worth ten million dollars. Dad made a little money on it. He was the pioneer. They seldom collect. That comes for others later. But by that time he'd moved back to Lubbock and started something else. The adventure was over by then, you see."

After graduation, Max decided to go to college and study archaeology. He was offered two scholarships, and met with representatives from those two schools.

"Those guys were so innocently dumb," he says, "I figured I'd be spending all my time trying to teach them something, so I said the hell with it.

"And I went back to the mountains and the wild and domestic animals, all its Indians, Hispanics and gringos, and the dead white men and women classic writers, of course. I read Dumas, who then was called colored, and Cervantes, who was Spanish."

> Andrews is one place I can't go back to. A few years back, Pat and I went to San Angelo, Texas, to accept the Levi Strauss Golden Saddleman Award. We came back through Andrews.
>
> It was terrible. Big pumps, big wells, little wells, little pumps. In some places they had four wells on forty acres. And even though we get a $100 a month from those wells, I just couldn't stand it. All those places I'd ridden and hunted. All oil wells now. Everything was gone from my days there. Gone! The prairie chickens. Everything. They've had (high school) reunions, but I can't go back. Even to honor the Roberts family. Wesley and James Warren Roberts were some of my best friends. Their father ran the newspaper. Their family did so much to hold that country together during the Depression and wars. And even to honor them I can't go back. I just can't do it. I'll have to write and tell them why.
>
> —Max Evans

A Nip In The Butt

"His name was Mr. S.," says Max, "and I despised him. Don't remember exactly why now, but I did. He owned the movie theater in Andrews, and about fifty other movie theaters in West Texas.

"Maybe he did something to my father, or maybe he did something to my mother's brothers. I don't even remember. But I despised him then. I remember that much.

"Back in high school, I was kind of outlawed there for a while. This other guy, we'll just call him Curtis—greatest second-story bastard that ever lived—well, we robbed some things. Robbed the movie theater once. How does the song go . . . you only hurt the one you love . . . or something like that?"

The newspaper in Andrews referred to this escapade as a practical joke, as we've seen earlier, but failed to mention any larceny in connection with it. But Max put that straight.

"I planned it so me and this other guy would put a bucket on the stovepipe of the coal stove, and then rob the place while everyone was confused with all the smoke."

"They heated that little thing with a coal stove. I told him to run up and put the bucket on the stovepipe, and then I'll run in and yell fire and we'll rob the box office money.

"Everything went just fine, except he ran off, so I had to go in and get the money. I scooped up all the damned nickels and quarters and dimes. Turned out it was either $27.80 or $28.70, can't remember which.

"That was an enormous sum of money in those days."

A nip in the butt to one who wronged someone Max loved.

Fast forward through ranch days, two weddings, three children, artist days in Taos, World War II, and publication of *The Rounders*. Go about thirty years into the future.

Put Andrews, Texas behind you, and you find yourself watching Max hustling his stories to movie people in the world-famous Polo Lounge in Beverly Hills.

"I walk in there," recalls Max, "and there sits this guy's son, Mr. S.

"He owned the land a huge shopping center was on in a city in Texas. He still owned some of the movie theaters. He was worth twenty or thirty million dollars. Cheap? He was just as cheap as his goddam sorry daddy was before him. Got to give him credit, though. He loved movies. See how silly and fun it all is? Every damn one of us.

"I'd met him three or four times. Now all he'd spend money on were these thousand-dollar hookers. He wouldn't buy drinks or anything. Well, the mob controlled the bar. They had their own private telephone line, and four of them sat there all day, including one high-class pimp. I've written about them before. They hated this cheapie. We sat there for a while, and he was making out like he wanted to be a big movie guy. He said he knew (director) Roberto Gabaldon from Mexico. And he did. He had him there in three days. We met there almost every day for three weeks on *The Mountain of Gold*. He'd done Mexican potboilers and classics.

"I liked Gabaldon, this great Mexican director, and we got along fine. Finally, "cheapie" asked how much I needed (for an option on *The Mountain of Gold*). By this time, I was determined to score on him. Nobody'd ever got any money out of the tightwad, and I was determined to do it.

"He wrote me out a check for ten thousand dollars, and then he celebrated by getting on the phone and calling one of these thousand-dollar hookers. He wanted everyone to believe he was this great lady's man, but everyone knew they were hookers. And he was paying my friends in the mob a thousand dollars a go."

Max showed the check to the mob guys and cheers and congratulations followed.

"I never had to buy a drink in there again," Max says, "until the mob got busted. You can look it up."

After the check cleared the bank, Max returned to the Polo Lounge and sat down with "cheapie."

"I asked him, 'Do you remember when I robbed your damned picture show?' He says, 'Do I remember? So you're the one? It was $27.80. It was you? I never would've taken that option on your book if I'd known that.'

"Well, the guys in there rawhided the Texas guy so much over that, he finally had to leave. We never did make that picture. The irony was that somebody stole (*The Mountain of Gold*) and sold it to someone in Mexico and they made the movie down there. Somebody made it, under a slightly changed title, but I didn't make a dime on it, he didn't make a dime on it. "Cheapie" was out the ten thousand and the $27.80, and some guy in Mexico made a little money on the deal. I hope he made a lot. Bless him."

The Ranch

❀ **There's probably never been** a cowboy who didn't dream of some-day owning his own ranch. It might just be a genetic revulsion against cleaning corrals, digging post holes and stretching wire. Cowboys are meant to ride horses and work cattle, and such mundane chores as patching windmills should be left to more mundane folks.

Then that would-be cowboy gets a ranch job and discovers he is the designated mundane folk. Blisters and swearing follow, in the normal course of events, along with the dream of someday being the honcho. The rancher. The guy who sleeps in the big house (usually with someone nice, too), the guy who gets to drive to town for supplies and eats at the diner while mundane folks are back at the ranch stacking rocks. The one guy on the ranch whose horse actually behaves itself during the normal course of the day.

So it was with Max, as we've seen. He'd been chore boy and basic ranch grunt and loaner cowboy for Ed Young, but he wanted a place of his own.

There are three ways of becoming a rancher, as any cow-hand will tell you. One: marry a ranch. Two: inherit a ranch. Three: make a ton of money doing something else and buy a ranch. Leave it to Max to find yet another way to do it.

Max and Helene share a moment at her relative's ranch in Wheeler County, Texas, just after Max returned from World War II.

It all began just as Max was finishing high school. He was working on the Rafter EY again when he received a letter from his Aunt Faye Wright.

"Come to Mama's," was the gist of the message. "Mama" was Faye's mother and Max's grandmother, Birdy Swafford, outside of Ropes.

He went there, wondering why he was being called in, and especially curious because it was Aunt Faye, whom he has always referred to as his "marryin' aunt."

She had four or five husbands throughout her lifetime, each one a well-to-do man, and she outlived them all. She was attractive, affectionate, and classy.

"I never knew what they died of," Max says, laughing, "but I think she probably loved them to death. She really knew how to treat a man."

At this time in history, Aunt Faye was married to a Dr. Harper Wright of Oklahoma City.

At Birdy Swafford's ranch outside Ropes, Aunt Faye said, "I hear you want to be in the ranching business."

Max admitted that he did, "but I realize I have to have land and cattle to do that."

"Well," she told him, "Harper got some land in northeastern New Mexico on a bad debt. It does have a bunch of springs on it."

Upon hearing of the water, Max knew he wanted the land. Aunt Faye asked him if he could come up with $500. If so, she'd make the rest of the payments easy.

"Well," says Max, "I got $100 from my dad, $100 from my Uncle Lloyd, and the rest from my friends."

Max says he knew he was actually being given the property as a gift, and that the money was a formality, a test. She had Max make payments on the ranch, even throughout the war, and then signed it over to him.

Then, owning 1,280 deeded acres plus another 1,200 acres of state-leased land in New Mexico, and some private-leased grass, he started off to claim his ranch.

"It was beautiful," Max says. "It had good grama and buffalo grass. It also had vega grass, which made good hay. It had

In 2002, almost seventy years after he built it, Max visits the rock tank he built on his former ranch in Union County, New Mexico, before World War II. David Bowser photo.

a beautiful malpais (volcanic) mesa. It had a large meadow with deep springs.

"I loved it. I could get up on that mesa and see four states. I could sit up there and study coyotes.

"I loved the hunting there," he says. "There was no radio, no water in the house, no electricity. And ninety percent of all the houses in that area at that time were exactly the same."

Max went to the bank in Clayton and asked its president, F. H. Chilcote for money to buy cattle.

"Chilcote was a poet," Max says. "He was president of the bank and broke all the rules to lend me money. I bought forty or fifty head to start up."

But Max wasn't the first one there, or the only one who claimed the land, and therein lies another mysterious tale.

Max is one of the great writers about spirituality. Not many people believe in witches, but Max does.
—James Gammon, movie actor in *The Hi Lo Country*

When Max drove up to the ranch to take official possession of it, his father came along, too.

"I remember it was raining that day," Max recalls. "I had this old van I'd made into a pickup truck, and my dad had his Chrysler. We got up there and Old Man Mahannah was packing up to leave. Dr. Wright had basically allowed him to stay there for nothing and he'd run sheep on the place."

They had coffee with Mahannah then, and Max noticed a bucket under a leak in the next room.

"It was funny," Max recalls, "because it wouldn't drip for a long time, and then it would pour in a long stream. Then it would stop for maybe thirty minutes.

Mahannah then told Max, "You know you aren't going to be able to stay here. You think you are, but you aren't. There's things here. . . ."

"Well," Max says, "I'd had spiritual experiences starting when I was ten with my grandmother, so I didn't worry about this. I just didn't believe him. I knew he didn't want to leave, so I just figured there was something wrong with this guy. He was jealous for sure, so I rang it up to that."

So Mahannah moved out and Max moved in.

Once that was settled, Max officially became lord of all he surveyed, and he reveled in it.

"I remember it was raining like hell the day I moved in," he says. "I was there three or four months, because I didn't have enough money to go to town, and I worried about Helene, my high school sweetheart, marrying someone else. We had mail service three miles away, and I had a truck, but it wasn't that easy. I had to tow the truck up the hills with horses, then coast down the other side and go like hell. Then it would die on me going up the next hill, and I had to walk back and get the horses to tow it again."

While there, Max found a way to combine a cowboy's natural revulsion to raising sheep with a need for raising money.

"Every now and then," he says, "I'd just rip out a section of that sheep fence and sell it, then replace it with barbed wire, which was a lot cheaper."

But then, there was that leak.

"I tried to fix this leak, but I never could," he says. "I spent a lot of time trying to run that leak down. Tom Cresswell, my coyote-hunting partner, was a carpenter and he swore he could fix any leak that ever was. He couldn't do it either.

"I'm going a little goofy with this leak now. It breaks out in places that have already been fixed. It'd break out in the bedroom or in the kitchen. By the time we got through with that roof, we'd put a new roof on it and it didn't stop."

Max says he didn't believe at first that the leak was part of what was spooky about that lonely little ranch house, but he's now convinced it was.

Max met Helene Caterlin in high school in Andrews. Her father was superintendent of some local oilfields and was someone Max liked very much. And he liked Helene (pronounced Helen) very much, too. They were sweethearts there, and he wrote to her often during the early months, when he was alone at the ranch, miles away from anyone else.

"She was a beautiful Irish redhead," Max says, "with a wonderful singing voice."

After a series of impassioned letters, Helene's stepmother drove her to the ranch and Max and Helene were married.

Max's first wife, Helene, and their daughter, Sharon, around 1943 while Max was away at war.

Their marriage lasted through the birth of a daughter, Sharon—now Sharon Bird, of Claude, Texas—and through World War II. It ended shortly before Max took up painting full time and moved to Taos, but those early days on the ranch were good for both of them.

But there were strange things about this ranch.

A short time after he and Helene were married, the two of them were walking along on a quiet, sunshiny day, looking for rabbits and quail for food.

"There was this old metal tank on this hill about two-thirds of a mile from the house," Max says. "'Who knows how long it had been there. It was big and it was heavy. But it had been up there on that hill for many, many windy days. The wind knows how to blow in that country . . . about 300 days a year.

"So we're walking along out there, and it isn't blowing at all, and that tank has tipped up on its side and starts rolling down the hill towards us. It'd hit clumps of bear grass and was bouncing to beat hell. We just stood there, stunned.

There was no one around. No wind. It was an impossible situation to explain. Helene wouldn't talk about it, but I knew what it was."

One day, not long after that, Helene and Max looked out the window and saw the henhouse on fire. The nearest neighbor was more than five miles away, and was a crotchety old guy, so Max figured it must be this fellow trying to make things tough on them.

"I grabbed my rifle," Max says, "and ran out of the house. There was an arroyo back there and I got in it to see if someone was hiding in it, but there was no one. There was no one anywhere. When I got back, there was no fire in the henhouse. There was no sign of a fire in the henhouse. Not a blade of grass scorched, even. I went in the house and Helene just sat there. I don't know what she was thinking."

When the strange noises began at night, Max began to understand the message old man Mahannah had been trying to convey. This was a strange house in the middle of wide-open New Mexico and it had a life of its own.

"The noises were really strange," Max says. "Moaning and taking on, and the closest house was five miles. Screams, too. I'd get up and take my gun and a lantern. Never anything there. After a while, we didn't pay much attention to them.

"Years later I wrote a piece of fiction about the place called "The Wooden Cave," which appeared in my first book, a collection of stories called *Southwest Wind*."

One night the darkness was splintered with flashes of lightning and the sky reverberated from the malevolent boom of thunder. The tall cottonwoods swayed against the white house and brushed back and forth like chained, lost souls.

Suddenly in a rare moment of silence, Tom gulped down a thick slice of prime beef and his experienced builder's eyes bulged from his head. Without a word he leaped up and dashed to the tool-shed. In a moment he was back, slamming the door into the wind and rain. In his hands he held a square. He dashed to an archway from the dining room to the kitchen and placed the square on the floor so one angle of it ran up the archway. There was a gap of several inches.

"My God!" he shouted, "The house has blown apart." It was plain for everyone to see.

"It must be the wind," whispered Harriet.

"Yes, it's just the wind," laughed Dewey. "The wind. Well, well," he continued, clearing his throat, "the old house ain't what she used to be. . . ."

As each took his place at the great oval of oak for the nightly repast, their glances went to the square where Tom had dropped it and where Arline had left it. . . .

Slowly, almost creakingly, Tom eased from his seat and slipped to the square. It dropped from his hands. The onlookers jumped. Then, with shaking hands he put it against the archway.

"It's . . . It's . . . at least eight inches off square . . . the other way," he stammered. . . .

—from "The Wooden Cave" by Max Evans

"There were other things wrong, too. Sometimes there were stains on the stairs going up to the attic. Sometimes there weren't. There'd be a step that would move. And a board would break off the outside of the house."

After World War II, and after Max returned to the ranch, he decided to sell the place to a man named Littrell, and buy two houses on 120 acres in the small town of Des Moines, New Mexico, fourteen miles west of the ranch. (In this case, the "s" on the end of Moines is pronounced.)

After some time had passed, Max ran into Littrell on the street. Littrell said he was planning to move the house to town.

"I don't know why I said this," Max says, "but I told him, you'll never move that house. He told me he'd talked to this house mover and there was no problem. But I knew he'd never move the house."

Littrell's mover jacked up the house and got it ready to go, and then slowly started out of the yard.

"And then," Max says, "he told me the entire house collapsed, right there. It just turned to kindling. In fact, that's what they did with it. They broke it all up for firewood."

Strange noises and shiftings in this house, Max's ranch house outside Des Moines, NM, epitomized a series of unexplained events on the remote ranch. This was the house that wouldn't be moved, and when the new owner attempted to move it, it collapsed in a huge pile of kindling on the ranch and was later used for firewood. Max first began painting in the attic room of this house. This photo was taken during the winter of 1946.

Max smiles. "Actually, none of this puzzled me, but it sure puzzled everybody else. That was a strange house. A very strange house. You know, for some reason you couldn't get Helene to talk about it, either."

One of Max's shooting tricks came to perfection there on the ranch, too. Witnessed several times by some of his friends, Max would hunt quail with a .22 rifle. He'd wait until the covey ahead of him got lined up on a certain rock, and then shoot. One shot, if all went well, took the heads off two or three of them.

War

War is an actual entity. It eternally roams the earth and spews its poison in the most susceptible places. Anyone who thinks they're gonna cure war is full of shit. It's here as long as we are, and the sooner we face it, the better off we'll be.

—Max Evans

❦ **When the Japanese bombed Pearl Harbor,** two things were bound to happen: Max would join the Army, and Max would be in trouble with his superiors.

What couldn't be foretold, at that time, was that it would take an act of Congress—literally—to get Max Evans promoted to private first class.

Married ranch owners with dependents were exempt from the draft, but Max decided to join. He sent Helene and tiny Sharon to live with his parents in Lubbock, leased out the ranch, and joined.

He went through boot camp at Fort Walters, Texas. But even that was not without controversy.

Max ran into trouble with superiors fudging on his marksmanship scores to make their friends look better. To someone used to settling matters like this with fists, Max simply became frustrated.

"I shot one point from a perfect record (in rifle marksmanship) in boot camp, " he says. "I was very, very proud of this. When the scores were in, the names were switched. Another guy got my score. Truth is, I missed shooting a perfect score by one little bitty bull's-eye.

"It really made me mad, but it taught me something. I was dumb enough to walk in the captain's office and say, 'I shot the best score, where's my name (on the list).'

"He said, 'You shot a 280,' and I said, 'I shot a 299, one point from perfect.'

For some reason, they sent Max to train with some other guys on the 60mm mortars.

"Well, I couldn't wait until the end of training, because I knew about the forced march. You have a forced march of thirty-six miles carrying a minimum of sixty pounds on your back.

"In the first place, I'd hunted my whole life, and not just horseback. I bet I'd walked a million miles by that time. I was just a natural good walker.

"So here we string out for thirty-six miles. I was passing guys out there. This captain was in there. Finally, there were only about ten of us in this thing.

"I walked up to this captain, the same one who had changed my shooting score, and I passed him.

"Finally, at the end of the thirty-six miles, there were jeeps and refreshments and things there, and I got there thirty yards ahead of anybody. But somehow that never got on my record, either.

"Of course, now I realize I was good at shooting and such, but I never did learn to take orders from those I didn't respect. Now, I learned a humbling lesson. The guy who switched score cards on me was trained as a sniper. A sniper's life expectancy in World War II was about two weeks. If a dogface survived the first two weeks of combat, his odds of making it all the way jumped way up. After the war, I never forgot that what gripes you today may taste sweet as chocolate truffles tomorrow."

Max was a real guy. If you needed help, he was there. If you came looking for a handout, forget it. I saw Max carry a kid in on his back several miles. This was Max. Don't

*Herman Eubank's handiness with his fists led promoter
Max Evans to capitalize on that skill during Army training days
in World War II. Here they recall old times in a 1998 photo.*

mess with him when he is in that mood. If you do, he
might kill you. I never tried to find out.

—Herman Eubank, Army buddy

Max liked the way this other Texas soldier, Herman Eubank,
handled himself fighting those "Yankees," so he decided to
become Herman's "manager" in the regimental boxing matches.
Naturally, it became a lifetime friendship.

We would get weekend passes if we won the regimental
fights. We lost (the big fight) in the ninth round. Boy,
what a beating we took! I don't remember how many we
took on, but it was bloody. First time I ever fought in a
ring. What a deal. I can say Ol' Max really worked hard
trying to keep me in the ring. He really wanted those
weekend passes. I wonder why? Still do.

—Herman Eubank, Army buddy

After basic training, they sent Max to the 28th Infantry
Division in Bridgend, South Wales.

Max became friends there with Charlie Grove, from Alabama, nephew of famous baseball pitcher, Lefty Grove; and with a man named Panucci, one of many soldiers of Italian ancestry in the outfit who hailed from Pennsylvania.

"All Grove could talk about was getting back after the war and getting his professional golf career going again. He said he was going to be the greatest golfer in the world, and I believed him. He sure was strong," Max said. "We had a fun fight one time and he whipped the shit out of me."

The 28th Division was shipped overseas to Wales to continue training before making the invasion of Hitler's Europe. Max was in camp in those Welsh mountains, and he loved mountains, but he wasn't happy.

"Well, hell," he says, "I had to figure a way to get out of that camp. My name is Evans, and I had relatives living within thirty miles of there. Every other store in that part of Wales

Max's army buddy, Charlie Grove, nephew of the baseball great, Lefty Grove, saying goodbye to his wife just before shipping out for Europe. Grove was killed in late August of 1944 in the Ardennes forest.

Max leaving home for his new pre-invasion posting in Wales in 1943.

was Evans Ltd. Or Evans and Sons or Evans Brothers. Hell, I was in one of my ancestral homes.

"Plus, I always liked sweets and they wouldn't give us any damned sweets. Well, I found a hole under the camp fence, and I'd go to town where they had a bootleg bakery. I'd get a bunch of sweet rolls or whatever they had, and then about midnight I'd sneak back into camp and sell them to the guys. I was making some good money there for a while."

The nightly doughnut raids didn't interfere with the long hikes and intense training each day, however.

"Everything was fine. We were drinking beer (in the local pubs). Of course, the good stuff they kept hidden away for their best customers.

"There was this lieutenant in the outfit I just couldn't stand, so in hand-to-hand training, I grabbed him and threw him and just knocked him colder'n an Alaska dog turd. Naturally. Well, that was the beginning of the end for Ol' Max, don't you know.

"A couple of days later, they put me up against a 240-pound sergeant, the biggest, most muscled-up man I ever saw in the infantry. He was a big target. I charged him and put him flat on his ass twice, and nobody had done that before. Then he figured out what I was doing and he slammed me to the ground so hard I thought I was dead.

"After that, they had us shooting for score again, and I'll be damned if they didn't pair me with a regular army sergeant. Most of us were plain ol' citizen soldiers and we looked at things differently than the regulars.

"I shot a perfect score. Now he was good, real good. He shot only three or four points behind me. And I'll be damned if he didn't switch the scores again. Impossible, I know, but it happened. They only posted the winner this time, which was him.

"He scored 'expert' and I scored 'sharpshooter.' By this time, I didn't trust the army at all. I outshot every sonofabitch and outwalked them, and did everything they asked of me the best I had in me. Of course . . . it was my fault. I didn't think smarter.

"As I said before, if they'd had any honor (the two regulars) at all, they'd have made a sniper out of me. Then I'd have been dead in two weeks. So you see, everything comes back to you. And sometimes you draw an ace when you've been dealt a deuce."

> Max could really shoot. One time we were throwing half dollars in the air, and I saw Max shoot two out of three of them with a .22 rifle. I still have one of those half dollars around here somewhere with that bullet in it.
> —Sam Hightower

With his buddies, Charlie Grove and Panucci, Max found the opportunity to hit the local pub every chance he got.

"Panucci had to be a patriot of the first order," Max says. "He had been one of Al Capone's bodyguards and they had ways of getting deferments. He could drink more Welsh beer than Dylan Thomas and never reveal a wobble.

"We'd go down to the Bridge Inn there in the town of Bridgend, South Wales. Wonderful place. They had these beautiful carved glass windows and doors. Right on the main street. We were drinking and having fun.

"But there weren't any other soldiers in this place. Charlie kept asking for scotch and getting mad. Well, I understood that, because they saved it for the locals, but Charlie kept getting mad. Well, I agreed with the people there, but I had to back Charlie, of course. Then he started a fight. Now this was one time I didn't cause a fight, Charlie did. And that's when I discovered just how tough Charlie was. Somebody grabbed Charlie and it all blew up. Well, I had to get in it.

"All in all, it was a pretty rough fight. I said, 'Hey, we gotta get out of here,' and he said yeah and then—that silly bastard—he picked up a chair and knocked that beautiful carved window out. He carried a chair out the door and was fighting off these tough Welsh coal miners with it, and a bunch of them were knocking the crap out of me.

"Well then, out comes all these people, screaming for the MPs. Seemed like there were thousands of them, but there was probably only about a hundred or so. All these people had known each other for a thousand years, you know, and I looked back and the street was full of them, and four or five MPs were leading them.

"These people were just trying to protect their town from these crazy infantrymen, and I didn't blame 'em.

"Well, Charlie could outfight me, but he couldn't outrun me, by God, and I passed him like he was running backwards. And that was a mistake, because I turned a corner and there in front of me was a thousand-year-old rock wall forty to fifty feet tall. And right behind came Charlie with all these people and the goddamned MPs. So what did he do? He charged the whole bunch of them.

"I didn't charge them at all. I just tried to duck, but they knocked me down and hit me in the knees. They sure knew how to take the fight out of a feller.

"Anyway, we go to the brig, of course. The very next day here comes the colonel with some MPs to escort us to town. He doesn't say anything. We drive up to this bar and it's all boarded up.

"Finally, he says, 'There's only one reason I'm not court-martialing you. We need you for fodder. You're going to apologize to this man and you're going to pay him back.'

"I said, 'Sir, with all due respect, you could take my salary for a year and a half and never pay it back.'

"We really did apologize. I gave the most heartfelt apology I ever gave.

"I don't remember how the money part worked out. But we trained all day and then got KP all night. We got every dirty job they had, of course."

A few days later, Max was told he was being transferred, with about thirty others, to the 2nd Infantry Division. They were taken to Cardiff, Wales, to the camp there.

All thirty of these men had been problems to their former unit. There were between two hundred and four hundred men in this camp.

Max says, "Then I knew. Oh shit, I said, we really are nothing but cannon fodder. They broke us away from our units and scattered us out with strangers and are going to send us straight to the invasion, with the 2nd Infantry to support the 1st and the 4th on Omaha Beach. You won't read anything in the books about the army doing this, but I'm telling you how it is. They did it."

Then it was D-Day, and Max found himself offshore as the shore batteries at Normandy rained lead down on his ship. Bombers continued to pour in toward the coast, and good men were up ahead, dying and killing on this sixth of June 1944. And a lot of the 2nd Engineers were needed and were lost.

> The night of June 6 and the day of June 7, Bluefeather was so seasick, he truly did not care when they landed or if they sank. Surprisingly, the German air force that was supposed to have been knocked from the sky that day, staged daring night raids. The roar and explosion of bombs, the antiaircraft guns, the flaming barrage balloons and the clattering of flak falling like steel rain on the decks of the ships stretched out in a convoy farther than any eye could see, made the night a circus of power and death; a display so large and unimaginable in scope, it finally became indescribable.
>
> —from *Bluefeather Fellini*

"By the time we landed (the following day), it was over except for the artillery. It was still coming in. And they'd put us into these units where we didn't know a soul. Didn't have a single buddy.

"They dumped us out into the water, which was still full of guts and blood, of course, and I barely made it to shore. I'm a sinker, not a swimmer. I bounced. I'd find a sandbar and bounced up and down and finally made it to shore that way.

"We got some machine-gun fire, too, and lost a lot of guys coming in. By the time we were landed, it was almost dark. There were rows and rows of slicker-covered bodies, some of them engineers from our outfit.

"The only weapons we had were those little bitty 60mm mortars. No artillery. We took that crossroads, Sainte-Mère-Eglise, with what we had. They knocked us out and we came back three bloody times before we got our heavy weapons and held it.

"Looking back on it, the only way we took that beach was that we just had so much air power and navy power and we knocked out so many guns that they couldn't hold back the tide. That's something people don't like to hear, but it's the truth. They outfought us, outmaneuvered us, outshot us, every damn thing."

Bluefeather saw a lot of this, and none of this, as they moved out of the water into all of the above—up little canyons, in the cliffs with sniper fire and artillery harassing them almost every step. Every few yards this harassment also killed someone. But the stench of his own vomit and the excrement and urine in his olive-greens helped disguise that of exploded entrails and the vast nauseating blood smell strong as a thousand slaughterhouses.

The war was a blur. Like a barroom brawl. There were no great organized plans and brilliant military tactics, no inflamed thoughts of glory and winning of great battles, no patriotic images of heroics and the flags of one's country waving in victory. There was simply a moving blur of frazzled images in a twenty-yard circle. The war, the world, everything, was all in this very small twenty-yard circle. That's all he knew. All he felt. All he realized of existence and nonexistence. All.

—from *Bluefeather Fellini*

Max's new division moved inland to Treviers and lost a lot of men making this crossroads secure. In one case, Max was the first to enter a chateau that had just been evacuated by German officers. He found some golden bowls and a candlestick and stuck them in his pack.

"I was dumb enough to carry them on my back for the next two weeks. Somehow, I knew they were valuable and I was going to get some money for them and send it home and finish paying off the ranch.

"Finally," Max says, "I couldn't carry them any more. I marked an area between a farmhouse and a tree and covered them up in a fox hole.

"They're still there." He laughs. "I've seen pictures of that area and didn't recognize a thing.

"There's really only one thing I did in France worthy of note besides doing my job as asked and trained, and surviving," Max says. "About 2:30 each afternoon, everybody would be out of water and begging each other for a drink. For some reason, I could go all day on just a little bit of water. I know that gave me high blood pressure. I've always been able to do that, though. When I was cow punching I could ride all day without water. The same when I was climbing mountains and crossing deserts in four or five states, prospecting.

"All the guys in my twenty-yard circle would be out of water. I'd pass it around, and there would only be half an inch gone out of it. They caught on quick to that. I ended up adding an extra canteen. My one sacrifice. I couldn't get shot. I'd spoiled them all for a drink of water when they were parched from the loss of it. That's all the claim I have to anything, really, except for living through it."

Max and his outfit fought in each twenty-yard personal circle, and had to keep each circle alive and moving away from the ocean. They were told they had to take what was known as Hill 192 away from the Germans. There were 88mm cannons on the hill, with the Germans well dug-in, and the artillery would be focused on American soldiers trying to take the village of St. Lô. The big guns had to go.

"If we didn't take this hill," Max says, "the Germans would kick us right back into the ocean."

It was July 1944, and it was time to silence the guns.

"We heard this hum getting louder and louder and closer and closer," Max says. "And then we saw them . . . as far as the eye could see came these bombers . . . our bombers. We lay in our foxholes as the bombs fell (on Hill 192). The ground began shaking with the bombs. I didn't think anything on that hill could survive, but plenty of them did.

"I remember lying on my back in my foxhole and looking up and from the bottom of the hole you could see the earth moving in and out with each blast. That's when it occurred to me that the earth is really a skin, flexing in and out. Amazing thing to see."

When the bombing stopped, Max and the others climbed out of the foxholes and started up Hill 192. The Second Division (Max's) took half the hill and the 29th Division took the other half. There were tremendous losses on the American side before the Germans were defeated.

"We took the hill in one day," Max says, "and all day long the air is pounding your goddam brains out."

> I only knew one war lover. He was a sergeant, and I called him Peck in *Bluefeather*. Even while we were fighting the Germans, he was looking forward to invading Japan. This guy would kill the other guys, or get you killed . . . one or the other.
>
> —Max Evans

The following day, both divisions went down the hill to take the town of St. Lô. And that day Max remembers seeing the final seconds of one man's life.

"What affected me the most was seeing this guy's struggle for life when he's only going to live ten seconds. It really got to me. His jaw was blown completely off. You could see his larynx and the blood was pumping out. There was nothing anyone could do."

In a setting where sudden death was commonplace and violence was the order of the day, there was something about this one tiny slice of it that has stayed with Max all his life. In mere seconds, silent seconds, the horror of war and the onset of death mingled with the wonder of life.

"The medics with him were touched, too. They were on either side of him and keeping him in a sitting position, but I don't know why, really. He only had maybe ten seconds to live, and he knew it and we all knew it. But life was so precious and this man was struggling so hard to get the last seconds of it. That was something I'll never forget."

Also that day, an 88mm shell hit near Max and bounced out on the ground near a hedgerow. It failed to explode.

Max remembered this in detail in *Bluefeather Fellini*.

Then a shell came whipping in from the side. Bluefeather flinched down into the small space he had initially scooped from the earth. He knew that part of his body was revealed. The shell hit in the field with a dead thud. Bluefeather bunched all his being against the impact. It didn't come. It was a dud. He looked to the side where the shell lay. He could feel the powder wanting to burst apart the steel and, subsequently, his body. He stared at it like a field mouse hypnotized by a rattlesnake. It was a long, long time, in battle time, before he could pull his gaze away from the unspeaking shell.
—from *Bluefeather Fellini*

Images like these have stayed with him for more than sixty years.

In the three-day battle for St. Lô, the Allies suffered twenty thousand casualties—three times the number suffered on D-Day.

"The future of the whole world was at stake right there," Max says. "It was attack, attack, attack. We had the 8th Division on one side and the 29th on the other. The only way we knew this was by the markings on the dead men we found. We're really moving and attacking, and the Germans are leaving, but they can still set up their artillery."

Then Max's outfit topped a hill and found, in the midst of hell and chaos, a beautiful valley with rows of poplars, and no Germans in sight.

"Then here came a whole bunch of Germans toward us with a staff car out in front, coming across this valley," Max says. "Sergeant Rudio was trying to gauge if we can hit them with mortars, and we could, but we had to wait for them to get closer."

But that didn't happen. Before the lead vehicle was within mortar range, two British Spitfires dove down on them, then went around and came back and fired machine-guns and rockets and "just blew those German staff cars off the road into the bar ditch (borrow ditch)."

The next day's edition of *Stars and Stripes* told the story of the Spitfires and just who it was they'd taken out of action.

"The headline read, 'Rommel Wounded,'" Max said. "Another ten minutes and we'd have blown his ass all to hell."

Heading next for Vire, Max was thrown into a day of laughter and terror so complete that the images haunted him, unspoken, until *Bluefeather Fellini* was written nearly half a century later.

It was a land of fields rimmed by hedgerows, with young machine-gunners at the corners, catching Americans in a crossfire, and tanks hidden at ground level in the hedgerows with just the big guns sticking out. Farther out were the German 88mms, able to zero their death loads into tiny spaces. And the men of Max's mortar squad and the rest of the 2nd Division had to walk through this.

Max and the other men of Company G went through a wide-open gate from one field to the next, only to discover this was a one-way death trap. The field into which they walked was a dead end. The open gate was the only way in or out.

"All of a sudden," Max says, "the shells started whamming into that field."

While the men were frantically digging in, four American tanks came up to relieve them. As they passed through the open gate, the German guns killed the first tank.

"I was dug in next to a hedgerow," Max recalls, "and I was lying on my back . . . for some reason I always lay on my back, looking up. A shell hit six or seven feet from me and I was hit by rocks from the explosion. But then, all of a sudden, I can't see. My face was covered with bees. That shell had hit a beehive in that hedgerow and now I had them all over me."

If Max gets out of the hole to shake off the bees, he'll be killed by the Germans. If he stays where he is, the bees will probably kill him.

"I was more afraid of the bees than I was of the shells," Max says. "That's when I started horse trading with God. Can you imagine anything so ridiculous? Well, I made a prayer to the Great Mystery right then and there. I said, if you can let me get through this, I'll get through the rest of it. Someday, I promised, I'll write you a book that people with open minds can read and it will help them.

"That's what *Bluefeather Fellini* was. I was late on delivering, of course. The Mountain of Gold was an attempt to fulfill this promise, but it wasn't enough.

"Well, the bees just left me. They just left. Not one sting. And right then the shelling stopped. All this terrible war going on, and I was chickenshit enough to horse trade with God."

One of Max's buddies was an Osage Indian from Tulsa named Daniel Wind, who later shows up prominently in *Bluefeather*. He always wore his helmet at a rakish angle and was behind Max when they entered this deadly field that day.

"A shell," says Max, "went Whoomp! And Daniel Wind was buried under a hedgerow. We were digging with our hands, sure that he was dead, and we got to him. He looked up and said, 'What are you doing here, Max?' And that helmet was still sitting crooked on his head."

When the bees were gone and the shelling stopped, not one of the five dozen foot soldiers in that field was seriously wounded. But all the men in all four American tanks were dead, some half in, half out of the tanks, burned to death.

> Bluefeather crawled over to Daniel and said softly, "Hey, Wind, do you know what an old, worn-out cowboy from Taos once told me when I asked him what thirty years of that kind of work was like?"
>
> Wind said, "No."
>
> "He said it was just shit, hair, blood and corruption."
>
> Wind thought a moment and said seriously, "He left out canvas and leather."
>
> Bluefeather took a little time now, then speaking to himself he put their words together, "Shit, hair, blood, leather, canvas and corruption." He whispered it several times before he reached in the foxhole and patted Wind

on his perpetually tilted helmet. "Hey, Wind, you're a bloody genius. That ain't only a fine description of cowboying, but that's a damn near perfect description of this little old war we're in here right now."

—from *Bluefeather Fellini*

They fought across France until they reached the outskirts of Vire.

"This wonderful Sergeant Milton Rudio," Max says. "He was wounded slightly and was gone for three weeks. I missed him a lot, but I was glad for him that he was out of the action, all at the same time. He was what you'd call an honest man in every way. He'd never lie to you or cheat you. He was a truly good soldier, and we became very close."

The fighting was intense, Max says, and everyone on both sides became totally mentally and physically exhausted at the same time.

"The Germans had this railroad gun," he says. "I'd never heard one before. This thing shot a five-hundred-pound shell. They always say you never hear the one that hits you, but they were talking about a machine-gun or a rifle. By the time you hear the overhead snap, the bullet's already past you. But they weren't talking about a railroad gun. It arched high in the sky.

"Sergeant Rudio sent me, and another soldier, Randall, I think, back to the food depot (to get supplies). He knew he could depend on me. I didn't want to be a hero. I just wanted to do my duty, drink a little whisky with my comrades and tell a few jokes. That was all I wanted to do.

"So I went back. Soldiers from many platoons were crisscrossing on this trail all day. I got down there and filled this pack with food and Randall got that gas can full of water. Going back, I heard that railroad gun again. Going over, it sounded like a jeep or a boxcar flying, tumbling through the air. I never even thought about it. I was coming back through this rubble. Everybody was kinda scattered out at this point. My buddy had stopped to have a smoke on the steps inside a bombed-out basement.

"For some reason I slowed down, and that's what saved my life. I heard that sonofabitch coming. I'd heard enough shells going over that I said, 'Oops, that one's not going over.'"

In September of 1944, during the siege of Brest, France, Max's mortar squad pauses for a snapshot. Max is standing at far left.

When this happened, Max wasn't yet back with his own outfit, but was going through an area with a number of other soldiers around him.

"Somehow or other, not one of us hit the ground. You know, you've done that so many times you can just see it out of the corner of your eye. That thing hit somewhere near us. And I woke up in the corner of this basement. Some guy's guts are in my eyes. I thought I was dead. Then I thought I was blind.

"This new replacement from Texas was talking to me and helped me. Me and him are the only ones left. There were no bodies, just pieces. This kid had sat down to smoke a cigarette on the steps into the blown-out basement, and the concussion went over him."

The soldier from Texas got Max on his feet and handed him his helmet. Shrapnel had made a hole through it. The Texan removed a small piece of shrapnel from Max's skull and was wiping at the blood coming from his nose, mouth and one ear.

"I got back to my outfit," Max says, "and told Sergeant Rudio I was all right. He was going to send me back, but his staff sergeant superior said 'Hell, he looks fine to me. He's standing, ain't he? We're short of men.'"

The huge railroad gun was mounted on a special flat car and was pulled back into a railroad tunnel when not being fired. This, says Max, was why they were so difficult to eliminate.

In this case, however, Max's concussion did not go unavenged. About two minutes after firing the shell, the railroad gun was destroyed by American aircraft.

But the damage had been done. The concussion of a five-hundred-pound shell exploding at close range, if it doesn't kill you outright, can leave a man with long-term problems. Max's problems exist to this day.

"I was pretty numb right then. I didn't understand this for a long time. There's a part of your brain that has to do with your speech. There were some words I couldn't say. I started getting terrible dizzy spells and was throwing up. I got to thinking I had a bad stomach ulcer, because by the time we got to the battle of Brest, my head wasn't hurting any more. By then I was really having dizzy spells, though."

Max later learned he had also had the ability to speak and understand Spanish and French blown out of him by that shell. He hid the words in English that had also been lost with the concussion. It was years before they would come back. Some words are impossible for him to pronounce properly to this day, but as he said, "There are a surplus of words in English, anyway. Especially in books."

"That's perty fair fightin' goin' on around here, dear brudder."

After what Bluefeather had seen and survived in this single day, he was qualified to make a year-long speech if he so desired, but because he felt too weary to work his vocal cords so heavily, he simply said, "Hey, I learned something, Bear. Ground war made me realize that one can breathe blood . . . and nothing is unbearable."

—from *Bluefeather Fellini*

I remember one time at the dinner table when I was a boy, my dad asked Max, "Why do you always see them shaving (in war movies)?" And Max said, "That's the only way you could feel clean at the end of the day."

—Dr. Jeb Stuart Rosebrook, historian

The German

Newspaper editors know that the front page belongs to the stories people will talk about over coffee in the morning. So, when an earthquake wipes out 6,000 people on the other side of the world, and at the same time one little girl gets lost in the woods in Colorado, the story of the little girl goes up front, and the thousands of souls buried under rubble makes page three.

Why? Because no one can identify with 6,000 people. All of us know a little girl. And we want to know what she had for breakfast, where she went to school, what she was wearing, and what the weather's like.

It is one of the mysteries of human existence, but overwhelming events somehow have to become personalized before we can deal with them.

Max's World War II became personified by one man. To Max, he would always be The German.

"We had been sent to take Brest," Max says, "as it was a real strong point for the Germans. Hitler's favorite SS battalion was there. Our generals wanted them. Patton had bounced off the heavy fortifications and had enough sense to move on. Others didn't. Later, I got to thinking that we could have just ignored it and gone around it and there's nothing they could have done about it, but that wasn't how things were. And Brest cost us 10,000 casualties and six weeks. Terrible bloody weeks without let up.

"We were several miles out of Brest, fighting our way toward town. There were fields and hedgerows, and we just kept moving the best we could.

"Most of the Germans had already left the area, moving towards the city and the concrete fortifications beyond belief, but they had left three or four soldiers behind to delay us. I had been blown up earlier at Vire so by this time I was whamming into trees and bushes, and watching for things to grab for balance. The balance of life, of love, of effort. Balance is everything, I learned."

By this time, Max's group had lost so many people that Sergeant Milton Rudio was forced to fire mortars with them. There is a photograph of Max and Rudio behind a hedgerow, outside Brest, with a scythe stuck into the ground. Evidently some farmer had heard the battle heading his way and fled to safety, first sticking the scythe into the ground so he could find it again. What a symbol.

It was by this universal symbol of death that Max saw The German.

"Right at that point, with the mortars firing at us and the rifles firing, I peeked over the hedgerow and saw this German running away across the field. I picked up the lieutenant's carbine and shot that guy. Killed him deader'n shit. This really bothered me later, but if I hadn't killed him, he'd probably have killed me on down the bloody line somewhere. That's war."

The high moan of the German eighty-eights, and the flatter tone of the American 105s, drowned out the report of Bluefeather's M1. The German's knees buckled. He fell forward, then rose again.

Bluefeather eased off another shot, surprised at the sudden deep pain of guilt he felt toward killing a man who a moment earlier had been trying to kill him. The German whacked against the earth face down. One foot twitched and that was all.

—from *Bluefeather Fellini*

"I checked him out two days later," Max says. "I went out and robbed him. I took his billfold out and there were pictures of him picnicking with his wife and little kid. Blood saturated it, a line across half the photos as if it had been drawn. Maybe it had. The billfold was full of French money, too. I took that. And he had this hunting knife. Never saw one like it before, so I unbuckled his belt and took the knife, too. And I took the photographs.

"The knife turned out to be a Russian knife, and I wondered if this guy had been over fighting the Russians earlier."

The instantly identifiable stench was already there, aided by the summer heat. The flies had done their dirty work, and the body was turning the usual gun-barrel black. He could see the round holes in the German's back about three inches apart. Bluefeather was only briefly revulsed at his good marksmanship. He grabbed a shoulder of the

In a photo full of symbolism, Max and Sgt. Milton Rudio pause for a photograph with their 60 mm mortar several miles outside Brest, France. A farmer hurriedly leaving his field stuck the scythe in the ground to make it easier to find later, and it was here in September of 1944, beneath this universal symbol of death, that Max shot and killed the soldier he has always referred to as "The German."

uniform and pulled the German corporal over on his back. The entire front of the dead man's uniform was blood-covered—some dry, some sticky wet where it had been between the clothing and the ground.

He extracted the wallet carefully, for half of it was blood-soaked. He was later amazed at his disappointment because the man had no valuable ring or wristwatch or gold teeth. My God, had he become more vulture than human? Was he so jaded and empty that the man he had killed was meaningless? Was humankind just a big, bloody laugh for deities, war lovers, warmongers and eternity as well? If so, even memory itself never had been.

These thoughts came later. As for now he was more troubled by the little photos he found of the man as a civilian having a joyous-appearing picnic in a park with his wife and two small kids. They were all smiling, and one little two- or three-year-old girl was waving at the camera. The poor unlucky son of a bitch had loved and lived the same things as everyone else. Ah well, he should have had the sense to surrender instead of trying to escape across an open field.

—from *Bluefeather Fellini*

Taking the wallet and the money brought the war home to Max.

"You can call them Nazis or murderers or anything you want. This guy wasn't. This young soul was a young guy just starting out and he had a family and loved them just like I did mine. And I shot the bastard. He was just like me. I had a kid over on the ranch in *The Hi Lo Country*, too. He had two Sharons. I had one."

There was a poker game a day or two later, and Max used the German's money in the pot.

"It was (somber) like the Last Supper," he recalls. "I tried to clean this money. I borrowed money to buy gasoline to try to clean the blood off it.

"I'd throw this money in the pot, and I won every damn thing that day. They kept throwing my money back to me— that blood money. You could still smell it."

Now it was Bluefeather's turn to ante up, and he, too, pitched the stained bill back in the pot.

The three remaining players stared hard at the note. Bluefeather tried not to acknowledge it, but even he couldn't help noticing the pinkish stain across one end. His eyes kept moving from the dirty end to the clean one. Back and forth. He shuddered suddenly and felt like the pink stain was spreading all over his body. The other players got up and walked away. He sat alone. Jesus H. Christmas Christ! He was becoming immune even to the blood of the dead—by his own hand, no less. He had to stop this numbing of his soul before it was too late. Too late?

—from *Bluefeather Fellini*

"Finally, I took $20 (of it) and sent it to my wife (Helene). I told her to change this money into a good bill and just hand it to the first wino she came across.

I don't know if she ever did. She never talked about it."

At the end of the war, the pictures and the Russian knife came home with Max.

"The thing that bothered me wasn't shooting that guy so much as it was those damn pictures."

Fifty years later, Max gave the photos and the knife to Frank Dubois, the New Mexico Secretary of Agriculture and the founder of *The Rounders* Award.

"There'd never been an award like this, named for a book, and it was my book," Max says, "so one day I thought I'd give him something that was so precious to me that there are no words for it."

Max smiles. "Besides, I didn't want to be tempted to look at the pictures of that poor bastard going on a picnic with his family again."

All this time, the concussion of the railroad gun had been doing its work. Max's equilibrium would betray him without notice. He fell. He became nauseated. It was a private war inside a very public one.

"By November, the snow had come, and those goddamned cold winds, and that's when the cold hit those nerves in my head. I started falling into trees then.

"They finally took us back to give us a hot bath. I never said anything was wrong with me. I never bitched about it at all. Anyway, after that shower, we got hauled all the way back up to that damned snow in the Ardennes.

"We crawled into those shelters. During the day the snow would melt and run into the foxhole, and a night it would freeze, so each day you had to raise the level of the foxhole with sticks.

"We were shot at every minute. When we got back, there was a new lieutenant, named Evans. One of the strangest coincidences of my life.

"The world was whirling when I got up there and I was puking all over myself. I couldn't help it. I just crawled into one of those shelters.

"I couldn't talk much. Lt. Evans said you have to go back. I complained, and he said I'm giving you a direct order.

"This was embarrassing. I got back and was in a hospital. There were so many wounded men in there. I thought I was going to die."

In England, Max was first hospitalized. But this was kinda tame, so he and another guy "escaped" for a week on the town. They caught the other guy. Max sneaked back in. After that, they sent him out with a crew working on telephone lines. He was halfway up one of these poles and fell. After that, he was reassigned.

"I missed the Battle of the Bulge by two or three days," he says. "I would've been dead, of course. The medics gave me a test in England and told me I was going home. I agreed with them."

Max spent five or six weeks in a hospital in San Antonio, Texas, and then they discharged him and sent him home to *The Hi Lo Country*.

At the time of his discharge, Max was a private, first class. This was solely because Congress passed a law saying anyone who had been in combat four months or longer was automatically promoted. They also got the blue Combat Infantryman's Badge. The greatest of all medals, Max says. "It's for survival. Generals wear it above all their other noticeables."

But Max was at least a private, first class . . . duly promoted by an act of Congress. He laughs over it today.

When PFC Max Evans was released from the Army, he had been through three major battles, suffered from an inner-ear problem that would stick with him the rest of his life, and carried in his pocket the only medal he believed in: the blue Combat Infantryman's Badge.

Helene and Sharon had been living with Max's parents in Morton, Texas, during the war, and now he went to Morton to pick up his family. While there, his father gave him a brand-new Dodge pickup as a way of welcoming him back from the war. Also, typically, W. B. paid for most of it, but left some of it for Max to pay for.

He also gave Max the money to buy a pair of boots and a new hat.

"I knew, even then," Max says, "that Helene and I weren't going to make it, but I wanted to give it a real try."

So he took his wife and daughter, Sharon, hat, boots, and new Dodge pickup, and drove back to the ranch near Des Moines, New Mexico, in *The Hi Lo Country*.

Home Again

❧ **Before the war,** Max had hunted coyotes with hounds, and he did so after the war as well. But on his return to *The Hi Lo Country*, he discovered that one of his hound-dog-neighbor pals hadn't made it back.

"Daz Rankin was sure a good guy. Before the war, he had one hound and I had three, and sometimes we'd run them together.

"Daz got drafted, and I suggested we go on one final coyote hunt, horseback. Well, that sounded good to him, and to me, too. We mounted up early one morning.

"The way we did it," Max said, "you run a long line through a ring on a dog's collar and hold onto both ends. Then when you want to release him, you just let go of one end. The last thing you want a hound to do is chase rabbits. That can ruin 'em forever.

"Well, Daz and me were riding out there, and I knew our chances of catching a coyote that day weren't good. So I said let's let 'em run rabbits. We did, and we had a great time. Lots of fun.

"Well, ol' Daz got killed in Europe. Machine-gun caught him right in the middle. They put him in a body cast, but he died."

One evening shortly after his return to Helene, Sharon, and *The Hi Lo Country*, Max and Helene went to Daz's parents' home to play cards.

"Mrs. Rankin looked terrible," Max said. "and during the evening she started crying. Well, that's when I did something really stupid and it's always bothered me ever since.

"I was hoping to make her feel a little better, so I said, 'Miz Rankin, I hunted with Daz the last time we were together and I knew him well, and I can tell you that he'd rather be dead than be bad crippled like he was gonna be.'

"That was not the right thing to say. She began screaming and carrying on and crying harder, and she yelled at me that that just wasn't true, that he would've wanted to come home even if he was badly disabled.

"She just wanted him back any way she could, naturally. Well, we had to leave then. That has always bothered me. I'm gonna apologize to Mrs. Rankin when I see her in the next reincarnation. I hope ol' Daz is there when I do it."

Des Moines

When I got back from the war and was discharged, I wasn't in very good shape. That head thing bothered me so much. I could maybe get one good meal a day down, but mostly I couldn't eat because I'd just puke it up again. I was so dumb I just pretended I had a weak stomach. Hell, I could eat the hottest bowl of venison chile ever made and ask for more through the tears. I should have admitted it.

But still I had to run around and do things. I was just so dizzy. I couldn't really plan anything because I might run into a tree or a brick wall or fall down.

—Max Evans

The death of Daz Rankin wasn't the only thing that had changed during Max's three-year absence from *The Hi Lo Country*. Ranchers who had been nearly starving when Max went off to war now found themselves with a lot of money, a lot of cattle, and a very short memory.

"The big ranchers were trying to crowd me out," Max says. "All but A. D. Weatherly. They wanted my water. They hadn't wanted my water before the war because they were all so worried about keeping their ranches and paying for them. They were all about to lose their ranches then. Well, the price of cattle just kept going up and going up (during the war) and all they had to do was sell the cattle. So I get back from the war and all of a sudden they're all rich, brilliant bastards."

"I had to do day work for other ranches: breaking horses, fixing fence, that kind of work. Had to do it. I didn't like the idea of doing day work any more, so I decided to sell."

And there were other considerations, as well.

Things weren't the same between Max and Helene. As with many young couples separated by years, thousands of miles, and very startlingly different circumstances, Max and Helene had cooled toward each other. They tried to piece the ranch life back together again, but things didn't work.

"Basically," Max says, "we were out there in the middle of nowhere on this ranch, and things got to be difficult between us. I'm sure not going to blame her. It isn't her fault. And I was wild and crazy, and that didn't help any, either. But I think the real reason we drew apart is that I was just basically an artist in many different forms. I couldn't help it. It's a genetic thing, I think. And . . . and a spiritual one even more.

"I'd point things out to Helene about the house," Max says, "but she didn't understand. She got to where she wouldn't say anything. I don't know if she was blanking her mind to something she had no comprehension of, or what, exactly. As a matter of fact, that's probably where our separation began, right then. I couldn't communicate with her. There wasn't any spiritual communication, in addition to the art. Even though she was a helluva woman. She was my high school sweetheart and she had a beautiful singing voice and I got along real well with her dad. But I think a lot of the reason we got married was lust. I wasn't even eighteen when we got married. Now I still care for her and people still love her over there. They like her a lot better than they do me. You know where all the blame goes. And that's fine. It should be. I deserve it. Every bit of it. And I earned every bit of it having a helluva time. I mean I sure did."

Max came back from the hell of war with a burning ambition to paint, to express himself in the matters of life, death,

Max's first child, Sharon, playing in the ranch yard near Des Moines (Hi Lo), N.M., about 1946.

love, passion. It wasn't enough before the war to be content with watching cattle grow, and a long absence from the lonely plains and an immersion in the caldron of terror in Europe didn't help.

One day a half-Indian man named Bid Littrell rode his horse the eleven miles to the ranch and Max asked him in for coffee.

Littrell said, "I hear you want to sell this place." Max said, "Yeah." Littrell asked what the best offer for the place had been and then offered Max a dollar more an acre for it.

"That was it," Max said. "That's all the time it took. It was that fast."

So Max bought 120 acres on the edge of Des Moines with two houses on it. It was along the railroad tracks between Des Moines and Folsom, New Mexico

"It had good water on it," Max says, "and it was the perfect place for painting. I could live in one house and paint in the other. That way the painting wouldn't bother Helene. Some women are like that. Some accept the painting and some don't."

So now Max had come to town where he could concentrate more on his passion than his pasture. While there may not be too many people who consider a 120-acre ranch to be a town place, it was for Max.

In his fiction, Des Moines was always Hi Lo.

Hi Lo is a little cow town—population of about one hundred and fifty—on a long piece of pavement from way down somewhere in Texas into, and across, northern New Mexico. To the south of town is Sierra Grande Mountain. Some claim it to be the largest lone mountain in the world. It is forty-five miles around the base and about nine thousand feet high. It takes a full day to hunt around its edges. To the north, east, and west is rolling grama-covered rangeland broken now and then by a steep, jagged, malpai-studded canyon—the Currumpah. There were two grocery stores, Chick Johnson's small hotel, two cafés, an all-night service station and two bars. The bars are the busiest places in town. The ranchers, cowboys, and odd-job boys—like me and Tom C.—all hang out there when they come to town. They do a little drinking—sometimes a lot of drinking—and catch up on the gossip, find out who won the latest street fights, and other such sporting activities.

Not all the work of a cowboy takes place on a horse. Here Max and Ray Vigil fix a water gap near Kim, Colorado, in 1972.

The bars are directly across the street from each other: the Wild Cat to the south, the Double Duty to the north. It was very convenient for all concerned. If a fight started in front of one, the customers of both places had what you might call ringside seats. If a feller was a little wobbly on his feet and wished to change company, he could just aim himself right straight across the highway and he would be pretty sure to hit a bull's-eye as far as bars are concerned. There wasn't enough traffic in those days to worry about the odds of getting run over.

The wind blows in Hi Lo at least two-thirds of the time. It comes howling around the Sierra Grande Mountain in a grass-bending fury. I think the reason so many fistfights break out is because the people are all on edge from bucking this infernal wind. In fact, after all these decades I've had to think about it, I know that's the main reason.

—from *Old Bum*

During this post-war period, Max worked at painting, of course, but earned money by helping his hunting buddy, Tom Creswell, with stone masonry. Together they hunted coyotes.

One quiet day in Des Moines, Max was standing on the highway with "Uncle Tom" Creswell, and they saw a tall, wiry man come out of Waterhole Number One (directly across the street from Waterhole Number Two, Des Moines' other bar. Number One was remembered in Max's fiction as the Wildcat Bar). As they watched, this man walked up to an old Model A Ford, threw it into gear, and backed it up. He backed it up, says Max, "all the way around this huge block there, and just as hard as he could go. I was fascinated and said so to Uncle Tom at the time.

"Who the hell is that guy? I asked, with great admiration in my voice. That, said Uncle Tom, is Benny Padilla, from Folsom, my only competitor in stone masonry in this country. And I said, I have to meet this magnificent man someday."

Creswell told Max this would not be a problem, as they shared certain . . . traits, and favorite places, such as the Waterholes, and that a meeting would be inevitable.

"My admiration for him was almost endless after seeing him back that Model A clear around the block before straightening it out and heading for home," Max says. "I realize this was an alcohol-enhanced performance, of course, but my faith in Benny became so strong I just know he could've done it cold sober, too."

Naturally, the meeting soon took place and another instant lifelong friendship emerged between the soldier-turned-cowboy and the lanky Hispanic stone mason, cemented forever by alcohol, fights, and a deep and abiding love.

"Maximiliano!" Benny cried, each time he saw Max. It was always his name for Max.

"Now that could either be a real insult with Mexican people," Max says, "because they hated that French bastard so much down there in Mexico, or it could be a compliment. I always figured Benny meant it in a friendly way. He had a strange kind of dignity, and was maybe in his early forties then. He and I became drinking friends. I don't want you to think he was a drunk, because he wasn't. He was a hard worker and a dedicated artist with those stones, but he played hard, too. And whenever I heard he was in town, I showed up and the fun started. "

Benny, says Max, was one of the toughest men he'd ever known. At one time, a calf roper named J. C. King was made a sheriff's deputy and sent to Des Moines to pour cold water on some of the booze-begun battles. King would ask Max's advice about how to bring certain of the hell raisers to heel, and Max, who had fought about all of them at this point, usually had some suggestions. One time, J. C. asked Max about Benny, and how to best handle Benny in an altercation.

"I held out my trigger finger," Max says, "and I made a little ocean wave movement like this, like it was on a corrugated tin roof. I told him this is what Benny's head is like. I told J. C. I had absolutely no idea how anyone could handle Benny. About three days later, as brave as J. C. was, and as smart as J. C. was, and as understanding as J. C. was, he quit the job."

Benny Padilla had a favorite story about "Maximiliano." In a day and a place where a shot of whiskey cost a quarter, Benny always bragged about the day when he and Max went on an $86 drunk.

"Now that was one day, in one bar," says Max, laughing. "And that wasn't easy to do in those days."

So, the question obviously presents itself here. Did Max and Benny consume $86 worth of booze by themselves, or did they help other people out of sobriety, too?

"Well, hell," Max says, laughing, "I don't remember. You think I could remember anything after a day like that? I never did get that straight, and I never did want to get that straight. Benny had a great way of talking. I wish I could write as well as he could talk. But that one day in a little country bar cemented our friendship forever."

That one day must have been memorable to at least one bartender in Des Moines. And the friendship between Max and Benny never faltered, right on through the years and the fights and through Benny's first two deaths.

I'd never had trouble or had a fight in Des Moines until after I got back from the war. This guy from Capulin (New Mexico), about twice my size, was in there one night and we were having fun. I didn't know he was a bully.

He took his glasses off and came over and said something awful. Don't even remember what it was, now. So I said well, OK, if I'm going to have to do this the rest of my life, I'd just as well start with you.

I knocked that bastard up and down the sidewalk. Nobody there ever saw me fight before. A crowd gathered around there and I beat that sucker, slowly. Didn't want to hurt him too bad.

I found out he used to come over from Capulin and beat on people and get away with it. So I just beat the shit out of him. I told him not to come back to Des Moines.

It made me a lot of friends, but it also caused a lot of bad feelings with some people who wanted to challenge me.

—Max Evans

It Was Just a Windy Night
In a Windy Little Cow Town . . .

"I don't know how it happens," Max says. "I don't think anyone knows how it happens. Well, yes I do. There's a psychic thing that happens. I can't say I don't know about it but I can't explain it. You hit town and here'd come another guy. And it might be the middle of the damn week. Out there in that country, in those days, almost nobody had telephones. There wasn't any radio. Nobody really had any kind of communication, really, in those days. But no matter how it happened, sometimes the people just came to town. They would pick it up out of the damned air. And there ain't no other way about it. I saw it happen too many times. These people would all come in and the party would start."

The parties involved booze, laughter, card games, once in a great while some illicit romance, and fights.

"The boys were back," says Max, "the ones who had survived the war, and they were a little wild. The fistfights were mainly for fun. Most of them were caused by ducking the wind, playing in the wind, working in the damn wind. You couldn't really get out of the wind in those little ol' bars, 'cause some sumbitch would open the door and let it in. That wind drove us all a little crazy. So there was a lot of fist-fighting and hell-raising, but it was mostly in fun. I can't think of much else to do there. You can look up and down that street and it'd be like a gun barrel. You could stand out there in that damned wind on that street for an hour and not see anything at all except maybe a car from Texas headed to Colorado.

"So this one night the people came to town," Max says. "This time Big Boy wasn't there, but Luz Martinez was there, and Benny Padilla, and the bar filled up. Now people didn't bring women into the bars in those days. Hardly ever. But Luis Martinez, L-u-i-s, had a little sheep ranch out there and he was there that night with his wife, Temy. She was the sister of Emilio Cruz, a tough sonofabitch, who had fixed some guys pretty good.

"So here we are, raising hell and having fun, and Luz was having a good time. He was my art partner and later became a famous santero. Followed me to Taos. You know.

"Ol' Luz got pretty damn drunk and nervous and ran out there and grabbed Temy and they were dancing. Whirling all over that room, and Luz yelling and jumping about a yard high all over the damn floor. He tried doing one of those jitterbugs and let go of her, and she crashed into one of those booths. Luis thought Luz had thrown her and was going to start something, so I went over and told him it was an accident and to let it go. So he invited me outside. He wasn't mad, he was grinning, but he meant it.

"His mistake was he was standing out there by a curb about fifteen inches high, so I ran out there and whacked him. He went out there on that highway so hard it tore up his Levis, and his knees. Pretty bad, too. Well, then, things started to happen. Benny's still in the bar, watching. Luz is so drunk he doesn't even know what's going on.

"It was just a windy night in a windy little cow town. Benny came out and started yelling, and Emilio Cruz came out, and he was upset over what I did to his brother-in-law. I decided to leave, so I got in my car. But my window was down and Emilio came over and hit me right square in the teeth through that window. Chipped them both. Finally had gold put on 'em. I thought, how dumb . . . never leave the window down again.

"And the car door wasn't closed, so when I backed up, the door came open and caught Temy and dragged her all the way out on the highway. Peeled her pretty good. I decided maybe she was dead, so I circled the block just like Benny did. Only forward. I went around that block real slow, and when I got back around there I saw Benny after Temy's brother. And coming up behind Benny was the other brother, holding a knife, and figuring to stab ol' Benny in the back. Well, I honked the horn and stepped on the gas and went to run over the brother with the knife. He heard me coming and jumped out of the way . . . mostly. The car whacked him pretty good and the knife flew out of his hand. I slammed on the brakes and yelled at Benny.

"He recognized my voice and said, 'Hey, what's going on, Maximiliano?' I said I think I just killed your friend here. He was fixing to stab you in the back."

So about that time, the run-over, would-be knifer started moaning, so Max and Benny decided to take him over to the local doctor, Dr. W. This was the middle of the night, and both Dr. W. and his wife, who was also his nurse, were drunk and asleep, which was not an uncommon occurrence.

Mrs. W. made coffee for the doctor, and Max and Benny carried in what was left of the midnight miscreant and laid him on the examining table. Later, he regained consciousness and the doctor said the only thing he could find wrong was a broken leg. Max and Benny were happy about that and left him there with the doctor and drove back to town.

"And you know," Max says, "there wasn't one single sonofabitch on the street. It was all over. It was done. We just drove home. That was just a nice little night in *The Hi Lo Country*.

"I just thought of it as good fun. Nobody ever held a grudge over it, either. Except those brothers from Folsom."

An Irreconcilable Difference?

Now let's take stock a minute here. Max is now no longer a cattleman. He is an artist with virtually no customers. He has two houses, one of which he paints in because painting bothers Helene. He finds a friend in just about any kind of bottled spirits, and fist fights are considered—by Max anyway—as aerobic exercise and a lot of fun.

It was about this time, Max says, that he noticed his marriage to Helene becoming "somewhat strained."

There was one incident in particular, he says, that stretched the bonds of love between them just a little.

"I'd gone into Raton one night with a buddy of mine, Tommy Jones, and we had a helluva time, drinking and making the bars. Tommy was the son of Pete Jones who had a good little outfit about ten miles east of Des Moines. I did a lot of day labor for them as well as breaking out a string of broncs for their riding and working pleasure."

Max and Tommy tasted the liquid pleasures of Raton until the doors were locked, and then started driving the thirty miles back east to Des Moines. It was about three in the morning by this time.

"Now, normally there's nothing going on in Des Moines at that time of the night, but we were surprised to see a light on in one of the two bars. So naturally we stopped in to see what was up. And there was this old friend of mine in there who had come up from Santa Fe to go deer hunting. It was Robert Castner, the New Mexico State Auditor, and the bartender was Bill Malone, an ex-prize fighter from Denver. They'd been friends in college. First thing you know, they're buying us doubles."

*The morning Max shot up the little cowtown of Des Moines, NM,
his companion was Tommy Jones, shown here with one of Max's
coyote-hunting greyhounds. This was one of littermate greyhounds,
"the only registered dogs I ever had," Max says.*

Any bodily pain felt by any of the participants had been thoroughly anaesthetized by this time.

This bartender was willing to stretch the state bar-closing law a bit for friends (especially when one was the state auditor), but when the sun came up, he decided the party was over.

But Max wasn't through hoorawing yet.

"I decided to wake up the town, so I got a gun out of the car and shot out six or seven plate glass windows. Then we got in the car and I ran over seven or eight mailboxes."

But eight dead mailboxes and some glass shards and screams of terror hadn't sated this partygoer's thirst for fun. About this time, Max remembered the new guy down at the gas station. Nobody, he says, liked the new guy. Something, of course, had to be done about that.

"He was always open about this time of day," Max says, "so we figured to just drive on down there and run the sonofabitch over."

But when the car with the two drunks in it hove into sight, the new guy at the gas station dove for cover. They missed him.

"All I did," Max says, "was sideswipe the gas pump. This made the car kinda spin around."

While the car was busy spinning, it managed to take out a big billboard next to the gas station and careened right on downhill to the start of Max's own driveway.

"So I drove down the hill into the flat near the house before the car died. Then I climbed out the car window. And here came Helene. She's coming and screaming at me and yelling and running across that field in her nightgown. Now I had a .38 Special in the house, and she had that and was pointing it at me. I grabbed for it and got it just as she pulled the trigger. The hammer came down on the web of skin between my thumb and forefinger. After I'd got the hammer of the .38 loose from the web of skin, I followed Helene up to the house to meekly apologize for carrying fun too far. I said, 'Tommy, you might as well spend the night,' and glanced back. Tommy must have seen that the sun was rising clean and blazing pure, because my glance showed him just hitting the edge of town in a dead run. It had been quite a trip for Tommy. It was a quarter of a mile to town, mostly uphill.

"Years later," Max said, "Tommy made Greyhound bus driving a career, headquartered in Albuquerque. I heard he was recovering from a heart attack at St. Vincent's Hospital in Santa Fe. So I called him and said, 'Tommy, I know how you got that belated heart attack.' 'Yeah?' he said. 'It was that uphill run into Des Moines that set you up for it.' 'You're right,' he said, 'but I was unarmed.' Ol' Tommy Jones went on to live durn near as long as me."

In the meantime, Max had followed Helene up to the house, apologizing every step.

"So then she went into the kitchen and came back with a great big ol' butcher knife. She missed me and stuck that sumbitch right through the wall. I was trying to pull it out of the wall and she was beating me on the back of the head. I threw one elbow back to get her off so I could get the knife and throw it away. I didn't know it, but I'd knocked her silly. I carried her to bed, then went and hid all the knives in the house before I lay down for a nap."

Understandably, wrecking the community of Des Moines had not gone unnoticed.

A little later, a couple of state police officers came to take Max to jail. He asked them if he could appear before the local judge. They said he could if he would agree to abide by the judge's decision. He agreed. He had always liked the judge and whenever he was in town took him a half-pint of Kentucky whisky, which he relished.

"Now this judge was like one of them Kentucky colonels, a real gentleman, you know? Wore a long black coat even on the hottest day in the year," Max says. "So we go before him and they read all the charges and hell, I'm guilty all right. Then this judge gives a speech, telling these police officers that (since I had just returned from the war) I represent the spirit of the country and gives this very eloquent speech with this magical voice. I can't believe I'm hearing all these wondrous words. It became a kind of music to me."

The upshot of it was that Max wouldn't have to go to jail in the county seat in Clayton if he fulfilled certain conditions. He had to replace the billboard, replace the gas pump, replace the broken windows, replace the mailboxes, and apologize to everyone concerned.

"Which meant the whole town," Max says.

Two other things: Max had to get this all done by sundown, and the judge would accompany him to make sure he did it all.

"I guess they figured there was no way I could get it all done by then," Max says. "But he only said that for the benefit of the police, because he stayed and consumed a whole pint of Kentucky whisky that I bought him on credit before doing my sworn duty of putting the town back together. But I did. I mean, all of it. The whole thing. I had to hire and bribe and threaten several sinners to help get it done."

After that, he mostly walked back and forth to the bars.

"Luz Martinez, my artist pal, and I mostly just sang and yelled. I sorta settled down."

But that didn't stop the problems at home.

"That day," he says, "kinda became a dividing point between me and Helene. And justifiably so. The woman could not have been more right. I could have been a little bit more wrong, but it would have taken a better man than me to do so."

There were so many wild sonsabitches in that little bitty place that I didn't really stand out. I don't think I was that different. (The residents) kinda put up with us.

Some of the other guys got killed and died, and I just got wilder.

—Max Evans

And, while his marriage to Helene became more and more strained, he found a lifelong friend in Luz Martinez. Luz, Max says, "was the only other person in that country who gave a damn about art at the time."

Luz had begun his career as a "primitive santero," one who depicts artistic images of the saints for religious purposes. The art form goes back to before the Spanish first arrived in what would eventually become New Mexico and quickly became respected in the Roman Catholic Church. Later, it was discovered by the Santa Fe art community, and collecting santos became the "in" thing to do. Luz was very good at making santos. Very poor, but very skilled.

Max laughs these days about the naïveté both these young artists shared when they first met. All they knew was they wanted to paint and were best friends. Luz was doing mostly cartoons when they met. Max had almost no training in art at that time and was still trying to find his "voice" in the medium.

Levi Gomez (the character Max created based on Luz Martinez), a part-Spanish, part-Apache, part-French, part . . . I don't know what . . . artist friend, was showing me some santos (standing figures of saints) he had carved from cedar. He told me that some people knocked down as much as twenty bucks apiece for such like. I was somewhat amazed at this. A few days later I read in the Saturday Evening Post about a cowboy artist called Charlie Russell receiving thousands of dollars for just one painting. This seemed like a good idea to me. Why shouldn't a rock mason/coyote/coon hunter have just as good a chance at getting rich and famous as a dumb-ass cowboy? I know it sounds stupid now, but during those old times at Hi Lo I believed almost everything was possible.

So Levi and I discussed things over a quart of good brown whiskey and decided we would set up a studio and get rich. We sure did the first, but we missed the last by a country mile.

Next door to the Double Duty bar (that's the one across the street) was an ugly old building held together by a bunch of brown rusted tin. We rented one end of this for fifteen dollars a month.

I bought a lot of paint in little metal tubes, some brushes made out of camel hair, a sketch pad and a few canvas boards, and started painting horses and cowboys. You talk about going crazy. For a while it was hard to tell which was the horse and which was the cowboy. Whenever I finished a picture, I would tack it up on the wall at a fancy price. I had gone that silly. No one else in that country did any serious painting. We soon found out that the citizens of Hi Lo didn't have much interest in art of any kind, so we went it all alone.

We got an idea that we might attract a little tourist trade if we had a sign. So Levi painted us a fancy one, and we nailed it up on the front of the building. We called our place "Ye Olde Masters Art Gallery." Nobody ever stopped by. It took a while for us to catch on to the dearth of cultural interest along Highway 87 at that time.

—from Old Bum

The Two Deaths of Benny Padilla

"Luz and I formed a little company," Max says, chuckling. "We signed everything he did and I did 'Evans and Martinez.' We didn't know you couldn't do things like that, so we just did it. We were just partners."

Max moved Luz into the spare house, the one where the painting was taking place, and these two friends lived a strange life of art in the middle of a vast grassland where most people couldn't care less. It must've made for interesting stories around Des Moines.

One of the more interesting stories around Des Moines took place one hot summer night when Benny Padilla died the first two times.

"Me and ol' Big Boy," Max says, "were standing on the corner there, waiting to get into a poker game, and this kid comes running up saying Benny Padilla is dead. We followed the kid down there and there was ol' Benny. I thought somebody had knocked him in the head or he'd died of a heart attack or something. I felt him for a pulse but couldn't find any on him. I told Wiley we'd just as well take the body over to Folsom to Benny's brother, Felix, who owned the local bar there."

Felix had a peg leg, Max says, but was bigger than Benny, even, and had "guns and clubs all over the place and wasn't afraid to use them."

Max met Felix one day when he was driving through Folsom and heard the sweet Texas swing music of Bob Wills and the Texas Playboys singing "San Antonio Rose" coming out the open door of the bar.

"I don't know what there was about that song," Max says, "but it always touched me. I thought it was the most beautiful song. My leg jumped over on that brake and that pickup threw gravel around, and I stayed there five days. Never left that bar. Me and Felix wore that record out. He got a cot for me. People would come and go but me and Felix were still there."

So this was the guy who should be receiving the dead body of his brother, Max thought, and he was already dreading having to tell Felix of the tragedy. So Max and Big Boy picked up Benny's body and kinda (since he was already dead) tossed it into the back of the pickup and drove to Folsom.

"In those days that was a real crooked corrugated old road," Max says. "Before you got to Folsom there was a creek with a little ol' bridge over it. Just as we got to that creek, I happened to look back and there was Benny sitting up. I yelled at Big Boy. 'Benny's alive!'

"He slammed on the brakes just as we hit that bridge. And when he did that, I heard something hit the cab. When we got out, Benny was gone. He just wasn't there. Ol' Big Boy takes off up the creek to the west, circling, just like any old cowboy would do, looking for tracks. I checked, too, and we couldn't find any sign of him.

"So we started looking back east on the creek. And evidently when Benny hit that cab, he flew out of the back of the truck and landed in the creek. We'd gone the wrong way. We found him lying there face down in three or four inches of water and he wasn't moving. We went over there and got him by the heels and drug him out.

"We felt around on him for a pulse and couldn't find any. I told Big Boy I think he's really dead this time. And Big Boy said he figured it that way, too. We drug him off up the hill to the truck, but we did turn him over so it wouldn't scar his face, anyway. He never moved. Never kicked. Nothing. We got him in that truck and I thought, my God this is awful. We misjudged this and that poor sonofabitch was alive. Somebody was going to get away with knocking him in the head, and we killed him. And what were we gonna tell his brother? We weren't even armed.

"So anyway we drove up there to Folsom and got out, and ol' Benny crawled out of the truck and went in the bar with us. We just followed him right in there.

"He yelled, 'Hey, the drinks are on me for my good *compadres* Maximiliano and Beeg Boy!' in that wonderful accent of his. I didn't know what to do. He either never remembered what happened to him in Des Moines, or wouldn't tell, and he didn't remember us drowning him in the creek, and we never told him.

"That Benny Padilla was tough. You just couldn't kill him. The Good Lord finally decided to make an angel out of him one day, and in a way he already was, because he'd been dead twice in one day."

Benny Padilla was immortalized in *The Hi Lo Country* as Delfino Mondragon, both in the novel and in the movie.

The Coyote's Brother

Coyotes have staked an enormous spiritual claim on me, because I realized that, all through my life, I've been surviving just like a damn coyote.

Different people have actually nicknamed me—for a few months at a time—"the old coyote." I was honored, deeply honored.

—Max Evans

✂ **Tell a Max Evans fan** that the first story he ever had published was about coyotes, and there will just be a smile and a nod. Naturally, they'll think.

Ironically, it was about hunting them, over near Des Moines in *The Hi Lo Country*, and it was for *The Denver Post* for June 11, 1950, and was called "The Killer On the Currumpah."

Max, along with his hunting partner, Tom Creswell, had earned extra money by ridding ranches in the area of coyotes. Coyotes aren't very big, but they are very smart and almost always hungry. Sheep and calves, they learned, are often much easier to catch and pull down than antelope and deer. Max and Tom hunted the coyotes with dogs. Ranchers paid them for each coyote they killed, and they also sold the hides for extra money.

When I think of the Killer now, I see red. You will understand my deep and abiding hatred for this coyote when you know some of the events that preceded our meeting. The irony of this is that I admire the hell out of the coyote's cunning and courage. . . .

My heart was beginning to race now as I thought of the chase ahead. We burst over the top of the little hill. I saw him not over a hundred yards below. Evidently he had never been run because he stopped quickly and turned broadside to us. I slammed on the brakes and Tom jumped out to turn the dogs loose.

We had a wooden crate in the back of the pickup with a team of dogs in each of two sections. Tom chose the side that held Pug and Brownie, our two best. They both hit the ground running straight for the coyote. The coyote wasn't standing still now, he was running for his life.

In an instant, we saw that he was headed for the rocks of the Currumpah. Tom jumped in the pickup, and we

Ol' Pug was more than a great coyote hound, he was Max's favorite. Together with other dogs, Ol' Pug rid the Hi Lo Country of many coyotes after World War II. This photo was taken of Max and Pug in Union County, NM, around 1946.

tore off after them as fast as we could without endangering our lives. The other dogs in the crate were barking to get out as we raced across the prairies.

"Ole Brownie's gainin' on him!" Tom screamed. Just when it looked as thought the coyote would make it to the canyon, Brownie seemed to put on an extra burst of speed. He was right on him now. The coyote's tail was whipping from side to side, a sure sign he was straining to do his utmost. Brownie came upon him then, right up to his neck.

He reached over and locked his powerful jaws just behind the ears and threw him. Brownie turned a somersault as he and the coyote hit the ground together. The coyote never had a chance to get up again, for he hardly hit the ground until ole Pug was on him too.

He was dead when we got there, but the dogs, in their rage, were still working on him.

> —from "The Killer On The Currumpah"

Later in this story, the reader learns that one particular coyote, dubbed the Killer, inadvertently causes the death of Max's dog, Brownie. It is a fairly straightforward outdoor story about this strange little side industry in cattle country. And it was the first pickle out of the writing jar for Max Evans. It brought him $25.

Max wrote several more non-fiction coyote-hunting yarns over the next few years, too. This was, after all, an exciting kind of adventure, and Max had been a pro at it. And with even the very first story, his respect for the coyote is obvious. Later, that respect would change dramatically into a lifelong kinship.

And even when Max first broke into novels, the coyote was there, too.

In *The Rounders*, Max has Dusty convincing his friend, Vince Moore, that buying a horse named Old Fooler is just the thing for an old coyote-hunter like him.

> "Now, Vince," I said, "You know how it is when one of them old hound dogs of yours, especially the one that can kill by hisself, gets in hot and heavy after a coyote."

"Yeah," Vince said, wiping his mouth with a creased, rough hand. "Yeah, I know."

"Well," I said, "you want to get in on the kill worse than anything else in the world. Ain't that right?"

"Yeah," he said, scratching his chin and blinking them little pig eyes that was something like Wrangler's, only redder.

"You haven't got any more worries about being there when you ride Old Fooler. . . ."

"I ain't got a dime to my name," said Vince, moving that big rusty hand back up to his hair. "Not a penny."

"Good Lord, Vince, you didn't think I was wantin' money, did you? Here, hit me another slug of that wonderful stuff. All I want would be eight jugs of this stuff. It's gonna be a long winter down at the lower camp."

"Yeah, and dry," Wrangler said.

"Jim Ed said it was dry as a snuffbox down there. The snow don't stay on the ground a tall," I raved. I could see them little red eyes just strainin' with the effort to think.

"Well, I don't know, boys," he said.

I had one of them sinking feelings like I had been fell on by a thousand-pound bronc. I knew if I waited till morning, and Vince sobered up, he would never agree to the swap. I was a desperate cowboy. Just then nature lent me a kind, helping hand. About a mile to the north a coyote let out a howl, and all the dogs jumped up and went to barking and raising hell. I saw quick-like that Vince's blood was really pumping and singing him a song. Yes sir. The old coyote fever was on him.

That's when I put the clincher to him. "Vince, you can catch that yappin' son of a gun an hour after sunrise tomorrow and be right there when the old red dog puts the big bite on him." For a minute the red eyes went blank. Then they shone out real bright.

"It's a deal!" he said. . . .

After a while Vince said it was time to turn in, and slumped forward with his head on the table and went to sleep, the proud owner of one hell of a piece of horseflesh.

Me and Wrangler stumbled out to our bedrolls and said good night to the stars.

—from *The Rounders*

Max's brotherhood with the coyote didn't happen completely in one day. It grew slowly through observation and through the closeness any hunter sooner or later begins to feel with his prey.

"One day I was horseback out on the ranch, on the edge of a long malpais mesa, and I saw this coyote loping out across this big pasture," Max says. "Just loping, loping along.

"Finally I saw this jackrabbit, maybe a hundred yards ahead of him. Did that coyote think he was going to run that born runner down? He was letting him get too far out in front there. He'd never catch him that way.

"Then I saw he was actually running that rabbit in a circle. Great big circle. And that rabbit didn't even realize it.

"Out there a long ways was this other coyote, lying behind a yucca. Just lying there, waiting. Well, here comes that rabbit, running along, and when that rabbit came about thirty feet away from that yucca, this other coyote gets up and starts loping along behind the rabbit.

"Now that first coyote, he goes and lies down behind that same yucca and rests.

"That old rabbit was really beginning to weaken. There was some kind of radar going on between those two coyotes. They ran that rabbit down and killed him without ever getting in a strain.

"Now I thought this must be a (mated) pair hunting for some pups, but it wasn't. The two of them ate the damn thing right there. Shared the meal. Just one of those magical things that happen sometimes."

As the years passed, Max's respect and admiration for the skills, the instincts, and the sheer nerve of coyotes increased. But still he hunted them.

Until one day.

As with nearly everything in Max's real life, it shows up in his fiction. His epiphany with coyotes was no exception. Max explains what happened in a novella entitled Old Bum, where he resurrected his dog, Brownie, for the hunt.

The wind was whipping the grama grass in golden rhythms. The electricity that generates somewhere in the brain and the heart was sparking fiery impulses through the flesh of my entire being. Old Tom C. was leaning stiffly forward with both of his huge, knobby hands gripping the dashboard with desperate force. They looked as strong and hard as the thousands of rocks they had shaped into beauty and usefulness. His eternally weakening, blue-gray eyes seemed to project tiny rays of light ahead, trying to call back the sight of his younger days. I nearly always spotted our prey first, but when the ancient hunter's blood started pulsing and pumping, Tom C. never quit trying. In these few moments out of eternity, it seemed that we were separated from the usual progression of earth, moon, sun, and stars. It was as if our limited chunk of this hard, wind-agitated land had been removed to another time and galaxy for our own special events of life and death to occur.

I spotted the mother coyote's ears. They were shaped wider, different from the swordlike blades of the large yucca clump she watched us through. I drove on silently, trying to keep all the tearing turmoil in my body from exuding out so the dogs would not pick up the silent message and start raising hell too soon. . . .

The coyote had four pups, three-quarter grown, lying low in the tall grass, but I spotted their outlines because their bodies created a motionless little void in the ocean of wind-dancing stems. She was sure we were going to drive on by and miss her, I knew. We were very close to that point you can never return to or from. That immeasurable portion of space where everything will happen.

I kept my foot easing up and down delicately on the accelerator trying to keep the mother coyote from noticing any untoward movement. I wanted to get exactly between her and the canyon, hoping we could catch her and maybe one of the pups before she could head for the canyon's safety.

Just a few more yards now. The world was a blur of red. There was no breath. The wind had no air for that moment. Then it all exploded at the same precise instant.

I hit the brakes. The mother coyote knew we had spotted them. She whirled, racing east, followed by her scattering pups, who looked back at us in a quick hesitation as they tried to follow their mother's lead and at the same time satisfy their curiosity of our movement. It was a fatal half-second of hesitation. Tom C. jerked the cage rope, and one team of the hounds leapt upon the ground. I jerked the other rope, and now two teams were stretching full out. Their long legs were just graceful, ground-swallowing blurs.

Our timing had been exact as a dagger tip. The first team downed a pup—one by the neck, the other at the brisket. The wind had whipped the battle-dust away by the time Old Pug and Brownie had caught the mother. . . . They rolled completely over twice before Brownie would stand up still crushing the neck. Before the coyote had a chance to rise, Pug was there to secure the prone position and demise of the coyote by crushing the ribs right into the heart and lungs. . . .

I raced afoot across the rolling world towards the kill, driven on by things so old, so deeply rooted, that I would have dived off a twenty-foot bluff without hesitation to be there at the moment of the ultimate. The kill!

Tom C. stumbled along behind, his old heart unable to supply enough air to fuel his movements any faster. Then it happened. My eyes, trained so long to seek out the tiniest form and movement, flashed uncontrollably to the three pups racing for safety over the crest of a hill perhaps an eighth of a mile distant. Two of them disappeared, and thereby lived as their many millions of years of genes instructed them. But one stopped. The universe stopped. Then, as always, it exploded again. The pup, without any hesitation, charged back down the hill gathering speed in its descent heading straight for the trio of Pug, Brownie, and its dying mother. It charged with all the speed of its body, with all its ancient fury, into the two hounds whose combined weight and bulk was at least eight times that of the pup. Its momentum knocked both dogs loose from the mother. It bounced over the dogs in a complete flip, rolling over several times, stumbling up stunned.

The hounds were also momentarily numbed. The pup's action had no place in their world of directed instincts. For an unmeasured space of time, they hesitated. Then all their millions of years of trained genes took control, and they downed the addled pup and killed it almost instantly.

All this had happened before our eyes in just under two minutes. But somehow in that tiny space of clock time, a millennium had whizzed by.

I was still standing motionless, except for the wind pushing me. The act of the coyote pup was beyond any scientific knowledge in existence. I knew I had witnessed a true sacrificial event against all human knowing. I was numbed and humbled beyond speech.

Old Tom C. finally stumbled up beside me, gasping. He, too, had extended his heart's strength as far as it could be crowded without its own final explosion. He hesitantly reached one of his great old hands out to my shoulder for support. It was trembling so that it shook my body, and myself, back to awareness of this present world. His painful, breathing body struggled to keep him upright one more time, through one more hunt. Finally, he was composed enough to stand without using my body as a brace.

Then he said, quietly, "I never saw anything like that in my whole life. Have you, Mark?"

"No," I answered, and the single word was taken away by the wind.

We loaded our dogs and the three dead coyotes—when there should have been, by all the laws, only two. I drove back to town. Neither one of us talked for a spell. We just stared straight and far down the road. I knew I could never hunt coyotes again. Not ever. I didn't.

—from *Old Bum*

"I've had ranchers get angry at me because I can't kill a coyote any more," Max says. "I'll hunt other animals for chile meat, but since that day in *The Hi Lo Country*, I can't kill a coyote. It would be committing suicide.

"At the very best, I'm killing my brother.

Saw an old coyote run across a meadow the other day and I was with Brent (Bason, Jimmy Bason's son). I thought to myself, 'Why, there's my old uncle running across there.' And I instantly started making prayers that Brent wouldn't do what he'd been raised to do. You know he's seen those coyotes eat those calves right out of their mother's womb. As a kid, he'd seen that plenty of times.

And when you see that happen, you know . . . there goes that new hat, or a trip to town, or a Christmas present, all those special things that keep you alive in the world.

I knew that's what was going on in his mind and I made that prayer instantly to try and overcome his thinking. I knew what he was thinking. And it worked. He drove right past that ol' coyote, and I'd never seen him do that before.

—Max Evans

Taos

✿ **Max has a way** of wearing out his welcome in small communities, and Des Moines was no exception. He wore out his welcome and his marriage at about the same time, and by identical methods, and decided to move to Taos: away to the west of the high mesas and windblown grass of Des Moines, over the pass to the west above Cimarron, through the pines and down the other side. That's Taos. Helene and the baby had already left for a life without Max in it, anyway. And there were other reasons.

Taos is a story, a segment of history, a cluster of ancient blended with the new, rituals a thousand years old somehow mixing with wine-and-cheese parties. It is the final resting place of Kit Carson and the birthplace of new ideas.

Taos is one of the Meccas of any artist. Paris . . . then Taos. Taos has air that is unlike anything anywhere. It has a crisp sweetness in the fall, like the first bite of a good apple, that causes people to stare at the sky and be thankful they can live for this moment. The leaves have a starkness in Taos that artists try to capture, make a lot of money in the trying, but still fail. Because Taos, crouching in thick adobe seclusion along a shady creek, is a work of God that man is allowed to share. And the best of the artists come there to try to hitch an artistic ride on this masterpiece.

The handful of famous artists who came to Taos before it had wine and cheese became known as the Taos masters. They made money, had fun, and partied a lot.

So here's Max Evans, who is struggling in Des Moines where art consists of photos in girlie magazines, his marriage has ended, and he's given up the cow business.

He's looking west toward the Sangre de Cristo Mountains, that southernmost spur of the Rocky Mountains, and he's thinking of Taos, naturally. The place to go to be an artist, right?

Well, not exactly. Max heard it was a party town and had a lot of gambling in it.

"So me and Wiley (Big Boy) Hittson had to get over there and see what Taos was like," Max says. "Ol' Wiley, he finally got a few days off together, and we drove over there together. Well, first thing you know, we're in the Sagebrush Inn, the gambling run by Curly Murray, who took over the gambling in Taos from Long John Dunn. We went in to the craps table there and I saw the dealer was palming crooked dice.

"I watched this guy, and he wasn't very good at it. He was giving you passing dice, then he'd switch 'em to crap-out dice. And I caught him. I told Wiley I'm going to let him roll a couple of times with those passing dice, and then I'll grab 'em and keep going. I told Wiley to stand right up against the stick man and stare at him like he was going to tear his head off like a chicken. He did. The guy was afraid to switch the dice. Wiley whispered he'd do it. Well, he grabbed those dice, and this kid couldn't say a word, and Wiley'd roll 'em and I'd win. Couldn't miss. I guess I won some four thousand dollars there. He had to give me the money. We had him. I said, 'Oh, this is my lucky day.'"

Max laughs. "Hey, he couldn't do a thing about it. Well, I guess he could have called Curly Murray and had us shot."

But an old coyote like Max knew that a move to Taos had to be planned carefully, especially when a guy's den was already filling with rain. So Max rented a house outside of Taos before the move. Then he had the local Des Moines mechanic work on his car. Max confided in him that he would be moving to Taos.

"When you get over there," he told Max, "just don't fool around with my niece."

Wiley "Big Boy" Hittson was one of Max's closest friends during the post-war years in Des Moines (Hi Lo). His untimely death became the theme for Max's book (and film) Hi Lo Country. *Wiley's horse in this photo is "Blackie," who Max called "Old Sorrel" in the book. Max Evans photo about 1946 in Des Moines.*

His niece was Patsy Jo James, who became Max's wife.

With the car ready to go, and the house rented, all there was to do was pack up and go, but they had to be a little slick about this.

"There were people there in Des Moines who loved me," Max says, "but there were also some people there who would've loved to kill me, too. It just so happened that these particular people had done so to others and gotten slick away with it. I had a tendency to wear out my welcome. I was a little worried about those guys ambushing me, so I told Wiley (his buddy, Wiley "Big Boy" Hittson), let's move at midnight. Just for the hell of it.

"We took a pickup truck and a car. He had a helluva load on that pickup and we drove real slow. The sun was coming up as we got over Flechado Pass, where it was twisted, going downhill to Taos."

The rented house, which Max called "a slab shack," was on the outskirts of Taos and just two blocks from a combination store, garage, and motel owned by Amos "Doc" James and his wife, Floye.

"I went over to the store," Max says, "and met them, and goddam we got along good. They had a grand sense of humor. He was a great mechanic. None of the old masters (famed Taos painters) would let anyone else work on their cars. They worked hard and played hard. (Doc James) was a smart sonofa-bitch, but he was also a mean bastard."

The "mean bastard" was to become his father-in-law, but that story comes a little later. These first few months in Taos, Max was settling into a routine of painting and partying.

The move to Taos meant saying goodbye to marriage. Goodbye to Helene and the baby, Sharon. Goodbye to ranching.

But not goodbye to Luz Martinez.

When a major film company is going to make a movie about a friend of yours, based on a book you've written, it's time to go pay a visit. That's why Max was in Des Moines (Hi Lo) to visit Wiley "Big Boy" Hittson's grave, bringing him a medicine pouch made by Woody Crumbo the Younger. David Bowser photo, 1998.

Max was worried about leaving Luz behind in Des Moines. "I knew someone was trying to kill him," Max says. "I'd already saved his life twice."

So, after Max was established in Taos, and after he and Pat were married, Max brought Luz to Taos, too. He lived with Max and Pat the first sixteen months they were married, then found a place of his own in Taos.

"Later, he remembered this girl from way over in *The Hi Lo Country*," Max says. "He never dated her or anything. He just wrote to her and asked if she would marry him. And she

In this rare photo, taken by Pat Evans sometime in the 1950s, Woody Crumbo, left, and Luz Martinez are shown with Max at the Evans' first house outside Taos.

did. She met him in Raton and they were married. They were in their late thirties or forties at the time."

And in Taos, Luz Martinez became a noted santero. Once, after Max and Woody Crumbo made some money in the mining business, Woody commissioned Luz to do some carvings. Up until then, Luz had been a modernist painter and had never done carving, but "those carvings were so powerful," Max says, "that Woody took Luz aside and told him he was meant to be a carver. Woody bought Luz a set of carving knives to get him started."

Luz Martinez's reputation spread.

"Luz had such a mind," Max says, "that he could not contain it by just being a santero. He started doing figures of the gods through history. His mind had many dimensions. I loved him very much. We got drunk together and had fist fights together.

"He had been commissioned to do a piece for President Kennedy," Max says, "but he put the order in a pile with the others because he wouldn't put the President ahead of his other clients. Luz fell dead shoveling snow before he could do the piece for the President, but that's how close he came to being world famous.

"The other Pope John had already blessed his work," Max says. "All he needed was the pope's fine Catholic friends, the Kennedys, and Luz would have been launched like a rocket to Mars."

Woody Crumbo

"I started going out to the Sagebrush Inn.," Max says, "which was four miles out of Taos in those days. It was a great pueblo-type place. Had a huge picture window in the lobby and you could see the whole town from there, and those massive mountains. They gave art shows in there. It was like a gallery.

"I'd been going in there and met Dal Holcomb, a magazine illustrator. He started working on me, helping me out, teaching me a little about design. Very interesting man, and he had the rest of the art community scratching their heads. He could live there and make a living, out of New York, and nobody else could do that. He was a fine artist as well as a commercial artist.

"So one day I walk into the Sagebrush Inn and I see paintings hanging there, big oils. And I'd never seen anything like it in my life. I knew it was from an Indian artist, and I also knew all Indian artists were painting in watercolors at this point. And I thought, 'Who is this painter?' Look at how he piled on that paint. It was an eagle dancer. The light hit it and it looked as though that painting had been set in a gemstone.

"I asked the bartender, who is this guy Crumbo. He said he's the greatest Indian artist who ever lived.

"I said, 'I'm going to wait here.' So I sat there and had a few drinks. I didn't care how long it took. I knew I had to meet this guy. I was looking out the window and here comes this Indian. Had his hair cut short. Looked a lot younger than his age. He started talking to me and I asked if he'd painted these pictures. He said, 'Yes. I'm Woody Crumbo.'

"I asked him if he wanted a beer, and we became friends forever.

"He lived at the pueblo and had come to town through Thomas Gilcrease, a part-Indian collector and had sent Woody to Taos to buy art for the great Gilcrease Museum in Tulsa, Oklahoma."

Woodrow Wilson Crumbo was a heavy-hitter on two fronts. He was a pioneer in the field of Indian art, and he taught and promoted Indian art throughout his life. But he was also a powerful name in all art circles throughout the world.

Woody's father died in 1916, when Woody was four, and Woody's mother, a Potawatomi Indian from Oklahoma, died when he was seven. For several months, this young boy lived in a cave on the reservation and made out the best he could, according to his son, Woody Max Crumbo, of Los Lunas, New Mexico.

Then one day he was "caught" by an older Creek Indian man and taken home with him to be raised. He was sent to the American Indian Institute in Wichita, Kansas, and later to Wichita University. By the time he met Max Evans, he was a renowned painter, a well-known crafter of Indian jewelry, a flute player good enough to solo with the Wichita Symphony, and an accomplished dancer. He had already received national acclaim at that point for painting the murals in the Department of the Interior headquarters in Washington, DC. Most of the Indian art collection in the Thomas Gilcrease Institute was collected by Woody. Woody moved his family to Taos in 1948, just in time to run into Max.

Woody's paintings hang in many of the world's museums, and were collected by Queen Elizabeth, Winston Churchill, and the Metropolitan Museum of Art in New York City.

Given this background, however, Woody Crumbo's work was largely snubbed by other Indian artists, because he painted in oils, and Indian art at that time was considered to be limited to watercolors.

"Woody," says Max, "wasn't allowed to even exhibit in the very Indian art shows he used to win."

According to Woody Max, this meeting between them was much more than two artists running into each other and sharing a beer.

"They'd known each other before," young Crumbo says. "They knew each other much too well right away. It was as though they had known each other in other lives, and when they met it was a case of 'Oh . . . here you are again.'"

"Yes," says Max. "That's pretty much how it was. Well, Woody found out I had this metaphysical thing and he wanted to talk about it. He was a great teacher of the metaphysical. He even taught the great medicine man, Joe Bernal, from Taos Pueblo, but Woody wasn't able to do it himself. After we got to know each other well, I told him about my grandmother and what she gave me. We were deeply involved in the mystical. Woody couldn't live without coming to my house (for tea-leaf readings) sometimes twice a day, and I lived four miles out of town.

"He took me on as a student of painting right away. He's the one got me started on nocturnals (painting night scenes). He's also the one who showed me how to work with a pallet knife, where they just gleam. Now I never had finished that. I was just getting really good at it and selling paintings when I decided to become a writer. That shows how smart I am."

Woody ran a studio and gallery in the Old West town of Cimarron, south of Raton, later in his life. In February of 1989, Max paid him a visit.

Here is Max's remembrance of that visit, in print here for the first time.

The Last Earthly Meeting

We were at Cimarron, New Mexico in the northeastern part of the state at the foot of the mighty Rockies, altitude over seven thousand feet. It was mid-February, windy, icy, and cold. Exactly the proper conditions to sit in a warm room and have the visit of one's life. It lasted from six in the evening until six in the morning. It was a joyous time of remembrance, of laughing at the ridiculous as well as the sublime. Woody Crumbo and I were putting the wrap on the massive spiritual, earth-dirt, and artistic worlds we had shared so intensely in our youth. We both knew it. Woody's wife, Lillian, shared many of the laughs and I was amazed that she could still believe in our dreams. Dreams are limitless to those who have reached the state of knowing.

Woody and I had plunged at our dreams with force strong enough to make windmills turn, and when one failed another was instantly ready to take its place. A lot of them were fulfilled and then taken away so we would, in all destiny, move on to others.

Even now I can remember that feeling of the times at the Taos Pueblo when Pat and Lillian would visit in the kitchen laughing, having dreams with us and those of their own, and Woody and I would use the table, causing it to talk by tapping, deciphering messages with great fun, and discussing all sorts of wondrous things to come. Minisa (Woody's daughter) and Woody Max were an undivided part of the movement in the ways of beautiful, bright children. Later our twins, Charlotte and Sheryl, would come along, and we would all share in this rare bounty of friendship at the Crumbo's new ranch at Llano de Ranchitos, south of Taos. The creative force was enormously powerful here. Michael Martin Murphey, the famed western composer/singer now lives there with the creek,

*Max visited his mentor Woody Crumbo, the Elder,
at his Cimarron, NM art gallery for the final time
about a month before he died. John Sinor photo.*

singing old soul songs right next to the great adobe house whose walls are full of good and helpful spirits.

We remember our times of discovery that night at Cimarron as we had roamed the mountain tops and searched their canyons for treasures, absorbing the scents, sounds, the music of ancient things. Sometimes the mountains—for a fleeting moment—would pull back the shroud of chance and let us have a peek at her mineral riches. We recalled the wondrous insanity of our buried treasure hunts, mirthfully even, with a little nostalgia of two old men still planning more searches. Isn't that what we're all meant to do—search? And when we find something of value, whether it be a solid substance or an often intangible spiritual one, search on.

I think so, and I know Woody did. We laughed until breathing was painful at our overcoming, defeating, and sometimes making fools of ourselves in the midst of the limited social and financial worlds. We shared worlds without counting. We covered them in those twelve rare, precious hours with mental and spiritual implosions and explosions of caring, sharing the great risks and the small winnings.

I remembered how he taught me to use a palette knife with only one spoken sentence. He showed me by painting with the knife, then he said softly, "Now at this stage you stroke the knife and let the paint spread where it wants to." In other words, let the art spirit take over at that point. Though I didn't paint but a few years longer, this simple-sounding advice carried over into my writing in an even stronger force. Woody Crumbo, the master mentor, is in effect all over the world, his teaching spirit carried on by numberless hands and souls right today and as long as those things of beauty have any value to us.

At six in the morning I was awake as I had ever been in my life, but it was the time of parting. I said I'd walk the two long blocks to the motel. Woody insisted he drive me. I didn't protest. I knew. He started the car in the freezing, dark morning. We had to wait a bit for the frozen windshield to thaw. Then he drove me ever so slowly to the motel. Neither said a word. Then he spoke and I could tell it was tremendously important to him, "You remember me showing you the sacred Kiowa flute back in Taos? Well, I returned it to the Kiowas with the proper blanket to sit on. I played it for them for the last time and completed the circle."

I didn't speak. I didn't need to.

As we pulled up in front of the motel, I asked Woody to wait a minute. He nodded okay. I had signed a copy of my book The Mountain of Gold to Woody and Lillian, but in the excitement of seeing them I had forgotten to take it with me earlier. As I returned to the car, he had the window rolled down, waiting in a cloud of frosted breath. I handed him the book, saying, "Woody, at least this story came out of our mining adventures. It didn't sell real big, but several different religions have preached sermons with it."

He smiled in the indescribable way I'd seen so many times under most of the circumstances that one can handle. It was fleeting and forever. We shook warm hands in the freezing cold and wordlessly I went into the motel, and wordlessly he drove away. It had all been said and done between us.

A few weeks later, Woody Crumbo was dead.

Pat

Paint and party. Paint and party. And the partying often involved Doc and Floye James. They would visit at the store, then go to the house and party. It was there Max heard about their daughter, Pat, who was away at school. He heard so much about her he got kinda tired of it, in fact.

"I got so sick of hearing about her, I didn't even want her to come home," he laughs. "Her dad would drink and dance to the record player and yell and have a great time. We got along great."

Max says he dated two or three girls over there, because the word got out in the small town that, as an artist, Max had "a future." But he wasn't interested in them.

So he settled in, began painting in the slab shack, met Woody Crumbo, and "was getting along all right. No fights or anything."

"Now ol' Doc James had the coldest Cokes in town," Max says. "There was something about the way he chopped up the ice or something. They were just the thing for a hangover. So one morning after a big party the night before, I went in there and there was ol' Pat, home from college. I introduced myself and she said, 'Yeah, I heard about you.'"

Despite Pat's striking beauty ("When Pat walked in a room, everybody's head turned," Max says), Max tried not to be impressed by their first meeting.

"Next time I had a hangover, I went in there to get a Coke and she was there. She looked at me and said, 'I can tell you saw a lot of pink elephants last night, but have you ever seen a purple bubble?' And she blew this big bubble-gum bubble. It was the grandest goddam thing I ever saw in my life, and my whole opinion of her changed just like that. I fell in love with her right there and somehow it would last through all the stormy deserts to this day.

"I didn't say anything then, but I came back later and said, 'I have a painting hanging in the juried Harwood Show.' Now I didn't think there was anything to that. It was that mortar picture. I was the only one accepted into that juried show except for the old masters. So she went up there with me. It was our first date. She knew how special my acceptance and favored hanging in this show was. I didn't. She'd modeled for most of those artists and some of them had tried to capture her strange beauty in portraits. They'd all failed. I even tried later."

> (Pat's) held the fort for him so many years. She's held off the arrows and stabs of so many people for him. Evil people. And done a real good job of it.
> —Chuck Miller, one of Max's closest friends

"I'd heard all about Max from my parents," Pat says. "My mother came over to Highlands University (in Las Vegas, New Mexico) where I was going to school. And oh, she told me all about Max. Max this and Max that. She said he is real cute.

"My father liked him because he was funny. My dad had a great sense of humor."

Pat was engaged to another guy at college at the time, but said it really wasn't that serious. Being around Pat Evans, then and now, is always fun. Her voice, and her life, are filled with laughter.

"I sure wasn't interested in getting married at all," she says. "I wanted to go back to school."

Pat and "Chimmy," Max's all-time favorite house dog, shown here around 1985.

When Pat met Max in the store, "I thought he was OK, but I had no idea of dating him. He was cute, but pretty wild. We kinda stayed away from each other."

But then came the purple-bubble-gum incident and things changed for her, too. She agreed to go to the art show with him.

The painting Max had of the mortar men, a rather violent impressionistic piece, was the only painting he'd brought to Taos with him from Des Moines.

"He didn't even realize how prestigious it was to exhibit with those old masters," Pat says.

Max was supposed to pick Pat up at one P.M.

"He came at noon," she says. "The show didn't open for two hours, so we just drove around. We weren't holding hands or smooching or anything, just driving around and talking.

"We just knew. This was it. It was just automatic. This was it, no matter what you had in mind before.

"And we went down to the old plaza and parked, and we finished each other's sentences. We had a real meeting of the minds. We've always had it."

Then they began dating, and it was something that was only popular with the two of them.

"Nobody in town wanted me to marry him," Pat says. "Especially my daddy. Max was quite a rounder, you know. And I wasn't a drinker. I'd go have a Coke."

But this was obviously serious right from the start. Max let no grass grow under his feet.

"I bought this little place about three or four miles went of Taos before I asked Pat to marry me," he says. "It was eighteen acres of wonderfully subirrigated land and had a little ol' adobe house on it. It had electricity and there was this well in the front yard with a rope and a bucket.

"Pat wanted to go to college and become a dress designer," Max says. "She was always drawing, been around all the artists all her life there in Taos. Knew the old masters. So she planned to go to O.U. (University of Oklahoma).

"I said no, hell no. 'We either get married now or forget it. 'Cause I'm going out in this world. I can teach you more in three months than you'll learn over there in ten years.'

Pat told him she wanted to wait. He didn't.

Max and Pat's first home in the Taos area was out of town a couple of miles and even had its own ghost until banished by Woody Crumbo's hurried Indian exorcism. This photo was taken about 1949, before the Evans family moved into Taos itself.

"I told her I'd give her three days, and if she didn't want to get married then, just forget it. Well, a couple of days went by and I thought she'd decided against it. Then I was driving to town to get the mail and here she came in her car. She waved me over and told me she'd decided to marry me."

They met at the end of May 1949, and were married August 4, just three months later. They drove to Raton, and Max's old pard, Wiley "Big Boy" Hittson, served as best man.

"We met Wiley at the race track, where he was working some horses," Max says, "and were married by a justice of the peace. We went to a picture show and stayed in a little motel there. Then we bought this yellow-meat watermelon and drove on up to Raton Pass with Wiley and a horse trainer friend of his, and had a wonderful picnic."

"It just upset everybody's world," Pat says. "My daddy was not agreeable, but he was going to try not to do anything about it. Daddy thought Max was a great friend, but he didn't want him for a son-in-law. His main objection was that Max had no visible means of supporting me. And he also knew I wanted to finish college, and he wanted me to.

"Max was an artist then, and we were both searching. We were just kids then. I was twenty, he was twenty-five."

"He forgot," says Max, "that I had that subirrigated land and house bought and paid for. I wasn't a starving artist yet. However, he'd seen so many of them come and blank out in Taos that I never blamed him."

One little side note here, because it was important for both Max and Pat. Before marrying Pat, Max wanted to take her back to *The Hi Lo Country* to meet his old partner, Benny Padilla, he of the two deaths in one day.

"I took her over there to Folsom to meet Benny. He had this little ol' house right on the street, and it was right on the street. No sidewalk, just a curb. Benny came to the door and greeted me. 'Maximiliano!' he cried. I introduced him to Pat and I really did want to see what he thought of her. It was a kind of test, really. Well, he threw his arms around both of us and said, 'Come around back. I want to show you my garden.'

"We went back there and there was the greatest small forest of marijuana that ever grew in the world. My God, it looked like the Santa Fe National Forest, in its prime! He was so proud of that, you can't believe it. That was his great gesture. He showed her that he was breaking all the laws of the world right here on the highway.

"I decided I'd marry her, right there. I didn't tell her for a few days. And of course, before we left, he had to tell Pat about what great times he and Maximiliano had had. He did just exactly what I wanted him to do. It was a full-blown test. It was the finals. That's how it all came about."

For a honeymoon, they drove to Texas to visit Max's family. And there, one big turning point in their lives was followed almost immediately by another.

"At that time," Pat says, "Max's father owned gas companies. He was an amazing man. Always clean and well dressed. He'd get out there and dig ditches with a shovel, but it was always with a white shirt and a tie. Very clean. Very friendly. Very honest. He's where Max gets his honesty.

"Well, while we were there on our honeymoon, Max's father offered him the gas company in Plains, Texas. We could've paid him back a little at a time. And at that time, Plains was a going concern. We talked about it. I looked at all that flat country around there and I said, 'You know, I think we can figure something else out.'

"Max wasn't going to do it, anyway."

Turning down the gift of a steady way of earning a living and supporting a family didn't sit well with W. B. Evans, but he accepted it. He'd always known Max was different.

"Just think," Pat says. "If we had done that, we'd have died on the vine. Right then. There'd be no paintings, no books. Nothing.

"We both had wonderful parents, but we are totally different from them. They were business people and we aren't. They were highly respected in their communities, and," she laughs, "as I say, we are different."

So they drove back to Taos and moved into the house about two miles, as the crow flies, from town.

"He'd bought this place," Pat says, "in this delightful little old valley, under a mesa. Everything was just clean and fresh out there. We didn't even have running water the first year. We added the bathroom on the next year. People said our marriage wouldn't last six months. They said there's no way she's going to live without a bathroom. Well, I'll tell you what . . . we had a grand three-holer and it had this great view of the magic Taos mountain."

She laughs. "And Max could cook, some. I sure couldn't. All I could do was bake a cake. That first year, we lived on canned tamales and corn. Oh, I kinda learned to cook a little bit. I burned the toast every morning. My first present from him was a toaster. I still have it."

Max says, "Besides Pat being a model, she was a damned fine water colorist. She quit both fields after she was successful in them and became an artist at gardening, especially tomatoes, and one of the best cooks in the world. Ask anyone who has tasted it."

But back then, life for Max changed to Pat and paint and party.

There's one other thing about this house that's worth mentioning. Max and Pat weren't the first ones to live there, nor were they the only ones. The previous owner was described by Max as "a seven-foot-tall bootlegger." He not only died in the house under mysterious circumstances, but it was quite a while before his body was discovered.

To make matters worse, he refused to leave.

"He'd shake you when you were asleep," Max says. "He never bothered Pat, but he'd pull the covers off me sometimes."

One night, Woody Crumbo slept over with them. In the middle of the night, the ghost grabbed Woody's foot and shook it. Max and Pat were awakened by the yelling, and Woody spent the rest of the night in his truck.

"He came back and had a ceremony," Pat says, "and I saw Woody rubbing some feathers together. That was it. That was the last we saw of the ghost there."

Close friends who have known Max and Pat for many years smile and sigh when they mention Pat's name, because Max Evans certainly isn't the easiest man to live with. Certain words, like "sainthood" tend to creep into the conversation when Pat is mentioned, but Pat would just laugh at that. There has been at least one separation in their more than half a century together, but they've managed to tough it out.

"It would take almost all the adjectives in a dictionary," Max says, "to describe our fifty-four years of marriage, but dull, boring, uneventful certainly wouldn't be there. I have to admit that a few times, things were really on the rocks. Since we don't easily give up on anything we want badly enough, the issues were resolved."

I think one of the reasons we've lasted is that I'm pretty self-sufficient. I was alone quite a little bit. So he was free to go and be Max. He overdid it a few times, but I know he loves me.

We never have been mad at each other very long at a time. Fifteen minutes, maybe.

—Pat Evans

I'm the only thing that ever affected her (Pat). And that's because I'm a natural born sonofabitch.

—Max Evans

A World of Art

It's really hard to paint a sunset without making it corny, I don't care if you're a world master. You have to have a subject with a sunset to make it work.

—Max Evans

In the small world of art, things were going along very well. Max was studying with Woody, and his paintings were getting better each time. Max's life was divided between painting and hustling.

"I'd take them to the bars and sell them when they were still wet," he says. "I had to. We needed the money. Selling them wasn't really hard. You just told the people to consider how much they'd be worth someday when I got really well-known. You appealed to the greedy bastard in all of them, and they bought them."

"I can't speak for other artists . . . but I like money. I never believed that old saw that the two can't mix. Ever since Van Gogh the world had decided that genius can unfold only if it's undernourished. This attitude is a fine excuse for the rest of the world, but does little for the man with an empty gut."

—from *The White Shadow* by Max Evans

Then things got even better there for a while.

"This rich couple came in the Taos Inn and met Woody," Max says, "and they decided they would finance him to make all these silkscreen prints. And now they are all over the world. And then they wanted him to go set up a school where Indians from all over American could come to be trained to make silkscreen prints.

"Woody told me to make six nocturnals and he'd make prints out of them. Everything was so goddam wonderful you just couldn't hardly stand it.

Sometimes a mining office is more than a mining office,
and when Max Evans and Woody Crumbo went into mining,
the office naturally doubled as art studio when this
photo was taken in 1955. Woody uses an easel that once
belonged to famed cowboy cartoonist J.R. Williams
("Out Our Way") that Max procured from the guy who
stole it from Williams. Crumbo's The Death of Spotted
Eagle became famous years later. In the background
is one of Max's paintings called The Family.

Woody Crumbo in front of the Taos mining office and the camper along with portable drilling rig used to prove up a vast premium perlite deposit.

Woody Crumbo broke new ground in art with his stylistic portrayals in oils of Indian life and legend, and maybe no one symbol of his is as noticeable today as this Spirit Horse. Over the years many Indian artists have copied the style of the blue spotted horse, but Woody was the original. This silk screen print enjoyed massive circulation.

"These people had hired a public relations guy who could really dish out the propaganda. And the propaganda guy talked Frank Waters down at the Taos News into doing a full page on his work. Well, Frank did. He was part Indian and liked Woody, and he gave Woody a hundred tear sheets when it came out.

"This propaganda guy was getting hold of every paper in the United States about Woody and said he'd write anything they wanted.

"Now at this time, Pat was running Woody's jewelry store, I was painting those nocturnals, Woody's sister-in-law, with help from Pat, was training all the people at the pueblo how to do silk-screening.

"It was wonderful . . . it was helping everyone . . . and here we were, right in the middle of it."

At first, the first house Max and Pat had outside Taos wasn't much to look at and lacked many basics. But things were looking up by the time Luz Martinez took this photo in 1950. Max won enough money using crooked dice in a craps game in Taos to put in plumbing and a well, and a floor and another room. When the plumbing was installed, it inspired Max to write Xavier's Folly.

Max's oil painting Normandy Night Fire, was an expressionistic piece about his job with mortars in World War II. He painted it in Des Moines and was the only painting he brought with him to Taos. It was accepted in a juried show, alongside the work of the Taos masters, and led directly to his first date with Pat. It still hangs in their home in Albuquerque.

This painting of the Wheeler Peak area of New Mexico Max calls The Top of New Mexico. It was one of the last paintings he ever did before turning to writing. This one was painted in 1957. Collection of Kibbe Anderson.

And then the couple who were financing this backed out and left town, and took the reproduction rights to Max's paintings and Woody's work with them. And nobody ever knew why.

"There we were, flat on our asses"

All of a sudden, the world of art wasn't doing as well as it had been.

I went with Ol' Max down to Santa Fe one time in May of 1960 to help him peddle some paintings. We had these friends who owned the Highway House out on the old Pecos Trail, and we ended up out there.

He did okay, hustling down there. These guys ran the restaurant and lounge there and we planned to stay there Friday night and Saturday night and come back Sunday.

We headed to town to get something to eat at Don Hammond's place, Maria's Mexican Kitchen, but we didn't get there. We found a truck coming at us in our lane, and there wasn't much of a shoulder, so the car went into an arroyo and flipped end over end about seventy feet almost straight down. I was driving.

Damn near killed us. In fact, it would have killed me if Max hadn't got me out. I was crushed behind the steering wheel. Had my head all caved in. And I wasn't breathing.

I'd had it, no question about it.

He said, "Chuck, we gotta get outta here, the car is saturated with gas."

I told him to get out, but he said he was going to stay and get me out. He must've spent half an hour kicking that car door until he could get me out. He had a concussion and was bleeding real bad. He dragged me up that steep slope, and I weighed about 250 lbs. then.

We flagged down a Santa Fe policeman and he took us to St. Vincent's Hospital.

They set my leg and sewed him up and put us to bed. We had beds next to each other. This sister came by and said, "Well, gentlemen, you've had quite an evening. Is there anything else we can do for you tonight?"

And Max said, "Why yes there is, Sister. Bring me a great big hammer."

Max's painting Meeting by Moonlight *was painted in 1951.*

Max's nocturnal paintings became his trademark,
back during the painting days in Taos, such as this one,
painted in 1951, and called Ghost Rider in a Ghost Town.

Max's painting The Edge of Taos, *now in the Jeb Rosebrook Collection.*

The Lonesome Land, *by Max Evans. Painted around 1950. The Mattie Field Collection.*

Max painted The Blizzard *in 1951 in Taos. It's now in the collection of the Hugh Mitchell Ranch near Roy, New Mexico. "They despise my guts," Max says, "but they bought this before they started disliking me so much."*

"What do you want with that?" she asked.
"I want to break this sumbitch's other leg."
      —Chuck Miller, one of Max's closest friends

Yep, that was a helluva car wreck. But it was fun, too. We turned it into fun.
      —Max Evans

The Evans Family Grows . . .

Max and Pat had been married five years before Pat gave birth, on Oct. 16, 1954, to identical twin daughters.

Pat went down the highway a few miles to Dixon, New Mexico, for the births, and stayed at a maternity hospital there.

Charlotte was born first, weighing four pounds, four ounces, followed twenty minutes later by Sheryl at four pounds, eleven ounces.

"They were teensy-weensy things," Pat says, "and had to stay in an incubator until they reached six pounds. It was six weeks before they could come home. Max and I just about wore out the pavement every day, driving up and down the highway, going to see them. It seemed like forever before we could take them home."

In a photo taken by Pat Evans about 1954, Max is playing with their twin daughters, Charlotte and Sheryl at their home outside Taos.

*A devoted father, Max never drank around the twins,
Charlotte (left) and Sheryl, here in a 1963 photo by
Pat at their home on Ledoux Street in Taos.*

Mining

So there Max was, about 1953, drinking beer on credit in the
Indian Hills Hotel in Taos owned by Terry Monihan, brother
to the famous senator. Shorty Kendrick, an ex-cowboy, was the
bartender.

There were three of them on the suds dole that day: Max
and Woody Crumbo and some cowboy out of Trinidad,
Colorado, and now Taos, named Marion Minor.

As part of the service of the Indian Hills Hotel's unofficial
employment agency, Shorty suggested to Monihan that this
trio of subsidized suds suckers might be able to help a certain other patron of the hotel. A light bulb blinked in
Monihan's brain.

Since he was furnishing the beer on credit, Monihan asked
Max and Woody if they knew anything about mining, because
a rich man was staying there and he had a geologist with him
and they were looking to buy mining claims.

"Hell yes," said Max. "I didn't know shit about mining," he laughs now, "but I had always loved rocks. All kinds."

"So the next day, Woody and I picked up some mining claim papers and we drove up to Penasco. We stopped out there and walked out away from the truck and we staked out fifteen mining claims. It took us until dark. Then we went back to town."

As far as Max and Woody knew, their mining claims had some dirt and rocks on them, along with a squirrel or two.

But the next day, they went back up to their claims with the investor and his geologist. These were the days of the cold war and atomic secrets and everyone was crazy to find uranium.

"Well, I walked out there on that mining claim and saw this heavy black rock. I didn't know what the hell it was. But I handed it to the guy. He put the Geiger counter on it and it just burned that apparatus plumb out. That rock turned out to be columbite, the purest form of uranium, and rare earths.

"Later, I learned a lot of things about mining and minerals, but at the time, I didn't know diddly."

Later, Max bought a couple of mineral books and really studied rock. He learned that the area they staked out was full of pegmatite streaked with fissures of feldspar, called pegmatite dikes. The heavy black rocks were columbite. It was a real find.

"Why we went to that particular place to stake claims, I have no idea," Max says. "We just did. The geologist made a mistake that was all in our favor, not his client's. He thought the heavy chunk of columbite was pitchblende, the purest form of metallic uranium. That triggered the greed buttons."

The investor was so greedy he didn't even let them wait until the next day to contact an attorney. He pushed a contract on them that night, they signed, and received $10,000.

Presumably the beer bill was paid and they were drinking in the black after that.

"We learned we had to do assessment work on the claims to make them legal," Max says. "You had to do $100 worth of work on each one. So we hired that cowboy from Colorado and a couple of retired miners and sent them out there with a bottle of whisky. He was happy and so were we. We ended up clearing $8,000 on that deal."

So Max and Woody had become instant miners, and they liked it. No, they loved it.

Now $8,000 for an afternoon's work appealed to both these artists, and they decided to study up a bit on mining and see what they could do. Quite a bit, it turned out.

The 1957 edition of *Who's Who in New Mexico* lists Max Evans as the president of Solar Metals, Inc.; vice president of Evans Minerals, Inc.; and manager of Taos Uranium, Inc., and identifies him simply as a mining executive "mainly responsible for large discoveries of copper, gold, silver and uranium deposits in North Central New Mexico."

At its peak, Max and Woody's mining operation employed about 150 men. They shipped railroad cars full of ore to be processed at Moly Corporation in Red River, New Mexico, and at El Paso, Texas at A S & R (American Smelting and Refining Company).

"There were a couple of things Woody and I learned right away about mining," Max says. "This was a crazy time. Maybe almost as crazy as the gold rush in California. First of

The Red River mine was one of Max's biggest finds, running five percent copper "mine run" (throughout all the ore). The ore was shipped to El Paso for smelting.

all, the Atomic Energy Commission put all the power to buy and process uranium in the hands of a few powerful politicians. If someone had a good claim, and they wanted it, they'd just refuse to buy his ore. Then what's he going to do with it?

"We also learned to go easy on the assaying. It cost a lot of money (to get the assay done) and then the word got out and prospectors were all over those hills like ants.

"So what we learned to do was just to keep a good claim to ourselves until we sold it to someone. When the Geiger counter would go crazy as hell, we'd just take someone out there and sell it to him.

"Another thing we learned—learned this the hard way—we also got a few big hot checks. They were kiting these checks in hopes they could turn a deal before the checks cleared the bank. We didn't have the computers in those days, so it took a while to clear.

"The excitement of that machine (Geiger counter) making that fast gargling sound really did something to you," Max says, chattering like a Geiger counter. "So I learned how to write a mining contract on one page—it wasn't really hard—and we'd make a deal right on the spot, for cash. We made some good money and had some good fun for a while, too."

The mines produced copper, gold, silver, uranium, and perlite.

One of the big finds Max made as a prospector was a hefty mineral find on Frazier Mountain, across from the world famous Taos Ski Resort.

"We opened the old mines at the same time they were bulldozing the ski slopes," Max says. "We shipped some pretty good ore. The price dropped from 48 cents a pound to 24 cents in a hundred and twenty days and we couldn't afford to operate. Homestake Mining tried to take it over from us, on a drilling program, royalty deal, but I kept looking at Twinning Creek and turned them down.

"It's a beautiful, shimmering creek," Max says. "My favorite fishing hole. A real paradise. I didn't sell out to Homestake Mining because of what that would do to that beautiful canyon. That's the dumb-ass truth of the whole thing.

"I was born an ecologist, really," he says, "in spite of what terrible things are done to my rancher friends. I don't go around

The Red River mine was so rich in minerals that there was literally no waste. Bob Cresswell (brother of Max's old hunting partner, Tom Cresswell) was foreman and is standing by the truck, while Woody Crumbo is at the head of the chute in this 1954 photo taken by Max. The ore was taken by truck to Santa Fe and put on train cars for El Paso. Before the mine was closed (because there was too much alumina in it to process), Max and Woody had run a 1480-ft. tunnel into the mountain and "were looking at a billion dollars" worth of copper ore. But then the price of copper went from 48 cents to 24 cents a pound in 90 days. "We weren't meant to do this," Max says. The mine is right across from the city of Red River, and the area is now a wilderness area. One time Max and Bob Cresswell were back in the mine and hit a pocket of dead air. Cresswell jerked Max back and saved his life.

espousing my beliefs, I just was. So nothing happened up on that creek."

Well, nothing happened because of Max and Woody's mining interests there. But today Twinning Creek is in the center of the Taos Valley Ski Resort.

"Now I go and see what that ski resort has done to the canyon" he says, "and I wonder which would have done the most harm. At least we wouldn't have changed the course of the creek."

Max and Woody made nearly three million dollars in the mining industry scattered over about five years, "but we pissed it all away," Max says. "Well, that's not quite all; we did give a ton of it away. We were suckers for every starving artist in five states."

And there were other problems, too. Legal problems. A lot of the operating capital was raised by selling shares in the various mining corporations. They prospected, staked claims, and then either developed and worked the mine or sold it to someone else.

After a thorough examination by a court of law, Max and Woody's mining operations came to a halt.

"We were proven innocent by what amounted to ignorance of anything but charging ahead," Max says, "but . . . I ended up $86,000 in the hole. Woody was just dead-even broke."

One of their big finds, however, was a perlite mine located west of the Rio Grande Gorge, not far from Taos.

"The government suggested we sell it and give the proceeds to our investors. We did just that. The buyers were Alva Simpson, oil man, uranium man and partner with Gen. Patrick Hurley, former ambassador to China, father of the famous painter, Wilson Hurley. They split up their friendship on that

Miners from Questa, NM, work Max and Woody's Frazier Mountain mine across from the Taos Ski Lodge.

Tailings are all that is left these days of Max's Frazier mine, across from Taos Ski Lodge. The mine was rich in copper. Photo by Dennis Dutton.

deal and sold to Western Milling. That mine produced twenty-four hours a day," Max says, "for forty years."

But not for Max and Woody.

The Rounders, Max says, "finally pulled me out of debt."

You know, Max being able to earn a living at his writing, without having to become a teacher or get a job . . . working on his own terms, is a goddam miracle when you think about it.

—James Hamilton,
author of *Cross of Iron*, essayist, screenwriter

Max's discovery, the perlite mine west of Taos, was incredibly rich. After Max and Woody sold it, it was continuously mined and milled 24 hours a day for more than forty years. "Its taxes," Max says, "put innumerable New Mexico kids through college." Nature is slowly reclaiming the mine these days, Max discovered in a recent visit with actor friend Josh Bryant. "After he complained that I'd torn a hole in the desert," Max says, "I told Josh that I'd simply moved two square miles of White Sands National Monument a few hundred miles north so they'd have a white beach to sunbathe on."

The site of Max's perlite mine, before it was mined.

During the mining days, Pat and the twins wait at the Taos Ski Lodge during a stockholders meeting for the mining company. Martin Shaffer took the photo around 1956.

The Move Into Taos

During the five mining years, Max and Pat and the two girls lived in the little house about two miles as the crow flies out of Taos.

"Then the water heater blew up," Pat says. "So we put in another one. It blew up, too. That did it for me. I said, "We are moving into town.'"

This came right at the end of the mining operation. Though Max was $86,000 in debt, Woody came out of it owing nothing.

"But he figured he owed me money," Max says. "He said he was going to move to El Paso and take a job down there as director of the El Paso Museum of Fine Art, and he said if I wanted his house in town, we would consider his debt as our down payment, assume his mortgage at the bank, and we'd call it even."

Woody's house in town was a huge two-story place on an acre, with carved wooden doors. It was at the end of Ledoux street, in a fashionable area (for Taos) and was right next door to the Harwood gallery, scene of Max and Pat's first date.

And the water heater worked. The deal was done.

"It was a beautiful place," Pat says. "We loved it there. The girls could go out in the back yard to the irrigation ditch and play. They were always bringing home snakes and toads and getting flowers for bouquets."

Max, Pat says, was a devoted father. Both parents enjoyed their children. The children enjoyed it, too.

Charlotte remembers one evening at the dinner table when the girls were small. "We were in a mood, I guess," she says. "We didn't like anything on our plates and didn't want to eat. So Daddy asked us what we wanted, and naturally we said ice cream. 'Well, OK, then, let's go!' he said, and we drove down and ate ice cream. He was a lot of fun."

Max's propensity for booze and brawls worried the girls, however.

"I can recall," Charlotte says, "seeing Daddy come home with his face all smashed up, and it hurt us to see him like that. I especially remember that time the man hit him in the face with a rock."

The upstairs window in Max and Pat's house on Ledoux Street in Taos looked out on the world. On the other side of the window, Max wrote The Rounders, One-Eyed Sky, The Hi Lo Country, Mountain of Gold *and* The Great Wedding. *Max and the girls, Sheryl and Charlotte, are in the backyard here about 1958. Photo by Pat Evans.*

The house on Ledoux Street in Taos was where Max wrote
The Rounders. *Max and Pat bought the house from Woody Crumbo*
when Woody moved to El Paso. Here are Max and the twins, Charlotte
and Sheryl, in the backyard around 1958. Photo by Pat Evans.

Max had come out the back door of a bar in Taos on his way
home. It was winter. A jealous artist hiding there smashed him
in the face with a rock and left him unconscious in the alley.

"I would've froze to death if some people hadn't found me,"
Max says. "They almost ran over me, too."

And, Pat says, Max would never allow any drinking around
the girls. That was one hard-and-fast rule at the house.

Honest Max Evans: Used-Car Tycoon

✂ **They say luck occurs** when preparation meets opportunity. So here is Max, ensconced in the famous art colony of Taos. He has been well-trained to raise cattle and fight wars. He is a classy calf roper, can find mines where no one thought to look, and is becoming a fair hand with a paint brush. Naturally, then, he jumps at the chance to own a used-car lot.

It all came about, grew to fruition, and subsided—much as the Titanic subsided—through Max's good-ol'-boy network there in Taos. Marion Minor, the old cowboy who staked those mining claims for Max and Woody, was given a chunk of mining stock as a payback, and he used this to go partners with a guy named Chet Mitchell in a used-car lot on the southern fringe of Taos.

"They went broke fast," says Max.

This would have been around 1955, Max thinks. The property consisted of a rented lot down on the highway leading to Santa Fe, about a half mile out of Taos; a sign that said something like "A-1 Used Cars"; and what Max called "a little bitty bastard of a trailer on it for an office."

You need cars for a car lot, too, of course, and they had them. There were "twenty-five or thirty used cars and eight or ten trucks," Max said. None of them ran.

"Some of them," Max said, "were leaning like this."

Naturally, since the place went broke, Marion and Chet set about selling the place to Max. The price was cheap enough to be interesting to Max, and he soon came up with a plan that would carry them all gently down the road to becoming hundredaires.

"But my plan would take cooperation," he said. So he bought the car lot, dead cars and all, from Chet and Marion, causing them to laugh like hell.

That was simply because they weren't acquainted with The Plan.

Now before The Plan unfolds, it is best to take a lesson from Agatha Christie and list here the cast of characters involved in The Plan. And perhaps the term "cast of characters" has never before been as appropriate as it is here.

At a branding at Slim Evans' place near Taos around 1952 (scene of the used car graveyard), Max has a heel rope and rides Brownie as Slim flanks calves and Crow Indian cowboy Donn Davies wields the iron.

Slim Evans's old ranch house west of Taos still stands with Max in front (2003). Many kids slept in the attic bunkhouse and went on to make a good run at the world because of Slim's tutelage. They include David Evans, top PRCA roper, and still a cowboy. Sonny Jim, National Indian Rodeo Association World Champion Bulldogger. Woody Crumbo, the Younger, roper, rodeo producer, and realtor. James and Bill Evans, top cowboys who later headed computer and construction firms. Photo by Woody Crumbo, the Younger.

Cast of characters:

Sam Grinder—an old, toothless prospector who didn't stray far from a bottle of booze. Made immortal in later years in Max's Bluefeather Fellini.

Marion Minor—an ex-cowboy from Colorado who knew how to stake claims but couldn't sell used cars if they belonged to him. "Others folks' cars," Max laughs, "yes."

Slim Evans—Max's cowboy uncle who owned a small cow ranch outside Taos with a sagebrush-covered hill on it.

Ol' Snaky-Looking Girl—Slim Evans' wife, Rema.

Monster Kid—Slim's stepson and son of Ol' Snaky-Looking Girl. Good mechanic. A close friend to alcohol and given to fits of strength. (Real name forgotten.)

Reno—An Arabian roping horse.

Max Evans—The Boss. Expert at playing the radio in a used car.

Max held a meeting of most of the cast of characters out at Uncle Slim's place. He had a plan, he told them, but to make this plan work, he needed their cooperation. The Plan consisted of Grinder and Slim's stepson, Monster Kid, going to work on those old wrecks down at the car lot, cannibalizing them and getting at least some of them running. Max would then sell the running cars to those in need of them. The chewed-over hulks of what was left would then be hauled over to Slim's ranch and dumped behind this little hill he had, out of sight, to rust in peace.

This was fine with Slim and his wife, Ol' Snaky-Looking Girl ("a hard worker and a good one"). Monster Kid ("Slim kept telling me what a good mechanic he was, and I knew he was anxious to get rid of this seven-foot monster for at least part of each day—that bastard could tear a railroad tie in half with his hands") and Grinder went for it, too.

"Ol' Sam Grinder," Max says, "was the ex prospector and miner I loved and wrote about in Bluefeather. He was getting old and just wanted something to do so he could drink, you know."

Normally, being a mechanic at a used-car lot doesn't necessarily equate with an opportunity to drink, but this wasn't your average car lot, either.

So The Plan went into action. Monster Kid and the little drunken prospector went to work tearing those cars apart and putting some of them back together.

"We actually got a few of them running," Max says.

The first thing they got running was a truck, so they could use it to haul the carcasses to Slim's little sagebrush-covered hill.

"This little truck would only go between three and five miles an hour," Max says, "which was a good thing."

It was a good thing, it turned out, because it was never driven by a sober human being.

"If that truck would've gone fifteen or twenty miles an hour, we'd have had some hellacious wrecks. Those two were drinking all the time they drove it. But as it was, all we had were a whole bunch of little bitty wrecks because they went so slowly. Sometimes they wouldn't make it there at all. They'd miss the middle of the road, miss the turn off down there. Maybe they'd argue with a rancher or somebody about their fence being torn down and wrapped around their car."

But when the gods smiled down on the daily delivery of rusting Detroitus to Slim's ranch, and obstacles were unmolested by the drunks behind the wheel, they could make the six-mile trip in about an hour and a half.

So, with a few dead vehicles coughing slowly to life, it was time for the boss to find homes for them. When you're in a new field, you start easy. Max, who could sell suntan lotion in Carlsbad Caverns, sold one flatbed truck to his mining partner and pal, Woody Crumbo.

"He was sure proud of that truck," Max says.

Max says he didn't even know the truck had one wheel that wobbled until after Woody bought it.

"You could see ol' Woody coming for miles," Max says. "He didn't seem to mind much about one wobbly wheel because everything else on it ran okay. He just took the back roads and it was all right."

His next customer was none other than Marion Minor, who had sold the car lot to Max. Monster Kid and Grinder had managed to breathe the exhaust of life back into a slick-back Chevy.

"I traded it to Marion Minor for a helluva nice Arabian roping horse named Reno," Max says. "Real nice horse. Had him a long time. Only thing wrong with him was it took him about fifty yards to stop. Otherwise, he was great."

The deal was made, and hands were shaken. Between guys like these, that's as good as any contract ever drawn. In this case, it's probably a good thing.

After the handshake, Max took Minor out in his new car "to show him what a deal he'd made."

"He was driving the thing around Taos Plaza," Max says, "and I showed him how the radio worked. That's about all I knew about those cars."

Minor, the proud new owner of the slick-back Chevy, approached the junction with the Santa Fe highway with the intention of turning south on it. Well, that almost happened.

"It must have shocked him (to learn) how well the radio worked," Max says, "because he jerked the gear shift and the steering wheel come plumb off in his hand."

Fortunately, no one was coming along the highway at the moment, because the slick-back Chevy scooted right through the intersection and was heading for a building on the other side.

"I thought we were going to run into it," Max says, "but it hit a little ditch and bounced up and it died right there with its front wheels stuck in the ditch."

Max recalls being happy that the trade was already a done deal.

"I told him, 'Well, maybe you can get that mechanic of mine to look at it for you. I don't know."

At this point, Max had barely entered the world of pre-owned transportation, and he was feeling really good.

"The way I figure it," he says, "I'm way ahead of the whole game. I mean, I sold my buddy, Woody Crumbo, a flatbed truck with a wobble and traded a Chevy for a helluvan Arabian horse. Not too bad. Woody later bought him a fancy place in Sedona, Arizona, and made the entire move with this beautiful truck."

And still the commerce continued. The drunken miner and the well-lubricated giant tore into car after car, sometimes making things fit through sheer strength that Nature and engineers in Detroit had no intention of fitting together. Monster Kid, Max says, was so strong he could put a nut on a bolt as securely as though it were welded.

For that reason, and others, Max referred to him as Monster Kid only sotto voce, and when the wind was blowing his voice away from Monster Kid's location.

Now the daily, ninety-minute cruises of two drunks to Slim's ranch, carrying along car carrion they were handling less than deftly, did not escape the notice of the Taos constabulary.

"Those guys were either straddling the white line," Max says, "or in the ditch."

At three miles an hour, everyone in the area had a good opportunity to check out the condition of both occupants. This included the police.

"Those Taos cops were real good guys," Max says. "Otherwise, they'd have shot me long ago. But they were real tempted to arrest Monster Kid and Grinder for drunk driving.

I had to buy them some lunches and talk them out of it, 'cause I needed to move those dead cars. The guy who owned the land the car lot was on was trying to get me to sign a lease for six months or a year, and I sure didn't want to do that. I wanted to clear that off and get out of it."

Max explained that he "couldn't watch those bastards every minute. Please don't throw them in jail, because we have to get that trash off that car lot or it'll ruin the tourist trade."

With the deadline for Max to sign lease papers approaching, The Plan had to be thrown into overdrive. The guys worked hard at it. Every day. Toward the end of this three-month expedition into steel-resuscitating commerce, Max says, "We were really whipping up. Sometimes those guys could get up to five miles an hour. Everything got faster because I quit paying them every day and they couldn't buy booze."

And at one time in the short life of Honest Max, Purveyor of Quality Transportation, Max tried to get insurance. He should've known better.

"That," he laughs, "was a goddam joke. That insurance guy, Emmitt Somebody-or-Other, came out to the lot to see about it, and here comes these two drunks driving out of there. That kinda took care of that."

Out of the forty or so vehicles, five or six were eventually put into running condition by Monster Kid and Grinder, and sold by Max.

But all wasn't beer and skittles on this deal. There was one other problem, too. The dead carcasses took up more space on Slim's place than Max had figured. The little gully filled with dead cars. Then the car bodies climbed to the top of the sagebrush-covered hill—the same one the famous Taos artists had painted for years—and then the dead cars went beyond that, even. Went far beyond that. Striving for more elevation as only a pile of dead cars can, they stretched their oxidizing souls up and up until no sagebrush could be seen on the scenic hill.

"It ruined the view," Max says, "from a mile out of town plumb to the Rio Grande Gorge."

Max's rust-ridden pollution of Taos's beauty didn't go unnoticed, either.

"The city fathers were mad at us, the artists were mad at us. We'd ruined the tourist industry forever, they said. Most of the suggestions people had for the police about me were like 'Why don't you throw that sonofabitch in jail and bury the key fifty-foot deep!'

"Taos County, in those days, had maybe 3,800 people in it," Max says, "and I'll bet you that, at any one time, I had at least half of them disgruntled."

This new landscape feature, Mount Max, also contributed to the total decline in ambience of this artistic community in another way, too.

"There was a helluva racket through there when the wind'd blow," Max says. "Like a symphony from hell. Fenders slapping, grinding and banging all at the same time."

What would today be considered a large piece of moving, grinding, functioning art—and an enlightened social statement on our reliance on technology—was then just considered an unsightly, rusting damn nuisance.

Max took care of the problem through the liberal use of beer on a local merchant. After a thorough lubrication at La Cocina, Max talked one of the Cohen brothers from the local garage into buying the entire mountain of dead cars for a hundred bucks, and paying for the beer, too.

"The upshot of this whole deal," Max says, "was that I came out of this whole thing with a pretty good roping horse and about $1,200. I'd have made more money if I hadn't had to buy so many lunches for the cops to keep those guys out of jail."

Six months later, the last of the car bodies had been dragged off to a foundry in Pueblo, Colorado, by the Cohen brothers and the sagebrush on the little hill could return to normalcy and be scenic again.

Thus ended Max's used-car caper in Taos.

"It was a disaster, of course," says Pat, laughing, "but for a couple of months there, all his pals had something to drive around town in."

And the big question: with Max's fiction being largely autobiographical, why haven't we read about the used-car lot in his stories?

"Well," he says, "I didn't think people would believe it. I didn't believe it myself."

Calf-Roping

Ol' Max done lots of things and I done lots of things, only mine didn't work.
                                —David Evans, cousin and cowboy

Taos was the place for Max's art work, but it was also the place for his calf roping. Few cowboys who can coil a rope haven't dreamed of making it big on the circuit.

If I just get the right horse. . . . If I draw the right calf. . . . If nobody really good enters . . . . Ah, the stuff dreams are made on.

And with Max Evans, he who can't ride broncs but can rope anything with hair, the dream went on and on.

Max at a team roping in Magdalena, NM.

"If you look very closely at the loop," Max says, "you can see this was a catch. It only looks like I missed the calf." The horse belongs to Woody Crumbo the Younger, the roping was in Magdalena, and the year was probably 1984, making Max 60 at the time.

Max roped in R.C.A. (pro) rodeos on a permit, he roped in semi-pro rodeos, he roped in amateur rodeos, and he especially roped in jackpots, that winner-take-all standby of people of the West.

He roped before World War II, he roped after World War II. He roped until 1959 when being a writer took precedence over nodding one's head for the gate.

Max's last rodeo was, coincidentally, the last professional rodeo held in Española, New Mexico There is no publicly acknowledged connection between the two events. But it is this last rodeo of his, and how he went about doing things, that best illustrates the Max Evans Way of competing.

For those not rodeo literate, calf roping is a timed contest. At a nod from the roper, a calf is released into the arena on a dead run. The roper and his horse then chase the calf, rope the calf, and the horse slides to a stop.

The roper jumps off his horse, runs down the rope to the calf, throws the calf on his side, and ties three of the calf's legs together with a six-foot length of narrow rope called a piggin' string.

The time starts when the calf crosses a start line. It finishes when the roper completes the tie on the calf and throws his hands in the air.

> That equilibrium thing really messed me up. I never told anyone this, but every time I roped, I had to take Dramamine to keep from getting sick or falling off my horse.
>
> —Max Evans

Back in the 1950s, any time under fifteen seconds would probably see you winning some money. Tying a calf in twelve, in those days, would often win it.

So, that being said, let's go back to 1959 in Taos, and Max's way of entering the calf roping.

Two legends of New Mexico swap stories at a roping in Magdalena. Max has been friends with top roper and cattle baron Buddy Major, right, for many years. Photo by Pat Evans.

"I really wanted to get in the calf roping real bad there in Española," Max says. "So I went around to the bars and promoted enough money for my R.C.A. permit and for the entry fee. Ended up owing at least half of anything I won, I believe.

"Then I borrowed a real good roping horse from Wade Miles, son of Governor John E. Miles. This was a horse named Ripper, who was out in Curly Murray's pasture just down from our place then on Ledoux Street. He had hair that long. It was winter, you know.

"You could see him from the window of my studio, there where I wrote *The Rounders* and *The Hi Lo Country*. Curly Murray had taken over the gambling in Taos from Long John Dunn and had all that pasture there, not three blocks from the plaza.

"Ripper was a good horse. I borrowed him the day before the rodeo. Didn't even have a chance to brush him.

"Didn't have any transportation, either. Finally I got ol' Horsethief Shorty to drive me and Ripper down there in his pickup truck. The bed leaned over like this. So we got that horse, didn't brush him or anything. Yeah, he was barefoot, too.

"So Pat drove the car down with the kids and I rode with Shorty. We just about didn't get there in time. We were just going chug, chug, chug down that mountain.

"But we got there and here was all these champions, including that Oklahoma Cherokee world-champion roper, Tom Ferguson.

"Well, about two-thirds of the ropers had roped before I came up, and I think I only had to beat 14.8 to win this thing. So here I was on this barefoot, hairy horse right out of the pasture, riding into the arena, and I said to myself, 'You know, I believe I'll just win this thing.'

"Then the announcer, who remembered me from amateur ropings and jackpots, says, 'Here's the Taos champion!'

"This was in front of the world champion. I tell you, if I wasn't such a dumb sonofabitch, I'd have just loaded that horse up and left right then, or rode him down to the Rio Grande, kept going, never to be seen again.

"Taos champion . . . what an embarrassing thing. Well, I backed ol' Ripper into the box and all of a sudden I forgot all of it. 'Course, his hooves were a little long. He might fall down, but he was ready and so was I. He came out of there so smooth, I caught that calf so quick, and you know that calf turned around and came right back by that horse. Even with that, I tied him in eighteen seconds.

"When he turned back I said, 'Well, I'm out of the money, but when I get to him I'm going to wrap this calf faster'n anybody in the history of the world.'

"You know, looking back after all these years, I believe I'd have won that (if the calf hadn't turned back). I felt it in the box and I can feel it now.

"Just got the wrong calf. No excuse. It happens to us all one way or the other."

Max began roping in competition back during his Hi Lo days near Des Moines. They were, he says, some "punkin' rollin's" he attended with Big Boy.

"I couldn't afford a good horse," he says, "so I mostly borrowed horses," in the early days.

The roping part of his life heated up when he moved to Taos.

"When I got to Taos, and got that little place out in the country, I got this little brown pony. We called him Brownie. He wasn't too fast, and it took him two-thirds of the arena to catch that calf. But that really speeded up my tying."

Not everyone can take a $30 horse and make a money-winning roping horse out of him, but Max did. This is Brownie, out in the pasture in Taos about 1950. Photo by Pat Evans.

Max says he could wrap one up quickly because he had to make up the time Brownie cost him by not getting him to the calf quickly enough.

"The best roping horse I ever had was an Appaloosa mare. Bought her down here in Corrales. I called her Raggedy Ann, after that other mare (of Ed Young's) This must have been 1954.

"They were roping on this mare in jackpots. Now those were marvelous fun. On any given day, you might beat a world champion. They don't do that any more, and it's a shame. Rules, you

In a practice arena in 1957, Max is roping a calf on "Sleepy Kay." He says he didn't get the slack on this calf, but it wasn't the horse's fault. He later gave her to his friends Sonny Jim and Woody Crumbo the Younger, who "made a helluva steer jerking horse out of her."

Max roping the heels on Jack, while his buddy, Sam Hightower ropes the heads at a branding on the Mariposa Ranch near Taos.

see. Rules rule us all now. Millions and millions of rules. That's why I broke a few of them—trying to thin them out."

"This mare could build to a calf just as fast as you could possibly get a loop ready. I found out later that some days she'd work and some days she wouldn't. She was part of Old Fooler (the unpredictable roping horse in *The Rounders*).

"I took her to Taos and worked her quite a bit. I'd ride her at least three times a week if I could possibly take the time.

"Used to ride that Raggedy Ann mare down past Frieda Lawrence's place. D. H. was dead by that time, of course, and she'd married an Italian fella named Angelino Ravalgi. Real nice guy. He was a potter. Had his potter wheel out in the yard. But I hardly got to know him because every time I'd stop, here would come Frieda. She'd ask me questions about that Appaloosa mare."

A little detour here.

"Funny thing about Frieda," Max says. "She rolled these cigarettes five or six inches long and always had one hanging on the edge of her lip. Damndest thing I ever saw. Never saw it fall. Not once.

"Not long after that, Frieda died and Angelino inherited all that money. D. H. Lawrence's books suddenly became popular again and sold millions. Angelino got it all. He moved back to the Italian Riviera and bought a villa, and I'll bet it's filled with beautiful women and champagne. There's one thing about him, though. No matter how much money he spends, no matter how long he lives, he'll never live long enough to break even. He paid for that inheritance many, many times over, being married to Frieda."

Max laughs. "She looked like she could knock out Mike Tyson with a left hook."

Back on the trail again: Max had to keep this Appaloosa mare "ridden down" so she'd behave herself.

"I won some ropings up in southern Colorado and some at Taos on that mare. I'd try to get ready so I could throw the loop on the third twirl. That was about as fast as I could do it. And she was fast enough to catch most calves that fast.

"She had the hardest stop I ever saw. She'd stop on all four feet and that was really tough. I was complaining about it once, and Pat told me that was because she was bucking with me!"

Max laughs. "A couple of times I'd tied the fastest calves in my life. She'd literally bucked me off and I landed halfway to the calf.

"There was a guy in Santa Fe named Red Boggs who was the toughest sonofabitch in New Mexico. I thought, this is the guy to buy this mare. So I took Red to Maria's Mexican Kitchen to talk to him about her, taking a chance on him getting drunk and knocking my head off.

"You never knew what she was going to do at a roping. She might be a great roping horse, or she might buck me off. I never was a hand at riding bucking horses. It got to where I'd take her out in the desert behind our house and lope her through that dirt to take the edge off her, and then ride her all the way down to that arena, about three miles away. And it still didn't do any good.

"Everybody thought they were cowboy enough to handle this mare, but they weren't. I loaned her to a top professional. He took her for a couple of weeks. Roped on her in the Cow Palace (in San Francisco). She didn't buck with him like she did me. She made a sliding stop and backed up and tightened that rope. So he caught his first calf and was leading in the first go-round. He figured he'd win the two-calf average.

"So on the second calf, he roped it fast, then bailed off and headed for the calf and something went by him. It was that old mare. She ran past him and kept running around the arena, dragging that calf, with everyone trying to catch her.

"Well, he was so mad, when he caught her he kicked her in the belly. You talk about an explosion! He just got out of there before they dismembered that poor sucker.

"So he brought the mare back to me. I took her over to let ol' Red try her out. He got on her and worked her, and she had a helluva rein. We were turning calves out and Red was working them. Well, Red bought that old mare.

"I said, 'Red, I want you to know, again, that the best cowboys in the world thought they could handle that old mare and I haven't seen anyone do it yet. And I don't want you to come after me and beat the shit out of me.'"

Max chuckles. "He said, 'I can handle that sonofabitch.'"

"Now he hadn't been around long enough to know that no matter how tough you are, how tough you think you are or how good you think you are, there's something out there that'll get you, that will beat you and make it look easy. There's something out there that'll smash you just to even your mind out. To level things out, to make things come flat once in a while.

"Next time I saw him was in Maria's Kitchen. I asked him, 'How are you and Raggedy Ann getting along?' He said, 'Well, I don't know what to tell you yet.'

"I didn't see him again for maybe six months. He said, 'Max, you were right. I couldn't handle her. But I admired her so much, I put her out to pasture for the rest of her life.'

"Isn't that beautiful? I can see her now, so fat and lazy she can't even remember how many dumb-ass cowboys she did in.

"I admired the hell out of her, too. I had her for, oh, about a year, I guess. 'Course, I was trying to get rid of her after the first couple of months. But she had this attitude. You know . . . 'You can knock me in the head or spur me, it don't make any difference. I'm going to do what I'm going to do, and that's all I'm going to do. I'll deliver when I damn please. ' I really admired that ol' gal. Still do."

Max's next roping horse was the aforementioned gray Arabian gelding named Reno, picked up in a used-car deal.

"He'd build to a calf pretty well," Max says, "but he wasn't as fast as that Appaloosa mare. And an Arabian doesn't stop on his hind legs like most cowponies do. This old pony was a good one. I'd trust him every way, but he just wouldn't stop (right). He'd take you to a calf where you could get him in about fourteen seconds, if he'd stop correctly.

"Next horse I got was my only top one, ever. I was getting older, but I could still tie one pretty swift. I just needed a good horse.

"There was a guy named Hamm, from Clovis, New Mexico. Big, husky guy. His hands suited his name, you know? He had this big roan blaze-faced horse. He won a lot of ropings on him. He'd just quit the circuit and was just jackpotting around the country. And he'd still beat you.

"Now I knew I just had one more year (of roping), and I thought I'd just love to have a good horse for that year. Just one year on a real good horse to see what I could really do, you know? So I started talking to him. I traded him a set of my cowboy prints, and all the money I had in the world, which was $300 or $400, and something else, too. Can't remember.

"Horse's name was Powder Face. He was a helluva horse. I won three or four ropings on Powder Face. Well, we had a lot of rain that fall and I had him out in our subirrigated pasture. He'd come up to the fence and play with the kids. Well, he got thrush standing around in that wet ground, and the vet said to get somebody to build an iron shoe so the hoof would grow back out.

"All of a sudden, I realized I wasn't going to rope any more. So about that time, I heard from my cousin, David Evans. He was a helluva cowboy and was still running the southern end of a ranch over by Tatum, New Mexico. I tried to get him to be a steer roper. I figured he'd win the world championship if he did. I mean, he was a top steer and calf roper. He'd had a match roping with (famous world champion calf roper) Toots Mansfield."

If David was a bit reluctant to do any horse trading with Max, it could have something to do with the last horse he got from Max. This horse tore down David's barn and corral.

"(That horse) was a pretty sonofabitch, though," Max says, laughing.

"But he took Powder Face, and renamed him Roanie. went to Post, Texas, and won a big roping on him. I just loaned him to him. Well, Roanie gained some weight and David didn't work him for a while, and damned if ol' Roanie didn't fall dead one day. Had a heart attack. Damn, he was a great horse! Broke ol' David's heart more than mine. He was planning to go win a bunch of ropings on him. I was done roping by that time.

"The only thing I did after that was to borrow old Ripper and enter that rodeo in Española."

A couple of years later, when two fictional cowboys named Dusty and Wrangler tried to get a blaze-faced roan horse named Old Fooler to stop bucking and attend to being a top roping horse, there were some good, some top, and some awful roping horses that lent their experiences to the story. Raggedy Ann, Powder Face, Ripper, Snip, Brownie, and Reno live on in *The Rounders*.

But there's something about calf roping. About the intrinsic partnership between a man and his horse. It's an affliction that can follow a guy the rest of his life.

One time, shortly after Max had won the Western Writers of America's Levi Strauss Golden Saddleman Award for lifetime achievement, he and I were having lunch and doing an interview for the Albuquerque Journal, where I was a columnist.

"Well, Max," I said, "what's next? You've won all these big awards now, is there something else you want to accomplish before you're done?"

I was thinking Pulitzer and Nobel, of course. Not Max. He was quiet for a minute or two, then said, "Well, I'll tell you this because you're probably the only reporter in the world who will understand it.

"Just once in my life, I'd like to make a perfect run in calf roping." He leaned forward in intensity and whispered. "It wouldn't have to be fast, even, but just perfect. You know how it is, the horse works perfectly, the calf runs straight, I do my job well? Smooth. Just like a dance."

A Little Wreck Among Friends . . .

Max and his pal, Sam Hightower, have known each other since "Ah hell, I can't remember," Max says.

They both ended up in Taos at the same time, Max painting and writing and doing ranch day work, and Sam running a large nearby cattle ranch.

Sam and Max went partners on a roping horse named Jack, and one day when they were both working cattle on the ranch, Jack had a chance to prove his worth.

"We were working these big steers," Sam says, "me and Ol' Max, and I just knew this one big ol' steer would duck off and run."

Sam had just bought his first nylon catch rope and was dying to try it out on something, and this steer gave him the perfect opportunity.

"Yeah, I couldn't wait to see if this new rope was so strong I couldn't break it. That was back when (nylon ropes) first came out. So this one steer, well, I gave him some slack and sure enough, he broke (back) and ran on me.

"I built to him. He was going down this lane, heading for a hog barn, and it had a tin roof on it about this high. Well, just as I roped that sonofabitch, he decided to go under that roof

A publicity shot for The Rounders *in 1965 features Glenn Ford, Hope Holiday, Sue Anne Langdon, Henry Fonda, and, of course, Old Fooler.*

and around the post. I wasn't going to go through there and cut my damn leg off, so I kinda ducked off."

Well, with the steer running full tilt on one side of the post, and Jack and Sam running full tilt on the other side, and a brand-new nylon rope connecting them, Max had a ringside seat to an Olympic-class wreck.

"Well," says Sam, "I tried to bail out but it was too late. When that rope came tight, it was like we was flying. Directly everything was popping. Ripped the D-rings off the saddle, broke the breast strap, broke the girth, broke the damn tie down. Max said it looked like we were up in the air for sixty seconds.

"Finally we all came down to earth and I went flying off and it turned that steer ass backwards and that saddle wrapped twice around that post, we hit so hard.

"I came down flat on my back. Wham! Well, Max saw all this and he rode off and caught my horse, then he came riding up and looked down at me and said, 'Sam . . . you all right?'

"I just said, 'Hell, I don't know.'"

The Rounders

If Max Evans had only written *The Rounders*, he would have assured himself a small niche in the history of contemporary American fiction. *The Rounders* is a raucous and wonderfully comic novel about the present-day working West.

—Charles Champlin,
book and film critic for the Los Angeles Times,
from his introduction to *Super Bull
and Other True Escapades*

Max, even while he was painting and hawking the still-wet canvases in the Taos bars, had kinda backed into writing stories. He wrote some outdoor pieces, then tried some short stories. His first book, *Southwest Wind*, was a collection of these early attempts at fiction.

Then he was asked by Long John Dunn—who had run the gambling in Taos and all of northern New Mexico for many

"Max is the kind of guy you can take anywhere . . . and still be ashamed of him," says famed book and movie critic Charles Champlin, shown here with his wife Peg and Max at a meeting in Studio City, Cal. Around 1998. Photo by Pat Evans.

years—to write a book about his life. Max agreed, and *Long John Dunn of Taos* was the result.

But he still didn't call himself a writer. That would come years later, after many hundreds of thousands of words had passed.

Then came *The Rounders.*

"Well," says Max, "there we were in the house in Taos, and I had no idea what in the world I was going to do.

"The mining was over, done. I didn't have any paintings left, right then. Now I was still roping calves, and I did day work on some of the ranches in the area, so I still had that cowboy connection."

Max had already written *Southwest Wind* and *Long John Dunn of Taos* by this time.

"So I figured I'd write a story about cowboys, but not like Zane Grey. He had those people doing things people would never do, but he sure described the country really well.

"I decided I'd write about ranch hands the way things really are. I'd tell the truth. There would be a book about cowboys that would be real, for once."

So, between doing day work riding colts and helping with brandings on local ranches, Max retired to his upstairs study and began typing his story on an old upright Underwood typewriter. In those days, Max typed the books and then Pat edited them and retyped them on the same typewriter, this time using three carbons.

After writing for about six months, Max finally had his book, which at first he called "A Taste of Horsehair."

Of course, writing a book is one thing and getting it published are two different things. He needed help with that.

Max is not about to sit back and not get a book in print. He'll go make sure it happens. There's his wonderful promotional

One of the more interesting things about Long John Dunn, the old Texas outlaw and king of Taos gambling, Max says, is that he was able to change with the times. When the automobile came along, he gave up the stagecoach business and started buying gasoline. This horseless stagecoach of Dunn's was used primarily to pick up Mabel Dodge Luhan's friends at the train station in Lamy and take them to the house in Taos. Photo taken in the 1920s.

skills and his personality. If he had to go to some publishing house he'd never heard of, he'd do that, too.

—James Hamilton,
author of Cross of Iron, essayist, screenwriter.

The man who finally had enough faith in what became *The Rounders* and in the ex-cowboy from Taos, New Mexico who wrote it, was Henry Volkening, a respected New York literary agent and partner in the firm of Russell and Volkening.

"Henry Volkening," says Max, "was a real power. He'd have lunches with the heads of the publishing houses. He was respected and when he believed in a book, the publishers took it very seriously."

"He got these deals," he says, laughing, "because he could out-martini any of them. For *The Rounders* he had to out-liquid them eleven times before Macmillan took the book."

He guided Max's manuscript into print, which really meant starting him off on a career, because this was really the first big step. And it took faith. This book had several things going against it. It was about cowboys, all right, but these guys didn't shoot anybody. They didn't win the girl or the ranch. In fact, they lost their butts every time they turned around.

The story did not take place in the romantic Old West, either, that shining time that society has now turned into the days of American knighthood, even though it wasn't. No, this took place in post World War II New Mexico. Not a very exotic setting for a story of two guys who could have made more money washing dishes in the nearest town.

But this was also a story of the courage of living by a code. The courage to try to earn a living by refusing to fit into society. And most of all, it was funny. It was hilarious. People who had never seen a horse thought it was funny. People who knew horses thoroughly almost choked from the laughing.

And so, when *The Rounders* was still a manuscript called "A Taste of Horsehair" and wasn't even a book yet, Volkening sent it out to Ned Brown, an agent at Music Corporation of America, the largest agency in Hollywood. He became Max's early Hollywood agent, says Max, "by default."

One of the greatest parts of director Burt Kennedy's legendary birthday parties in California was the opportunity for Hollywood folks to see old friends. Here actor Morgan Woodward and Max relive old times when both were broke and they shared Morgan's house with almost no furniture. But both enjoyed the occasional drink of P.M. bourbon, which they assumed stood for Post Mortem. During his long career as a "heavy" (bad guy), Woodward claims the record of having been gunned down by Marshal Dillon on Gunsmoke more than any other actor. Photo by Pat Evans in 2000.

"In those days," Max says, "they had what they called a slush pile. This was a table full of manuscripts which actors, writers, directors, and producers could go through to see if there was something there they liked. As it turned out, the title of the book caught the attention of Burt Kennedy, the director who finally made *The Rounders*. He took it home and fell madly in love with it.

"In the meantime, I had renamed it *The Rounders*, because of the old Western expression about someone who has a lot of fun being a rounder. And a rounder does have fun."

Friends of Max have described him, in fact, as being the original rounder, which he considers a great compliment. 'I've always tried to do my best to have fun," he says.

Kennedy showed the manuscript to actor Fess Parker, who also loved it.

"Fess was the most famous actor in the world at that point," Max says. "He was Davy Crockett on television, and every kid in the world had to get a coonskin cap like his. Then he had a couple of successful series on TV, too, and played Daniel Boone for five years."

The six-feet-five-inch Parker, who owns a winery and several hotels in Santa Barbara, California now, had money even then and was looking for a "property" that would increase the good times. *The Rounders*, he thought, would do nicely. He called Max, and they worked out a cheap option on the book.

But Parker and Kennedy really needed to meet Max and talk turkey about this project ("Which was a con job all the way," Max says), and they convinced Max to drive out from Taos.

"I wouldn't fly, of course," Max says. "In those days I didn't explain about my inner ear (trouble). I just told them I was scared to fly and let it go at that. I said, I have to drive out, and said I can make it out there, I have enough money to buy gas, but I just have four tires, and they're slick. I don't have a spare. And that's a helluva gamble. So when I show up, if I ever show up at all, you may have to feed me and my wife and twin daughters for quite a while."

They made it to Santa Barbara. This was 1960.

"I really got worried, going across that desert," Max says, "because it was 105 out there, it was fall, but what are you gonna do?"

Fess Parker had a big house in the hills above Santa Barbara, and installed Max and Pat and the girls in the guesthouse.

"He was just a fair actor," Max says, "but he had a certain irresistible charm that people liked."

Max and family stayed there a month.

"It wasn't fun all the time," Max says, flatly. "Oh, it was fun the first week, when the two of us would go off to town and go to drinking and raising hell, but the rest of it wasn't fun. All he was doing was conning me, all along. I don't blame him. He didn't want me to have anything to do with it. That was the con job."

In the meantime, famous director William Wellman (Wings and The Ox-Bow Incident) had read the book and decided to come out of retirement to make *The Rounders*. He had been volunteering his time in working with writer Tom Blackburn to write a script for the film. Wellman was so serious about this, Max says, that he went to rodeos and climbed down in the chutes to see what it was like for the cowboys. He was a fairly old man then, and a World War I pilot from the Lafayette Escadrille.

Having a man of Wellman's stature want to make the film was a tremendous feather in Max's cap. Here he had the most famous actor in the world, Fess Parker, to play the part of Dusty, and Wellman to direct. The sun was shining on his world.

Almost.

When actor Morgan Woodward tacked a publicity photo of himself, like this one, to the wall in his home in the Hollywood hills, it was natural that he and Max should have a shooting contest with it using a revolver with full-load wax blanks. The shooting contest was handicapped somewhat by both shooters consuming quantities of "Post Mortem" bourbon, which didn't endear them to the police when they arrived.

Fess took Max all over Hollywood and introduced him to lots of people in the film world, including Fess's old fraternity brother, Morgan Woodward, who became Max's lifelong friend.

"Fess really treated me right that way," Max says.

Then, about two weeks after arriving at Parker's house, Fess drove them to a meeting at Tom Blackburn's home in the hills above Burbank. And Max was finally able to meet the famous director, William Wellman.

"Fess did a strange thing that day," Max says. "He asked me what I was going to wear. I told him the totality of my attire consisted of two pairs of Levis and three white shirts. So Fess said he'd wear Levis, too. But he took a long box out to the car and put it in the back seat before we left."

Wellman took right to Max. These were men who spoke the same language. In fact, Wellman liked Max so well, it ended what could have been a magnificent working relationship.

"We were sitting outside looking over the whole world, having drinks," Max says. "Wellman took one look at my battered face, and he knew I'd been in World War II combat, and he kept looking at me. It was starting to make me feel uncomfortable. Then all of a sudden he blurted out, 'You're going to play Wrangler.'"

Wrangler is Dusty's partner in *The Rounders*, and Max's description of him pretty well tallies with Max's own description. The only problem was, Max wasn't an actor and here one of the most famous directors in Hollywood wants him to co-star in a motion picture with the most famous actor at that time in the world.

Yep. It was a problem.

"You're chunky," Wellman told Max, "and you've got a busted-up face. You'll be perfect."

"And Fess," says Max, "just turned white as a goose. He got up . . . and this was the weirdest damn thing I've seen in my life, and I've seen some weird things . . . he got up and went out and got that box. In it was a black suit and a tie, and he put them on. Now this is a casual, daytime thing, and what the hell was going through his mind, that he was going to impress William Wellman by putting on a shirt and tie, I'll never know. Pat was just stunned.

"A little later, Fess said I couldn't play the part, and Wellman said, 'The hell he can't. He's a natural. I'll tell him what to do when we get on the set. It'll be real.'"

"I didn't even want to do it," Max says. "Not at all. But here's the thing. I admired William Wellman so much, for him I would have done it. He busted his ass to get that script done, and went to Colorado Springs to the rodeo and got down in the chutes. Just to get the feel of it. So I would've done it for him. I sure would've."

That, said Max, was a very unpleasant night.

"I didn't know if Fess understood me or not," Max says, quietly, "but after dinner that night I went over and told him . . . well, I told him he was lucky to be sitting there alive. He was sitting there, and he was still real tall, sitting down, you know. It was that jealousy of his. He was destroying the picture and didn't know it. He should've known better. He is a smart and charming old boy, but somehow he went wrong here for all of us.

"So the next week we go to a meeting at United Artists. They didn't have studios then, just offices. I don't remember where this office was. Well, why would I?

"King Vidor died, and his widow, Doris Vidor, ran the place. We met and there was just her and some guy, big-time sonofabitch—don't know who he was—and us: William Wellman, Fess Parker, and me. We were there to close the deal.

"So she said, 'Well, let's put this together.' She ignored Fess Parker. Here was the most famous actor in the world, but she was talking just to William Wellman. She was going to produce the movie, and Wellman would direct. That's what was planned. Now you're sitting there owning the world, as a writer. For thirty minutes, you're owning the world. So they get down to putting the thing together. Wellman said to her, 'And here's my two leads right here,' meaning me and Fess. Wellman named Slim Pickens and some women who were going to be in it, and me and Fess.

"Then Fess said, 'Mr. Wellman, Miss Vidor, I'm not going to put my time and money in this—and this is no offense to you, Max, you're a writer—with you playing Wrangler.'

"And Wellman said, 'Are you set on that?' and Fess said 'Absolutely.' So Wellman stood up, turned around, and walked off. Didn't even go back in to tell them it was off. He turned around once and yelled 'Come see me!' And I did. It was a privilege to visit such a great man."

So here's the picture: Max and Pat and the twins are staying in Fess Parker's guest house with a car with four slick tires and no money to speak of, and the deal is off. So Pat put the girls in the car and headed for Taos. Pat ran out of gas and money in Grants, New Mexico, and called the wife of rodeo champion, Elliott Calhoun. She put Pat and the girls up for the night and loaned her gas money to make it to Taos.

Max decided to stay in Hollywood for a while longer, as long as the option lasted, to try and find a way to get *The Rounders* made. He'd met a lot of Hollywood people, thanks to Fess, and planned to see what he could dredge up through them.

To help out, Parker said he knew a hotel in Beverly Hills where Max could stay and he'd take him there. This turned out to be the Crescent Hotel, a fleabag place that cost $25 a week. It was right in front of the fancy MCA agency building that looked like Mount Vernon. Max moved in.

"Some developer was just keeping it open," Max says, "until he figured how to tear it down and make that Beverly Hills money."

When he dropped Max off, Fess stuck a folded bill into Max's pocket. Max had manners enough not to look at it until after Fess had gone.

"He was a rich sonofabitch," Max says, "so I figured it was probably at least a hundred. But it was a twenty. Well, that's fine. That's how he stayed rich."

The manager at the Crescent Hotel was very clear: you pay by the week or I put your bags outside and there are no exceptions.

"Well, I didn't have a knife or a gun to go mug somebody," Max says, "and I didn't even have a dime to make a call. It was tough. I knew I couldn't pay the rent, so I figured I'd get out a day early. The manager helped me tie a rope around my suitcase."

During a Hollywood visit with Fess Parker, Max met Parker's old school chum, Morgan Woodward. Woodward gave Max his number and told him to call him sometime. Well, this seemed like a good time.

Woodward is one of the most easily recognized "bad guys" in Hollywood. His most chilling performance, according to many, was as the prison guard with the mirrored sunglasses in Cool Hand Luke. He has also been gunned down numerous times in Western films and television series, and he holds the record for being killed by Marshall Dillon more than anyone else.

Now retired from acting, Woodward flies a plane and spends as much time as he can at his Paso Robles, California, ranch, and he reads a lot of books.

Back in the early 1960s, however, he was trying to get acting jobs.

"Max ran out of money at this cheap hotel," Morgan says, "so they threw him out. He called me and said he was going back to Taos. So I told him he could stay with me.

"I had a house, but I didn't have any furniture. I drove down to get him and—I'll never forget this—he was sitting out on the curb with a cardboard suitcase with a rope tied around it. We went to a second-hand store and bought a cot. He stayed with me several months."

("Now that," Max later said, "was Hollywood glamour, Pardner.")

Nor were these months dull. Max was writing and Morgan was acting, and when they took breaks. . . .

"We had a high ol' time while he was here," says Morgan. "We ate peanut butter and spaghetti, and when I'd get lucky and get a job, we could go out and get some Mexican food. He was finishing a book then, and I don't remember if it was The Hi Lo Country or The One-Eyed Sky.

"Now we both liked to have a toddy, and it didn't have to be after the sun went behind the yard arm, either. Our adult beverage was the cheapest whisky we could find called P.M. Bourbon. We decided it stood for Post Mortem.

"About that time, I got lucky and got a (role on) Wagon Train, and one day I gave a ride home to one of the other guys on the show. He was kinda sheltered, from back East.

"Well, we had a few toddies at the house, and I had this single-action revolver with full-load blanks with wax bullets. These aren't the loads we used for close-up work. These things hit the living room wall with a thunk.

"So we put one of my eight-by-ten glossies on the wall and shot at it. Had a shooting contest. Naturally, the police came. Scared this kid half to death. But the police were more tolerant of actors in those days."

On another occasion at Morgan's house, following the requisite downing of a few Post Mortems, of course, Max dared Morgan to parachute off the second-story balcony.

"I'm a pilot," Morgan explained, "and had this parachute. I don't really remember if it opened on the way down or not. About a thirteen-foot drop, I'd guess."

Max didn't jump. He said, "The way the house set on a tall slope, it was probably thirty feet down to the first hedge. I figured Morgan's parachute would open in plenty of time. He must have folded it wrong because it took him a spell to untangle himself from that hedge."

"Max has been my close friend for more than forty years now," Morgan said. "There are lots of things I like about him, but I think his most outstanding feature is how straightforward he is. He accepts you at face value. You can always depend on what he says.

"He's also the most positive person I've ever known, especially about his own work. He has an incredible amount of confidence about his work, and every piece he writes is better than the last.

"He doesn't look back with regret about anything."

Morgan laughed. "He also has a mind much greater than he'd like for you to discern. He gives the impression of having been in the bunkhouse for a long time."

It was Max who introduced Morgan Woodward to Sam Peckinpah.

Morgan got a call from Max to meet him and the famous director at a local bar.

"Peckinpah kept going on and on about how much he enjoyed my work," Morgan said. "After a whole lot of this, Max said, 'Quit praising him, Sam, and give him a goddam job.'"

Peckinpah was in declining health by then, and actor and director were never able to work together, but they were able to enjoy that evening with Max.

Five years later, and five options later, Burt Kennedy filmed *The Rounders* in northern Arizona, with Glenn Ford and Henry

Fonda in the leads. It was a rollicking success, led to a short-lived television series, too. But it also brought Max Evans and Hollywood together, and they stayed together.

His first successful book, *The Rounders*, brought Max more than $100,000 and a career in writing.

> The kind of writing Max does, the kind of truth he tells, he'll never make a lot of money. Oh, once in a while he'll hit a lick, but it's not like Louis L'Amour, you know.
> —Chuck Miller, one of Max's closest friends

> Everybody wants to be a writer. Isn't that the weirdest thing? But you either have it or you don't. You can go to school and study and work hard at it, but if you don't have it, you're never going to get it.
>
> Writing is a natural, inborn rhythm that flows and comes. And there's no way to teach that.
> —Pat Evans

Yaqui Gold

I was back up in that mining country in the Black Range recently. I had to be real careful, because I didn't want to get the bug again. I was all through with that mining business. It's infectious. There's no cure for it, you know, except to be planted plumb under. I'm not real sure that would work in my case.

—Max Evans

✀ **There is something about gold,** about the weight of it, the feel of it, the way the sun catches it. It is the oldest and most durable measure of wealth, and the search for it has caused the deaths of thousands, maybe millions.

Max was not immune to this, either. Not only did he search for it as a miner and prospector and speculator, but he crossed the lines of legality time and again for it.

Until the 1970s, it was illegal for any American citizen to own raw gold. You could wear it as jewelry, but not hoard it as raw or smelted ore. But in Mexico, people could have as much gold as they could handle, and in China and India, people wanted gold and would pay exorbitant amounts for it.

Max worked in mining in Taos with a man he calls (for reasons that will become obvious later) "Mr. R." Mr. R. was fluent in Spanish and traveled freely in Mexico. While down there, he found gold being hoarded and bought it. The problem came in getting the gold to its new owners in China and India. This conduit was a group of Los Angeles-area businessmen whom Max describes, winking, as "organized gentlemen." They were headquartered in Irwindale, at that time a sparsely settled area of rocks and brush against the San Gabriel Mountains that was famous for its gravel quarries.

Mr. R. bought the gold and brought it as far as El Paso. The Los Angeles gold smugglers picked it up a short distance northwest of El Paso and paid for it. And between El Paso and Taos was Max Evans, gold smuggler.

This all came about because of Max's friendship with Laddie Anderson, one of the most colorful and controversial characters he's ever known, a "seven-foot-tall" Colorado bush pilot with a scar clear across his face.

Anderson was a veteran of gold smuggling in India and China, and flew for the Irwindale smugglers in Asia. It was during that time that his plane went down in the jungles of India with a fortune in gold on board.

When a pilot disappears with a load of gold and is gone for weeks, the sponsors from Irwindale could be expected to think the worst, and they did. They put a worldwide contract out on Laddie. But they didn't know Laddie Anderson nearly as well as they thought they did. Severely injured in the crash (this is when he earned the deep scar completely across his face), he nevertheless managed to take care of himself, work his way through miles of jungle, and get back to civilization. And he brought the bosses' gold with him in two ancient carts pulled by Indian oxen.

After that, he could just about write his own ticket with the "organized gentlemen" from the gravel pits. As a gesture of good will, they bought him control of India Air Lines. After a few years, Anderson sold his interest in the airlines and bought a ranch in Colorado, and it was during this time that he and Max struck up a friendship.

"He was the nicest, gentlest guy you ever met," Max says, "but with that scar, and his size . . . well, after he'd visit me, people in Taos didn't mess with me for a long time. And this was a good thing, because I'd busted up my knuckles and hands so much by that time that I couldn't fight like I used to."

It was Laddie Anderson who made the connection between Mexican gold and the fellows in Irwindale, and it was his friend, Max Evans, who made a profit by being the middleman.

Max would meet the Mexican connection in the Del Norte Hotel in El Paso, which Max says was full of smugglers and cattle buyers, then take the gold to the designated exchange spot.

Thirty times, maybe forty times, Max made the drive to El Paso, paid Mr. R. for the gold, and then drove into the New Mexico desert and sold it to a representative of the Irwindale faction. All this came during a time when Max was struggling as an artist and a writer and was trying to put a living together for him and Pat and the two girls.

The last time this happened, Max had hocked everything he could find, borrowed from everyone he knew, and came up with $3,500 cash that Mr. R. told him he needed to get a really large stash of Mexican gold.

"This was really a fortune to me," Max says. "I had a friend in Taos at that time, we'll call him Mr. C., who had done time for murder. He was a tough man. I took (Mr. R.) and introduced him to Mr. C. in a hotel room I'd rented. I gave Mr. R. the money and I told him, 'If you cross me on this, this man will get you. Do you know what I mean when I say get you?' He said he sure did, and he took the money and went to Mexico.

"That was the last I saw of him for several years," Max says, as Mr. R. never came back with the gold.

There's more about Mr. R. and Mr. C. to come, but back to Max and his circumstances at that time.

He'd hocked his shorts to finance this final gold buy and now owed money to all his friends. But it was then that Laddie Anderson had an idea. He knew a doctor in Modesto, California, who had contacts with Hispanic people in the Mother Lode area of the High Sierra, and some of these families had hoarded gold and wanted to turn it into cash.

Max went to Modesto and checked out the doctor's reputation.

"He was highly respected by everyone I talked to," Max says, "so I made a deal."

The deal was that the doctor would get the gold from the people in the hills, two million dollars' worth, and would drive with it to Los Angeles where he would meet with Max in a motel room. At the same time, representatives of the organized gentlemen would arrive at the motel room with two million dollars in a suitcase. The transfer would be made. The Modesto physician would be given $100,000 for his cut, and Max would be given another $100,000 for setting this all up. Laddie Anderson was acting as a sort of director, monitoring the transfer of the gold and the money.

"Well," Max says, "on the day the gold was to arrive, Pat and I were in the motel room.

"It's hard to figure now, " Max says, "but it was the Orange Motel right across the street from a Copper Kettle café . . . right on Sunset Boulevard, where I'd later wage many wars for survival. My first trip to Hollywood had little to do with films.

"We waited and waited, but the gold didn't arrive. Laddie said, over the phone in code, that the doctor had left Modesto with the gold, so we were expecting it.

"Pat and I sweated blood 'til we ran out of it for four of the longest days and nights The Great Mystery in the Sky ever invented. The gold was moving closer with each call and I had to call and explain this to the boys at Irwindale until my throat rasped like the gravel at their headquarters.

"Then here come these four men. They brought the suitcase in and set it on the bed. It was a very hot day, but they all wore these overcoats, and I didn't have to guess what they were carrying beneath them.

"I was sweating like crazy. I told them the gold would be here any time now. We sat and waited, and I about went crazy. Here were these guys with guns, and no gold. And the worst part was, I'd gotten beautiful young Pat into all this. If that gold didn't get there, I knew they were going to kill us.

"You know," he says, laughing, "I was so desperate I started looking for a weapon. The only thing I could spot was a little glass ash tray. Can you imagine? As though it would do any good to attack four armed men with a six-ounce ashtray!"

The Good Lord has watched him, and there have been these few seconds of time every now and then when the Good Lord saved him and let him live.

—Dr. Roland Sanchez,
long-time friend and Max's family doctor

Well, several hours went by . . . more than enough time to bring the gold down from the last frog jump from Modesto, and there was no phone call to tell Max about car trouble, or anything like that. They'd been stood up, and they knew it.

"What can you do? I was scared to death, but I had to tell these guys it looked like the gold wasn't coming.

"Two of them walked outside and talked for a long time. I knew we were going to die. Then the leader came back in and said, 'You got lucky this time.' And they took their money and left."

Max later learned that the doctor had gotten within about fifty miles of the rendezvous, then got cold feet, thinking he would be killed, and turned around and drove home with the gold.

"I thought to myself, 'You idiot. You almost got yourself killed and Pat killed, the beautiful woman you love and cherish, and you have two precious little girls.' And that was that for the gold smuggling."

But that wasn't that for the craving for gold or the hold it has, and that sure wasn't that for the dealings with Laddie Anderson.

The Great Mexican Bat Guano Caper

Ol' Max ever mention The Great Mexican Bat Guano Caper? Well, he's quite the promoter and con man, of course. He had this idea that we were going into the Yaqui Indian country in Mexico and bring back all this bat guano. There was said to be a lot of money in it as fertilizer. So we got together this motley crew. There was a soldier of fortune pilot who would do the flying. Then there was this bandido who Max got out of prison. He was a terrifying old guy, about five feet tall, carried all kinds of guns.

Since I was there in the bar (as bartender), I was sort of the front man. We were all going to go down there to the Yaqui country, and then Max would take it over. The bandido would do all the talking with the Indians. But then things started going wrong. The bandido got arrested in Louisiana. Then in comes a seven-foot man named Laddie, who was some kinda key person. From that point on, the story gets murky. I never did get down there, but Max did.

—James Hamilton,
author of *Cross of Iron*, essayist, screenwriter.

Laddie Anderson came to Taos to see Max some time after the motel/suitcase/no-show-gold episode.

"He told me he had a chance for a very lucrative contract in Mexico," Max says. "There were these caves in the Yaqui Indian country outside Guaymas that were filled with guano. Laddie knew this Yaqui general (in the Mexican army), and he could get the contract to mine it if he was able to get some financial backing. He asked if I could find some of the money and come in with him, and I told him to go ahead and sign the contract."

What had really intrigued Max about this, however, was not so much hauling bat manure out of caves (they used it for everything from fertilizer to gunpowder) but of Laddie's mention that there was also some placer gold to be had in that Yaqui country.

"I figured we'd go mine that guano for a while and maybe get some of that gold in the deal, too,'" Max says.

Anderson signed the contract with then-President Lopez Mateos and the Yaqui general. The contract also called for the miners to hire Yaqui labor, since it was on the reservation, and to clear mesquite along the mostly-dry Obregon River and build kilns to turn it into charcoal.

"The Mexican government," says Max, "had the idea that if you cleared out a lot of that mesquite, the Indians could start farming along that river. But the river was dry most of the time. Still, that was in our contract."

Of course, traveling to Mexico meant flying down there, and Laddie was a bush pilot with a plane, but Max couldn't fly. Since being blown up in France, his inner ear flared up into fits of vomiting the minute an airplane's wheels left the runway.

"Laddie said he knew how to fix that," Max says. "He said he'd just knock me out and I could fly down there unconscious."

Seemed like a good idea at the time.

Max would get in Laddie's plane and drink chloral hydrate, history's famous "Mickey Finn," and pass out. He would then wake up hours later in Guaymas, Mexico.

"I could fly that way just fine," Max says. "I'd wake up in a motel room in Mexico, and I always wondered how Laddie managed to get me there from the plane. We hid this action from 'most everybody, especially Pat. I owed her that after risking her life in the Orange Motel on famed Sunset Boulevard."

The bat-guano caves on the Yaqui reservation were nearly fifty miles out of Guaymas by jeep on a four-wheel-drive dirt track. In the contract, Laddie and Max had agreed to hire Yaquis for eighty-five percent of their labor force, and they did. But they also had some "gringo" workers there.

"One of the things we told those guys was that in no circumstances were they to look at a Yaqui woman. Now I didn't see anything particularly attractive about those women, in the conventional sense, but those Yaqui men thought they were beautiful. But I forgot for a while what it's like for a cowboy to be out on the range for a few months without women. The same urges possessed miners as well. That would lead us to disaster."

Sir Max Ingalls

At about this time, one of the more interesting characters to cross trails with Max came along and joined the party.

"His name," says Max, "was Sir Max Ingalls. He was an internationally known con man. Smoothest sonofabitch that ever was. He picked up the Yaqui language just like that. He was quite a linguist, and he had a great sense of humor. And the first thing I know, he's in with the Yaquis. He was known all over the world, and he was a Brit, but I don't think he'd really been knighted, except by his own kind."

Max and Laddie had about thirty people working altogether, mining bat guano and selling it, and clearing mesquite along the dry Obregon River and making charcoal out of it.

"We were mining this bat guano and packing it on burros down to Guaymas and making a big pile of it. They'd load it on a boat down there. It was my first experience with packing burros and I sure developed an appreciation for what those packers could do.

"Now we were forty to fifty miles from Guaymas and they had to pack that all that way through those terrible dry desert mountains, but they were doing it. And we sold it as soon as it got there, and what they used it for after that, I don't know. But they were buying it wholesale, so there wasn't a lot of money coming in.

"Frankly, I didn't care about the guano, I wanted to get to the gold. I guess I was greedy. Well, no, not greedy, but it was the excitement of getting to that gold. I'd been in the mining business and that was what I'd always been after. We knew the gold was there. We had our geologist friend, Den Galbraith, come down from Denver and take samples, and it was sure there. We could get this guano out of the way, and take care of this charcoal stuff, and then get to the gold. There was a chance to make some real money there."

"Now here's a mystery I'll never understand. Somehow the Yaquis had some Spanish gold bars. There's all kinds of legends about Maximilian and Spanish gold and that the Yaquis had some, and they sure as hell did. These were poor people, half starving, but they had this gold with Spanish markings on it. And somehow this con man, Sir Max Ingalls, got the Yaquis to let him have one gold bar. It wasn't standard size; it had been smelted by the Spanish, and it was heavy as hell.

"He went off on his own and sold it, came back and gave the Yaquis and us a little money. I felt bad about it, because these people really needed the money, but we were running out of money, too, and I was trying to raise more any way I could."

Sir Max Ingalls got two or three more bars from the Yaquis, and went in a jeep, on his own, to Los Angeles to sell it at the gravel pit.

"During this time, Laddie and I were making trips to Santa Fe and to Denver, trying to raise money. The flying was really getting to me because I was so tired of waking up (after the flight) half dead. That inner ear was really bothering me, but I couldn't even tell anyone or complain. I especially wanted to keep any more worries away from Laddie. He was a big man, but the load was mountainous.

"Laddie talked me into making this last trip. Charlie Parker, a famous assay man in Denver, assayed the samples (of gold) brought back by Den Galbraith, and I went with Laddie on this last trip."

So once again, Max knocked himself unconscious with a Mickey and flew to Mexico with Laddie.

"We got us a jeep and started driving from Guaymas back to camp. I looked in the sky and saw a bunch of buzzards in the sky, circling around. I knew they had some kind of dead game there.

"So we got up there and found Sir Max Ingalls. He was just beginning to turn black. There were seventeen (bullet) holes in him. I didn't know what to think. To me, this was the end of the world. Laddie said, 'You know, we just gotta haul him back down to Guaymas and turn him over to the law.'

"So that's what we did. I thought we shouldn't move the body, but Laddie said by the time we got down there and convinced them, the buzzards would eat him. So we hauled him on down there. They sent representatives in another jeep and we went back to camp.

"When we got there, our gringos were in a little war. Of course I know there's no such thing as a little war if they're shooting at you. The Yaquis had these gringos surrounded and were shooting at them, and the gringos were shooting back. There we were in the middle of it. There was two of them shot up, and I don't know how many of the Yaquis were shot up."

It turned out one of the men had become too well acquainted with one of the Yaqui women, which started the war. ("Now ain't that one helluva dumb ending?" says Max.)

"So the lawmen went around behind the Yaquis, way behind them. And finally one of the cops started yelling and he'd managed to stop the insane thing.

"One thing's for sure, (the gringos) would all have been dead if we hadn't come back when we did. The gringos had all the guns we had in camp, which was maybe five rifles and a few handguns, and they were surrounded."

Laddie and Max drove back and got to the plane.

"That was all for me. I told him to fly me home and I was all through. He said he understood."

Max said he went around scared to death and looking over his shoulder for several weeks because of the death of Sir Max Ingalls and was worried about repercussions.

"Then there was this little wire-service report in the paper that said Sir Max Ingalls had been killed in the Yaqui country and had been found with seventeen bullet holes in him, and that was it. Nothing more."

Max and Laddie still had the contract to complete, but had run out of money. Besides, Max was finished with it. So the two of them drove to Amarillo and met with two businessmen and turned the contract over to them. The main man was an Amarillo, Texas, oil man named John Adams. He took in a wealthy irrigation farmer as a partner.

"You have to understand," Max says, "there really was a massive fortune to be made there, but you had to have the money to get it done."

The man from Amarillo and his partner spent $80,000 trying to complete the contract, but they were unable to pull it off. That was about like $400,000 would be today.

"Now that kinda wound it up," Max says. "But there was one more thing."

That was Mr. R., the gold smuggler who had double-crossed Max, taken his $3,500, and disappeared.

After that happened, Max asked his friend and ex-convict, Mr. C., about the elusive Mr. R.

"He told me he'd run into him in Juarez and took him into an alley and popped a couple of caps. I took that to mean he'd shot him to death," Max said.

By the time the Great Mexican Bat Guano Caper ended, Max and Pat and the girls were living in Albuquerque, but went back often to Taos, which they still considered very much home.

On one of these returns to Taos, he and Pat were in La Cocina on the plaza, and ran into Mr. R., very much alive and standing at the bar.

"I had to play as cool as Sir Max Ingalls," Max says. "There he was. And that sonofabitch, right in front of Pat, pulls up his shirt and there's a healed-up hole in his belly from a bullet. He turns around and the exit scar is even bigger. And he laughed and said, 'You told me the truth.'"

Mr. C. had shot him and left him for dead in the alley in Juarez.

"He did this right in front of Pat, and she sorta caught on then. I had a flood of emotions but I thought oh hell, you gotta give the guy credit for having the guts to come up here. So I said, 'Buy this sonofabitch a drink.' We had a couple of drinks and then he left and I never saw him again."

The Remuda Bar

Life is a collection of memories and flavors and tastes and smells and terror and joy, and for Max, one place will always stick in his mind. Its official name was the Remuda Bar, named for the many pack animals that rested here at the spring and in the corrals. But it was known by many other names, most of them deserved, and one in particular: the Outlaw Bar. Among the semi-blatant pushers of the law's envelope, the phrase was "I'll see you (up or down) at the Outlaw Bar."

The Remuda Bar was in remote country, roughly halfway between Guaymas and the "diggings" where Max and Laddie's men were mining bat guano. Accessible only by burro or jeep, the Remuda Bar sat just outside the Yaqui reservation, visited by Seri Indians and miners from the nearby hills. But it was more importantly not visited by law enforcement agencies from Guaymas and, because of that, was the hangout of smugglers of gold, mercury, and guns. Sir Max Ingalls, the great con man, was a regular, as were some of the organized-crime figures Max Evans had known in California. Max's notorious "Mr. R." also did business there from out of Sinaloa.

"There were also scattered about," Max says, "hovels of brush, sometimes with rock underpinnings. There was also a fancy—for the location—line of pickups, many with flat tires and useless engines that had what were called in those days 'campers' on the back. These were small portable rooms with a stove, sink, fold-out table, and two single fold-out beds. Every one of them was a different color, and they were lined up like Patton's tanks. Their permanent occupants included a few Indian girls and three or four gringas from across the border, but were mostly Guaymas whores who, for whatever reason, found it more profitable to work in the wild than in Guaymas."

The yard of the Remuda Bar, Max adds, hosted both the ugliest and the prettiest whores in Mexico in those days.

Food for this collection of misfits was provided by an old man and his wife and two helpers who spent all day making hot-chile tamales, which they sold for 25 cents apiece. Others provided burritos, lamb, and goat cooked in many forms.

"There were murderers, the aforementioned whores, thieves, and robbers beyond count and description," Max says. "But there was also information for sale there on anything, and the smugglers reigned supreme as they did in San Francisco and Chicago."

In the bar itself was cold beer, kept that way by a generator-powered ice box, and two kinds of hard drinks: good and very bad.

"Whether it was tequila or brown whiskey," Max says, "the good was very expensive. The bad was very cheap. Oddly, the gravity-powered water from a big spring up the canyon was cool and delicious. It made the worst whiskey better."

Standing seven feet tall, with an attention-riveting scar across half his face, Max's partner, Laddie Anderson, received great respect in the Remuda Bar. Max says he finally lost his fear of the place through being with Laddie.

"We had a lot of natural fun," he says, "and much of it simply by observing what people would call the flotsam of the earth. It was a place to play and do business at the same time, dual activities I've always had a preference for combining into a single entity."

This particular blend of humanity could be a recipe for explosion and fresh graves, but the man who ran this place prevented any such disasters.

"The boss of the Remuda Bar," says Max, "was called 'The Keeper' in Spanish. He was of average size, but had a big scar down his face. His face was perfectly like the tragedy/comedy masks in show business. On one side the muscles were cut perpetually sad, and the other side was smiling.

"These (bar habitués) were the worst bastards from all around the world, but somehow that man's face and personality were such that I never saw a fight in there. I never felt so safe in my life. It was—in itself—a whole world that I really miss. At that time it was a smuggler's paradise—the smuggling of metals and guns being a grand and respected American tradition."

The Remuda Bar may still be there in the foothills of Mexico's Sierra Madre, but Max won't go there any more.

"There's not enough money to get me back there and ruin my memories of that place," he says. "The dopers have taken over now, and have ruined it. They just shoot each other to be shooting each other.

"I always wanted to write a story about it, but somehow felt I'd be betraying something semi-sacred, if that can possibly be analyzed. But I'm not going back to check it out in this dimension," Max says. "I sure miss the 'ambience' of the place, as they say in Santa Fe."

I was staying at this little ol' motel in Beverly Hills that was waiting to be torn down. Twenty-five bucks a week to stay there. And Pat forwards me this letter from Laddie Anderson. It was from Managua, Nicaragua. He'd gone back to bush-piloting down there, and gold smuggling, too, probably.

Anyway, he'd crashed way out there in the unmapped jungles somewhere and walked out. Took him thirteen days. He said he wanted an agent to help him sell his story. I found an agent named Ned Brown at MCA who said he'd do what he could for him. Ned was one of the good guys there and a good editor. Ned got kinda excited about it, just the adventure of it. He told me to write him back and tell him he would handle it, and how would they meet?

I told Ned that Laddie could take his letter and use it to raise enough money to get here. Never heard another word from Laddie, to this day. Never knew what happened to him. Later, I put him in a dedication to one of my books, hoping he'd see it and get in touch with me. But he didn't. Guess he got killed somewhere . . . guy who lived like him. That's how that ended. A great man gone. I cried, finally.

—Max Evans

Sam Peckinpah

"Max was very attractive to people who were very serious (in films). People like Burt Kennedy and Sam Peckinpah. They were creative partners, he and Sam.

"It seems they were always horse trading. I was always just sweeping up the wreckage. They'd trade things back and forth.

"I was either selling something of Max's to Sam or buying it back."

—Bob Goldfarb,
Max's Hollywood literary agent and friend

Sam Peckinpah was a magnificent, terrible sonofabitch.
—Max Evans

✃ **One day in 1961,** up in Taos, Max got a phone call from a young agent in Hollywood. In an excited voice, he said, "I have some great news. The most brilliant young director in the world wants to meet you."

"Well," says Max, laughing, "I'd never heard of Sam Peckinpah in those days. But this agent said, 'He called me and said he'd read *The Hi Lo Country* and said he wanted to meet the sonofabitch who wrote that book.'

"I said, 'He said that? Well, I'll meet him then. You set it up.'

Benton Hot Springs, north of Bishop, Cal., was director Sam Peckinpah's favorite campsite. Here Sam (center) relaxes with Max and with his brother, Judge Denver Peckinpah (left) as the trio heads for Tonopah, Nevada, over the pass to the north in 1965. The Rounders *had just been released, as well as Sam's* Major Dundee. *Photographer unknown.*

"So he arranged a meeting for Sam and me at this Oriental joint called the Polynesian near Warner Brothers in Burbank, California.

"I walked in at noon and said, 'Hi, I'm Ol' Max.' And he said, 'I knew who you were when you walked in.'

"So we started visiting and telling lies and talking about all this hell raising we'd done and fun we'd had and then it was two o'clock in the morning and they were kicking us out."

Sam drove Max to a motel and dropped him off, and thus began a friendship that lasted nearly twenty-five years, until Sam died.

The parties, the dreaming, and the labor had begun. Our agents were working out details for Sam to option *The Hi Lo Country*. In the meantime, I went to a studio screening and saw that he'd already stolen part of it. It was a TV movie directed by Peckinpah called The Losers, starring Lee Marvin, Keenan Wynn, and Rosemary Clooney, a comedy about two cowboys who come to town in a battered pickup and get into trouble while trying to have fun. I didn't mind that the theme was almost identical to my book *The Rounders*; I was kinda proud, in fact. But in the last reel, I recognized an entire chapter lifted from *The Hi Lo Country*, down to almost exact dialogue. I was slightly disenchanted with Señor Peckinpah. Of course, I had no way of knowing that Sam and the studio had already agreed to cut that sequence so it would fit the time slot.

I eagerly anticipated our dinner meeting that night on Sunset. He beat me there. I walked up to our table and said, "Hey, you . . . I just saw The Losers, and you didn't even bother to change the dialogue."

He gave me that slow, impossible-to-understand, dark-eyed look with only a smattering of a smile he'd later become famous for, and said quietly, "Of course. It just shows you what good taste I have. What are you drinking?"

Well, what could I say to that? Besides, it was a really fine film (eventually it ran five times in prime time).

He did option the book in a few days at a fair price, and from his own pocket. He bought it several more times through the years. We horse-traded it back and forth until there was such confusion we had to hire a gang of lawyers to straighten everything out. It's mine now, and I'm sure going to miss our trading. One thing about Sam, he never played cheap. When he optioned a book or just asked you to dinner, he laid down his own money even if he had to borrow it.

—from "Sam Peckinpah: A Very Personal Remembrance," *Impact Magazine* (*The Albuquerque Journal*), February 26, 1985; reprinted in *Super Bull and Other True Escapades*

Peckinpah was brilliant and made movies that made cinematic history, but he was also controversial, mercurial, and sometimes about half nuts. He was almost constantly at war with the studios.

Major Dundee was to be his masterpiece, Max says, but the studios cut off his money in the constant war they were in. Charlton Heston volunteered to finish the film with no salary. Then the producer cut twenty-seven minutes out of the finished film and burned the negative.

It nearly destroyed Peckinpah as the twenty-seven minutes flamed to smoke.

"It was really hard for him to find work most of the time," Max says. "He had to do a lot of under-the-table work and do things under other names."

But he also got Max a lot of work the same way. He told Max up front that he would never get credit for his work, his name would never appear, he would never get any residuals, and that he would be paid in cash. Max was also bound not to tell anyone which of the films he'd worked on, and he never has.

But this under-the-table script rewriting fed the Evans family well for years. Sometimes Max wrote in Taos, sometimes in Peckinpah's home, sometimes in a rented house near Hollywood.

"It was a godsend to me," Max says. "It took me from a few weeks to a few months, and I got back to Taos, and later Albuquerque, with cash in my pockets. We could pay bills, get a nice Mexican dinner, and start another book.

"He did me that enormous favor. He was putting himself on the line, doing that, because he had to do that work, too. The McCarthy era was far kinder to those blacklisted than the system was to one of its own . . . Sam (wonderfully mad) Peckinpah."

Sam then decided he would try to get another book of mine called *My Pardner* made. He said if I could get it to Henry Fonda and he liked it, we could get it produced. I told him Hank had already read and loved it. We set a meeting for the three of us at a restaurant on Santa Monica Boulevard.

Hank and I arrived first and waited for Sam at the bar. Both Sam and I had great respect for Henry Fonda, but

Fonda had never met Sam. Sam finally arrived, and let me tell you that I was feeling good. Here I had two friends who were among the world's best at their occupations. We all had respect for the project. How could we miss? Sam didn't kick over the table or throw glasses at anyone and shout expletives as he'd done on several occasions at and with me. No, he was a perfect gentleman, discussing the project in the softest, most delicate terms with Henry all during the delicious luncheon. Hank grunted and smiled, nodding his head as if in agreement. I, too, tried to be a gentleman, only ordering one unnecessary drink and staring at the terrible paintings on the wall as if they were Van Goghs while humming silently to myself and feeling sure these two worthy companions were securing our future forever. Sam smiled. Hank smiled. I smiled. The entire world was full of golden joy and smiles.

The luxurious glow was maintained all the way until after the parking attendant had delivered Sam's car to him. He shook hands with us, smiling again with what seemed to me great and deserved satisfaction, mumbling something about getting together and making the picture. As we watched his car move away, Hank put his hand on my shoulder and said, "Max, I never heard one damned word that man said."

My whole body dropped down in my Lucchese boots and spilled out on the concrete. I knew I'd never be able to get them together again, and I never did. You see, Sam had developed this habit of talking so low the listener had to strain, I mean strain, to hear at all much less analyze what he did decipher. The director had developed this trait gradually over the years in dealing with the higher echelons of Hollywood. It was a protective trait. A tape recorder couldn't decipher his part of the conversation and the opposition could never pin him down to an exact statement. A clever and advantageous ruse for sure, but he'd used it so long it had become natural and he would sometimes confuse and put off people like Henry Fonda that he really cared for. A lot of interviewers were fooled by this, thinking he was shy and withdrawn, until those times when the whispers would instantly, shockingly turn into the roar of the tiger. Then you could visualize the birds and beasts of the jungle taking wild, erratic, and usually fearful flight. He was—ask some masters—a consummate actor himself. So, out of a strong survival instinct, he became a complex and deadly opponent, even those times when he deliberately appeared weak.

—from "Sam Peckinpah:
A Very Personal Remembrance"

Sam Peckinpah was able to make astonishing films despite himself. On one occasion, he left a studio executive stripped naked in the Mexico City airport. Sam mailed the man's clothes back to Hollywood. The studios needed his genius, and paid for it, but they made him pay for it in other ways, as well.

And, occasionally, Peckinpah let the madness show through.

For a short while he had a writer's office at MGM. I met him there one Thursday afternoon. We were looking forward to a long weekend at Malibu with a few good friends. We made one of those fateful decisions that seem to come so naturally to writers and other fools: "Hey, let's have two for the road." "Yeah, sounds keen to me."

One young executive who looked about like Rock Hudson in his prime, accompanied by two lackeys, entered the open door to Sam's office. As I recall, they came in peace with an offering of friendship. At least on the surface. I knew these brave power brokers were some other kind of symbol to Sam when he didn't offer them a drink but did raise his glass to me in a toast to them. He spoke softly, graciously, of the many wondrous attributes of the leader of the trio. How he would without doubt someday be the head of this great studio and oversee majestic productions that would reek of much gold and have the qualities of a Tolstoy. I barely caught his last few words: "Max, let's castrate these cats." I jerked the desk drawer open, yelling, "We'll use the bedeezers on 'em." (The burdizzo, an instrument used by cowboys on bulls, is a kind of a hand-clamp that supposedly relieves the male in question of his virility without blood or pain.) Of course, every studio desk should be required by law to contain one of these humanitarian tools. This drawer didn't!

The trio was running over one another, all hitting the door to the long hallway at once.

Sam shouted "A knife! A knife will have to do. Here's a good sharp one!" As we all thundered down the hall, as they say in the old-time westerns, Sam screamed, "Bulldog the one on the right!"

I yelled back, "No! No! I'll flank the fat one on the left." Just as in the movies they just barely got the office door shut and locked as we hit it. We could hear them shuffling furniture inside. They were safe. So were we, I thought, if we could get out before security got us. We did; and I'm sure glad we didn't catch them. The rest of this story would certainly have been different.

The executive very shortly quit the studio business and married a world-famous actress of stage, screen, and television. I hope in some way that Sam and I contributed to the executive's long and successful marriage.

We had a lot of ridiculous laughs that weekend, but on Monday morning Sam Peckinpah found that the lock had been changed on his office door. His brass nameplate had also vanished.

—from "Sam Peckinpah:
A Very Personal Remembrance"

When they first met, Sam Peckinpah lived in a fine house in Malibu. Later, he moved into a mobile home there.

"He liked the idea of living in a little ol' mobile home and having these people from *Time* magazine come see him there," Max said. "It kept them off guard. We'd just go off and laugh like hell and celebrate."

Sam went to Max with all his stuff: his ideas, his work. And Max went to Sam with his. They were very close.

—L. Q. Jones,
actor, *Ride the High Country, The Wild Bunch,*
The Ballad of Cable Hogue, and many other movies

Sam called from Mexico and invited us, my wife, Pat, and our twin daughters, Charlotte and Sheryl, to spend the summer at his Malibu place, called "the birdhouse," saying he would join us as soon as the Mexican disaster (the filming of Major Dundee) was complete. I was working on a new book, so we just loaded up the typewriter and took off.

These were great times. We became acquainted with Sam's family . . . his sister, Fern Lea, brother-in-law, Walter Peter, and their three small daughters, Stephanie, Suzanne and Michelle. Sam was recently divorced from Marie, mother of his four children—three daughters Sharon, Kristin, and Melissa, and one-year-old son, Matthew. All our children, and those of visiting friends, were in the seven-and-younger age bracket. Fortunately they were all simpatico. Sam loved them—all of them. No matter what else is ever written or said I will always remember Sam's love and vast generosity to his children and his friends.

I was now involved in many Hollywood projects, and commuting from Taos, New Mexico, became very complicated, so we decided to move to Studio City for at least a school year. Sam had moved to a house on Broadbeach. The weekends at Sam's picked up where they left off. We all went to Sam's—he, after all, was the one with the ocean—where the joy of youth, of creativity and a machete-edged lust for life were centered.

Regulars who dropped by these gatherings included Lee Marvin (who once magnificently played, in the kitchen, a scenario of two fighting roosters by himself and made it believable); Robert Culp; Warren Oates; Vera Miles; Jim Hutton; the master composer, Jerry Fielding, and his wife, Camille; stuntmen; crew men and women; and Chalo Gonzales with his relatives from Mexico. It was a circus by the sea gone happily mad.

—Max Evans

Once a bunch of us were out to dinner at a restaurant. We had hors d'oeuvres and drinks, but hadn't been served our meals yet. Lee Marvin jumped up and said, "Oh, I learned a new trick!" and he grabbed the tablecloth and pulled it off. The dishes were supposed to stay on there, but they didn't and it made a terrible crash. You never heard so much noise.

He said, "Oh . . . I guess I need more practice."

—Pat Evans

Many, many things worth telling happened at these pleasurable events, but there's only one little antic I was to detail. Matthew, Sam's son, had just learned to walk, and he also learned to remove any encumbering clothing almost as soon as it was put on him. I guess the sand was more comfortable to him when it wasn't trapped inside his training pants. He would play happily around the cooking area. I was standing watching Sam baste the meat with beer, when I felt a sudden dampness on my leg. I looked down to find Matthew calmly peeing on my pant leg. Sam noticed, too, and said just as calmly, "He's putting his mark on you. It's a sure sign he loves you." I guess it was, because every once in a while he irrigated Sam, too. Matt is six feet tall now and has been in the Marines, like his father was.

—from "Sam Peckinpah:
A Very Personal Remembrance"

On several occasions, Peckinpah (who understood the power of drama, of course) used his friend Max for more than just company.

"We were staying there at his house in Malibu," Max says, "and he was having some tough times with the studio. A lot of times when he'd meet them or their agents or lawyers at a restaurant, he'd have me around. Now I'm just a middle-sized guy, but my face is busted up so that he'd just have me come and sit and stare at them."

Max laughs. "They didn't know what to do. It'd throw them off. Only move I'd make is to have a martini. And stare at them. If he wanted to have me verify something, he'd say, 'Isn't that right, Max?' And I'd just stare at them and nod my head.

"We did this every time they had to talk business."

There was a lot of laughter and booze and fun, but there were serious things going on at the same time. It was a heady brew.

"Begonia Palacios, this beautiful actress from Mexico City, was the great love of Sam's life," Max says. "She was beautiful and tough. She could stand up to him and stand up to anybody. She did care about him. She did recognize the genius of his madness, or the madness of his genius, however you want to put it. She finally couldn't put up with his crap when he was in the madness. She left him, and he divorced her. Then they got back together and got married again. They ended up being married three times, and had a little girl named Lupita.

"I stayed there at what we called the trailer house many times. I wrote 'Candles In The Bottom Of The Pool' there, my most reprinted story."

And there was the trading, the non-stop trading, of stories and money. Particularly *The Hi Lo Country*, which had become something of an obsession for both Max and Sam.

On one of these trading trips to California, the clowning got a bit carried away.

I'd decided to take a nap beside a pool at the Holiday House. I felt the need of a small rest after having joyfully leaped a hedge which concealed, to my dismay, a cliff. I rolled, bounced and slid about forty feet into a concrete embankment and whacked two ribs in half. So, I was a bit spent.

Perry Nichols, an artist from Dallas, was there with me. Perry and Sam jerked off their clothes and dived into the pool for a midnight swim. It came to Sam that since I was not a swimmer, but indeed well-known as a sinker, that it would be great fun to roll me into the pool. He did, and I sank as usual. On the way down I thought that when I touched bottom I'd either have to make one hell of a big jump or learn to breathe water. With lightning calculations I decided to try the jump. It was a success. I came up out of the pool with not too much water in my lungs and clasped the tips of my wet fingers on the edge of the wet concrete. It was a precarious position with both hands in use, but when Peckinpah pried one of those loose the strain intensified. If Perry hadn't come to the rescue I'm sure I would have been thrown back upon my second choice. He did manage to talk, push, and otherwise get Sam out of the way until I could crawl out of the pool. I lay face down coughing and cursing but looking more like a water-logged baby whale than a mad human being.

After my recovery—that is to the point where I could stand and weave my way to the car—we retired to Sam's house for a nightcap. A couple drinks later I no longer noticed the water chousing about in my lungs. I looked at Sam and said, "You s.o.b., you tried to drown me," and I attacked. Now I was much younger then and had considerable strength for my size. My intentions were to pick him up about shoulder high and crash his head against the floor, cleanly breaking his neck. Well, it wasn't easy. He fought far better than he should have and it was with considerable difficulty that I got him even chest high. After all, he'd been trained by the U.S.

Max was able to write some of his best work while a guest at Sam Peckinpah's Malibu house. Max was writing Shadow of Thunder *when Pat took this photo of him and Sam sharing a cool one in 1965.*

When Max was given the opportunity to portray a stagecoach shotgun rider in the movie "The Ballad of Cable Hogue," it also gave him a chance to see his friend, Sam Peckinpah, direct a film in 1972. Max turned his experiences with Sam, (shown here seated) into a short book on the madcap, rain-crazed production on Lake Mead in Nevada, and furthered the volcanic legends of both friends as a result.

Marines. This was finally accomplished and I aimed at the floor with his head. I heard it pop and stood back with great satisfaction to observe the remains. I was deeply disappointed to find that I'd hit the floor with the wrong end. He was soon sitting up, his dark eyes glaring like a gut-shot bobcat's, and he was saying over and over,

"You dirty bastard, you broke my ankle!"

I apologized profusely, admitting it was a terrible mistake.

"I'm sorry, Sam," I said, "I meant to break your neck."

He laughed, and so did I.

> —from *Sam Peckinpah, Master of Violence;*
> *Being the Account of the Making of a Movie*
> *and Other Sundry Things*

Max wrote *Sam Peckinpah, Master of Violence* after Sam invited him to play a small part in what became a tender Western called The Ballad of Cable Hogue. Max played the shotgun rider on a stagecoach driven by Slim Pickens. But the main reason for taking this job was to get a look at the master in action. And he got all he needed.

"I'd wanted to see how Sam made a movie," Max says. "I wanted to see his genius at work."

And, in a stormy career that left broken dreams and careers in its wake, Sam Peckinpah didn't slack off for *The Ballad of Cable Hogue*.

Mother Nature contributed greatly to the film's problems by raining daily for weeks on end in the desert some fifty miles east of Las Vegas, Nevada, at Echo Bay, where most of the picture was made. This already had nerves frayed, and the entire cast and crew got a serious dose of cabin fever at the only hotel for fifty miles around as they waited daily for the record-breaking rain to quit. This was exacerbated by a liberal daily dose of adult beverages.

Max and Pat have some fun with Slim Pickens, the former rodeo bullfighter and clown who made it big in films. Max rode "shotgun" for Slim on a stagecoach during the filming of The Ballad of Cable Hogue.

In a publicity still from the movie, Jason Robards (with his back to the camera) talks with stagecoach driver Slim Pickens, and his shotgun guard, Max Evans, during the making of The Ballad of Cable Hogue.

The movie went way over budget early on, and the problems included most maladies known to medical and psychological science, now and then even putting a power sneak on homicide.

Out of an original rain-soaked crew of eighty, thirty-six had been fired by Peckinpah and another fifteen had quit.

But Max had his book at the end of it, a small book that is as much of a gem in its own right as The Ballad of Cable Hogue itself. It gives a glimpse into the making of movies that most people will never get to experience.

And Max spoke his lines perfectly and didn't fall off the stagecoach.

But most of Max's dealings with Sam Peckinpah took place at Sam's home in Malibu.

"One time I was there, about two years before he died," Max recalls. "Don't know what I was doing there, probably some writing under the table for him. And Bago was there. That was his pet name for Begonia.

"I really regretted then not knowing how to speak Spanish any more. I used to, but Hitler's five-hundred-pound blackjack knocked all languages out of me. How odd that I wind up with words being both my breath and blood."

"Lupita was about five years old then. I could just see in her eyes that she had all the beauty and grace of her mother and the deep sparkle in her eyes of her father. And she's got all this charm. In my heart, all of a sudden, I was wishing they'd get back together so they could raise this marvelous little girl together.

"Now Begonia wasn't paying much attention to me. She was kinda abstract to me. I don't know what it was. She had once been so openly friendly. Then it changed suddenly, out of the blue.

"Now this is kinda hard for me to tell, but Sam and Begonia and Lupita were going to go into Malibu to do some shopping. He said to Begonia, looking at me, 'You know, that guy right there is a brujo' (witch). 'He's a good one.' Then he talked to her in Spanish and I could hear the words (but couldn't understand but maybe one out of three). All of a sudden she was no longer abstract. For the next couple of days, until she left, she gave me this enormous respect. I don't know what he told her in Spanish. Whatever he said, it worked.

"It was almost embarrassing to me. She was asking, 'Is this meat tender enough?' 'Is this wine all right?'

"It made me uncomfortable, so I was mostly writing until she left.

"Sam really respected writers. I think he would love to have done fiction. When I was writing fiction, whether it was a short story or a novel, he'd do little things for me. Give me so much respect. He was kind. He just changed into a different human being. I saw that in him, but I've never heard anyone talk about it, and I haven't spoken of it until now, either."

It was a few days after Begonia and Lupita left for Mexico that one of the strangest incidents in Max's life occurred.

"Sam asked me one morning if I was writing that day, and I said no, that I was thinking about the ending of my story.

(I always think of the endings first. If a story doesn't have a good ending before I write it, I say to hell with it).

"So Sam says, 'Let's go for a walk down the beach then.'

"You have to go down this bluff, and then there's a canyon comes down there and runs down to the beach. Across this slight little gully was this little Peruvian woman wearing one of those little hats and a long dress, and she was skipping along.

"At first, I thought Sam was setting me up or something. Never saw anybody like this except in photographs, like in National Geographic or something. Little derby hat. Skipping along, smiling.

"Sam looked at her and smiled and started talking to her in Spanish and another language.

"I thought, well, Sam has really gone to some lengths this time. But I was going along with it and thought whatever this was, was worth doing.

"We go on and we get right to the ocean. She skips around in front of us. Now, whether you like it or not, makes no difference to me, but that woman just slowly disappears, just lifting up off the ground and disappearing over the ocean.

"We just stood there watching her. I'll bet we stood there for a full ten minutes. Then we just walked down the beach for a quarter of a mile without speaking.

"Then he said, 'That was an old friend of yours.'

'But you did all the talking,' I said.

'She knew you didn't know the language,' he said. 'But that was an old friend of yours. She said to tell you hexagonals hold the universe together.'

"He didn't explain this to me, and I can't explain this to you. Later on, it began to make some strange, strange sense to me. I've seen some weird things, but that one really got to me. We never talked of this again. But this was a beautiful experience and one of enormous importance, and I don't know how or why. I hardly ever think of it. And how can you tell anyone?"

Max wrote hundreds of these mystic experiences down once, but he says Pat refused to type them and he doesn't know where the manuscript is. They are bizarre and other-worldly, but they are part of his life. Nor was this the only time Max and Sam experienced strange things together.

"Sam and I were going to the studio one time and we were in his Corvette," Max says. "Never did like them, you know. I called them 'scoot-ass' cars. We're driving along the freeway and the phone rang in the car. It rang twice."

Max is quiet for a second, then continues.

"Well, there's no phone in the car. It was way, way before cell phones or anything. I didn't know if he'd heard it. I was sure hoping he had."

Then they looked up and saw a car coming straight toward them going the wrong way on the one-way highway. There wasn't enough time to swerve and avoid the inevitable head-on crash.

"Then that car went right through us," Max says, his voice dropping to a whisper. "Right through us. I was shaking real bad at this point and I didn't know what to think. Did Sam see this, too? I looked at him and he was shaking, too.

"Then Sam looks at me and says, quietly, 'I guess we should've answered the phone.'

Why did this happen? What was the message? Max has no idea.

Sam had the soul of a Mexican general wrapped up in a gringo hide. He was as mean and crazy as a gut-shot javelina, and as tender as a windless dawn.
—from "Sam Peckinpah:
A Very Personal Remembrance"

It was getting close to Thanksgiving of 1984 and Max needed to see Sam. He had no idea it would be for the last time.

"Sam had *My Pardner* then, but he couldn't get it made," Max says. "He'd hired three or four guys to write screenplays, but they didn't do any good."

He laughs. "He didn't hire me to write it."

But Max, in the meantime, thought he would be able to get the book made into a film and went to Malibu to talk Sam out of holding the story.

But he didn't go right to Sam's. Instead, he went just up the hill from Sam's mobile home and stayed for a few days with Walter and Fern Lea Peter, Sam's sister and brother-in-law.

"He was really playing games at this point," Max says, "so I decided to play his games, too. He'd call Fern Lea and ask how I was, and I knew he meant when was I going to see him.

"His old buddies had come down out of the mountains to see him, too. Finally, on Thanksgiving, I went over with some of his old cronies. I told them I needed to see Sam alone, so they could just stay for one beer and then they had to leave. And they did.

"So, when Sam and I were finally alone, Sam says he has to take a shower, and tells me to watch the football game on TV and let him know the score. He kept yelling to learn the score all through his shower."

When Peckinpah had gone to take his shower, Max said, he looked "two hundred years old and four feet tall."

When he emerged, he was standing tall and fresh and well dressed. His pallor was gone.

"He was carrying a plate," Max says, "and he held it out to me. It had two lines of cocaine on it. I told him no thanks, that whisky was all I could handle. I told him that was all he needed, too. He knew that.

"I said, 'Sam, I need *My Pardner* back and I want you to give it to me. No bullshit, no terms. You just write down on any piece of paper you got that you give it to me. You know I'll treat you right.'

"And he said, 'Max, I can't. I need it for collateral.' So I guess he'd borrowed money on it.

"About that time his daughter and son-in-law came to get us to take us back to Fern Lea's for Thanksgiving dinner.

"'Come on, Daddy,' she said. 'Fern Lea has it all ready.'

"He just stood there in the middle of the floor, all by himself, with those black eyes of his. And he said, 'I can't go.' That's all he said. And that was the last time I saw him.

"About ten days or two weeks later, he called me. He was real sweet to me. First time I'd ever heard him like this. He said he had to go to Mexico. He said he had to see Bago 'real bad.' He emphasized that. He said as soon as he got back he would give me *My Pardner*."

A few days later, Sam Peckinpah had a massive heart attack in Mexico. They flew him to Los Angeles and he died shortly after that in a hospital bed.

His friendship with Max lasted nearly a quarter century, which was almost a record for Sam Peckinpah.

"But what a beautiful gesture from Sam," Max says, "to want to give me that book. Still, the last memory I have of him is him standing alone in his living room with those black eyes of his. It's haunting."

Sure, he'd once tried to drown me and I'd broken his leg for it. He'd thrown a glass full of whiskey at me simply for speaking to a professional hooker friend of his while he had left the room momentarily. Even so, he once sent his secretary all the way from CBS in Burbank with cash when he heard I was broke. I was staying at actor Morgan Woodward's house in the Hollywood Hills when the hundred dollars arrived without my asking. You can forgive a person for many foibles when he makes gestures like that.

Sam admitted his plentiful sins and didn't apologize for them. I, too, have many sins. We were simply friends. No apologies needed.

—from "Sam Peckinpah:
A Very Personal Remembrance"

Hustle

I think a lot of the privation came about because Max didn't want to be a wage slave. He was stuck. If he wanted to be a writer, he had to wheel and deal.
—Dennis Dutton, writer and friend

By and large, Hollywood is the world's basic geographical mental illness. It feeds on the genius of people who don't live there and produces films that resemble the original creation enough to warrant bearing the same name after it has been run through a series of mediocrity filters.

But the writer can make money in Hollywood through basically having him rewrite his original work in several forms. There's the one-page synopsis, then the treatment, then the rough-draft screenplay, then the shooting script. At each step of the way, there is money. Increasingly more money. And then if the film is made, there will be thousands of dollars given to the writer in addition to the smaller payments made earlier.

But before any of that happens, there is the blessed, darling, gold-plated "option."

An option means "first dibs." Someone in Hollywood reads your book, thinks it would make a good movie, and wants to try to get it done. This involves using other people's money, lining up the actors, talking studio executives into it. This is also a process that can take years. But what's to keep the writer from going to someone else?

The option.

Max clowns around at the New Mexico State Fairgrounds in Albuquerque in 1974. Photo by Dick Skrondahl.

Most options run six months at a time. The producer pays the writer anything from several hundred dollars to many thousands of dollars for the exclusive right to that book while he runs around trying to put the "package" together. If he doesn't get it done in six months, he has to pony up more cash to hang onto the rights for another six months. This is a gold-bound, rock-ribbed financial blessing to a writer. He's already had the story or book published and has been paid for it. Now here's Hollywood waving cash on the chance that someday down the line they may give him a whole lot of money when they actually make the picture. If they never do, and the producer drops the option, there's always a chance another producer or director will pick it up.

A famous best-selling novelist once confided that the ideal situation was to have all your books optioned for films, and then hope they never actually make a movie.

"If they do," he said, and we won't use his name, "they'll bitch it up and then no one will want to option anything more of yours."

But selling options is only possible by surviving Hollywood's version of something called "lunch."

During lunch, which can last until closing time, people from Hollywood—sometimes a double team of both producer and director—order food and drinks and tell the out-of-town writer he's the next Hemingway and that buckets of riches lie just past the next studio approval; here, let's fill that up for you again, and please sign at the bottom.

Max Evans bought his beautiful Spanish home in Albuquerque largely on options. He fed his family on options. He pulled himself out of mining debt largely on options. And he had to go through the lunch system to do it.

When this first began, back in the early 1960s, we can only imagine the glee of the Hollywood crowd, who collectively sport fewer ethics than an El Paso used-car salesman. Here they are, going to talk to Max Evans, a cowboy, for God's sakes, from northern New Mexico.

Bartenders were primed for action, and the dotted lines were in the producer's jacket pockets. And here comes Ol' Max, wearing cowboy boots and a grin through a brawl-broken face, and a voice that came straight from the open range. And the guy can write . . . anything!

Feeding frenzy? Well, not quite.

In the first place, Max had been "promoting" the money to get there from friends, family and tourists. He was no stranger to sales. He'd promoted his paintings for years at that point. He'd promoted a roping horse and entry fees and a ride down to Española just to get in the calf roping.

What saved Max, however, and made it possible for him to sell his work in Tinseltown, was simple.

"I could out drink every goddamned one of them. Just flatfooted could do it. This gave me a helluvan advantage. Next thing you know, they wanted to option one of my books."

> When I first knew Max, he was still promoting Hollywood. And that's just what it was, too. He turned the tables on 'em. When he first went out there, they thought, 'Here's this old cowboy from New Mexico. What the hell does he know? We'll take him out and get him drunk and steal his stuff.'
>
> "But they were the ones who got drunk, and he was still standing, and they couldn't stand that.
>
> "Ol' Max hung tough for the things he wanted, and he got 'em.
>
> —Chuck Miller, one of Max's closest friends

Max sold literally dozens of options over a long career.

"I sold five options on *The Rounders* before it was made," he said. "One a year for five years. I finally learned to cut the options as short as I could. I had to learn the hard way because they're smarter than you are. They've been doing those tricks in Hollywood all their lives, and you are from out of town and they're home."

After a trip or two to Hollywood, and after learning some of the ropes of selling things there, Max got scientific about it.

"There was a hotel called the Sands, out on Sunset Boulevard," he says. "It was in the middle of the two-bit action. At one time, John Wayne had met people in that bar and made deals there. There was a great bartender and he'd been there for years. He was there until they tore the place down.

"He understood what I was doing and helped me do it. Hardly anybody had credit cards, in those days. If you had cash you could get in. Now every time I checked in the Sands Hotel, I had to make a deal. I mean, I *had* to make a deal, to get out of there. I had no goddamned choice. It was either rob a bank or a Safeway store or stay there and work until I got an option. No choice.

"One time my hotel bill ran up to $4,000," he says. "That's like a $40,000 bill now. I didn't have a dime. I'd been there a long time and I'd done my share of the entertaining. I'd met some big-time guys there and was trying to hustle some deals. Somebody would option a short story or a novel, whatever I could get. And I wanted to get back (to Taos) to work. There was another novel I wanted to write.

"Anyway, they slipped this bill under my door. And I knew the guy who owned this place, and he was a chickenshit, all right. Now you might think I did this out of bravery, but I didn't. I did this strictly out of desperation. The oldest instinct in the human being is survival. That's older than food and water and sex. So I just marched into his office and threw that bill on his desk. And I said, 'Why you sonofabitch! You insult me like this? You know I pay. I've been coming here three or four years now. I bring you more business than any guy in town. I don't even live here, and I bring you more business. Don't ever do that to me again!'

"He said, 'Why, I'm sorry, Mr. Evans.' And he never did again. I'd established credit. After that, I could run up bills of two or three thousand dollars and nobody said a goddamned word. I had a good restaurant there and a good bar, and I went there for nine years. And I never walked out on a single dime I owed.

"I met Sam Peckinpah in there many, many times, and a lot of other big names, and some that weren't big but deserved to be. I met little three-cent sharks and million-dollar sharks and was being hustled just like I was doing them. The only thing in my favor . . . the only thing . . . I knew what they were doing and they didn't know anything about me, except the fact I had endurance."

The thing about Hollywood is that you have to deal with so many chickenshits. The town is full of them. And some of them aren't even that good. Some of them aren't even up to chickenshit speed yet. At the same time, I've met and made some of my lifelong friends there. Great place, huh?

—Max Evans

Max is the most honest person I know. If he tells you he's going to do something, no matter what the sacrifice, he'll do it. He's honest in his opinions. There's just nothing phony about him. And that's the way his father was, too.

—Pat Evans

Moving to Albuquerque . . .

Max really kinda had to leave Taos, you know. There were people up there who had power, had influence, had money. They thought it was time that wildness should have gone out with the gambling. They were in a position to make it hard on him without coming out with an eye-to-eye confrontation. They could do things behind the scenes.

It was nothing more than jealousy. Here's this wild, crazy sonofabitch, but he was succeeding. They started stories about him and other women there in Taos, hoping, I guess, that Pat'd shoot him.

It got so he couldn't hustle, couldn't operate any more. And there was a real possibility of his getting shot, you know. He didn't want his family to be exposed to that, so he sold his place up there and came down and bought this place here (in Albuquerque).

—Chuck Miller, one of Max's closest friends

✂ **Pat says the decision** to move to Albuquerque from Taos was primarily because Max was traveling back and forth to Hollywood so much in those days, and it was much more convenient to live in the bigger city.

In good weather, it takes about an hour to drive from Taos south to Lamy, where you catch the train. Max doesn't fly, because of that inner ear problem. In Albuquerque, you've already cut off over two hours of travel time between Taos and Hollywood. But there is ample evidence that Chuck Miller made a good point, too.

The Taos den was filling with rain.

One early morning escapade can pretty much ruin a guy's reputation in a village the size of Des Moines, and twenty years of wildness can tip a town the size of Taos against a man, but it might take Max quite a while to get a city of a quarter million upset. So the decision was made to start looking for a place in Albuquerque.

As it turns out, one of Max's friends, Charlie Crowder, was instrumental in making this move. By the time the decision was made, however, Max and Charlie had quite a history of working together.

"Charlie's quite a guy," Max says of the land developer who founded and developed the entire community of Santa Teresa, on the Mexican border. "He was known to be the most successful human being in making land trades with the federal government, and no one knew how he did it.

"I found out, however. One night I was out drinking with Charlie, and he started quoting Shakespeare. He did that when he had too much to drink so people couldn't take advantage of him. Business talk would stop and here came Shakespeare. So I took Charlie back to his motel room and he kinda slumped on the floor against the wall. He told me he had to call the President and to hand him the phone. He dialed a number and I'll be damned if Lyndon Johnson didn't answer the sonofabitch. No wonder he came out so well on those land trades."

Max helped Charlie from time to time by setting up meetings and things like that, and Charlie helped Max out, too.

One time stood out in particular. Max was in desperate need of money. The bill collectors were hounding him.

"I'd already been to those bank bastards," Max says, "and these same guys I'd dealt with all those years would sit down and look at my assets and talk about this and that and collateral. I told this one guy, 'Aren't I worth something?'"

This exact line later showed up (and not at all by accident) spoken by Jason Robards in Peckinpah's film, *The Ballad of Cable Hogue*.

So Max drove to Albuquerque from Taos, thoroughly upset, and went to see his friend Charlie Crowder, who had an office several stories up in this building.

Max didn't waste time with preliminaries.

"Charlie," Max said, "I want you to pick up the phone and call your bank and I want you to tell them to give me five thousand dollars, in cash, and I'll go down and pick it up right now. I want to pay these bastards what I owe them in cash and look them in the eye when I'm doing it. If you don't call your bank, we'll just have to see if you know how to fly (pointing to the window)."

Charlie picked up the phone and called, and Max paid the bastards in cash.

"I was just kidding about throwing him out the window," Max says. "I'd never do that to Charlie. I've said it to some other people, though, and meant it."

One little side note here on that day. While Max was in Charlie's office, someone got into Max's car and stole a package containing a manuscript for a novel. Max was going to have it copied. There are no copies anywhere. It's lost forever.

"Probably just threw the pages in the trash when he found out there was no money in it," Max says.

This was the second manuscript to disappear. Max lost another one years ago. It has never been found.

The House on Ridgecrest Drive

In talking with Charlie Crowder, Max said he and Pat had been house hunting in Albuquerque and weren't able to find anything they liked or could afford.

"I knew I needed trees and brush to hide in," Max says. "Lots of trees. Well, Charlie said he knew just the place. He'd looked at it with an eye to buying it for his mother, but it was too big for her. He made me promise we wouldn't leave town without looking at it first."

So Max and Pat went to the house in Albuquerque's southeast heights, and found a two-story Spanish home surrounded by shade trees, an oasis of green in what was otherwise a busy neighborhood.

"Before we even got to the front door," Max says, "I knew this was our home."

The house was well beyond their budget at that time, but Max swung some deals and optioned *The Hi Lo Country* again.

"The timing worked out perfectly and we were able to swing the deal, just barely," Max says. "We were supposed to have this house."

They moved in January 1, 1968.

Today, after more than thirty years of Evans occupation, the pretty home on Ridgecrest Drive is shaded by even taller trees. Pat's efforts in the yard have made it more of an oasis for creativity. Max and Pat each have their own offices in the house,

Pat in the backyard of the house on Ridgecrest Drive shortly after moving to Albuquerque in 1968.

and the décor falls somewhere between Southwest art and the local public library.

When they first moved in, however, they discovered—just as in the first house in Taos—they weren't here first. Years before, a neighbor's teenage boy had gone into the basement and shot himself. When Max and Pat and the girls moved in, this spirit would hide things, turn lights on and off, and cause mischief.

"Finally," Pat says, "I saw that his parents were moving to Florida. I went in the house and told him his parents were moving away, and didn't he think he should go with them. And he did."

Both Charlotte and Sheryl inherited the love of art from their parents. Although they both have other day jobs, Charlotte is an accomplished painter, and Sheryl is a metal sculptor. Charlotte now owns a silk-flower business, Charlotte's Flowers, and specializes in weddings. Sheryl is associate manager for a huge HUD retirement community.

Pat is the one in the Evans family with a green thumb,
and is especially noted for growing absolute jungles of tomatoes
in their backyard on Ridgecrest Drive in Albuquerque. This
crop would probably be 1999. Photo by Max Evans.

The Evans girls live a few blocks apart, and get together each weekend with their dogs, Pat says.

"They just have the best time together," she says. "They were the cutest little rascals growing up. Cute as they could be. And you know, they're just like their daddy. They're dead loyal and honest.

"Max was gone a lot when they were small," Pat says, "but when he was here he was the best daddy. And there was never any drinking around the kids."

For a long time, Pat sold real estate for a broker who was a friend of hers. Now and then she kept her hand in at art, too, and illustrated the covers for both *Bluefeather* books.

"Everybody thinks . . . you know . . . that you're rich because you're not out there at a job," Pat says. "But we've had to work hard for everything we've got."

Bluefeather Fellini will last as long as people read. Except for it being prose, it's an epic, an American epic. Most writers dream of writing the Great American Novel. Well, there it is. It's been done. It's all been done by Ol' Max Evans.
—Robert J. Conley,
novelist and official historian of the Cherokee Nation

Bluefeather

On the beach were parts of men, and in the water were parts of men. A small percentage were whole, however, having drowned as their landing craft disgorged them in water too deep for solid footing. The beach was a caldron of chaos beyond the limbs and bones and scraps of torn flesh mingled with discarded gas masks, useless punctured canteens, broken and bent concrete and steel beach obstacles, erratic piles of smashed and destroyed equipment, and disabled and destroyed vehicles already being reclaimed by the sand and sea. Destruction incarnate.

Many of the seventy-two known elements of the earth, which were of such beauty and sparkle in their natural veined and disseminated forms, were here fused, amalgamated and alloyed into terribly efficient instruments of death. The same elements whose seeking and finding was Bluefeather Fellini's life's work were now particles of booming savagery just before the stillness of death. His sought-after beauty was trying to kill him, but of this he was mercifully oblivious. Violence violated violence. Piercing, screaming steel, twanging off hard objects and thudding, slicing, piercing softer things, and on impact, blood flying into the convulsed air and becoming a red mist before running in rivulets, sinking into the wet sand searching for the birthing sea. This was the ultimate exploitation of the human wholeness—its severance. The bodies floated facedown calmly now in the sea, moving only as the mother ocean did. On land, the living crawled through the motionless dead and paused over and over next to the nonmovement to gather a bit of sulfurous air into their heaving lungs, and another tad of courage. Then forward again. Again. Again.

—from *Bluefeather Fellini*

"Every book I've ever done is different," says Max. "I didn't set out to write any particular thing; I just couldn't help myself."

The idea of any book taking over a writer and forcing him to abandon a normal life until the task is complete is certainly nothing new. But with Max, the books take on lives of their own and dictate how his will be spent. Nearly all of them are strongly autobiographical, such as *My Pardner*, and *The Hi Lo Country*, but perhaps none as strongly autobiographical as the immense work known to Max as "Bluefeather," and to the rest of us as the two fat novels, *Bluefeather Fellini* and *Bluefeather Fellini in the Sacred Realm*.

In fact, *Bluefeather* is so autobiographical that Max often refers to it as though it were a history book. "His name was so-and-so in real life," he'd say. "I called him thus-and-such in the book."

"The book" has always meant Bluefeather Fellini.

When he gets in the writing spirit, he doesn't know if it's day or night. He has this large vision, and he often doesn't think of his immediate needs.

—Elia Sanchez, family friend of Max's

Max at age 57 in the backyard of their home on Ridgecrest Drive in Albuquerque. Pat took the photo for a book jacket.

From the day I wrote the first line which is: "It was a time of youthful jubilation, and *Bluefeather Fellini*—the chosen one—knew that never, never, never, before had anyone been so blessed," until five-and-a-half years later, when I weakly scribbled "The End," I can't remember, but I'm sure I crawled to a bed and slept a week or so.

During those eons I lost contact with all my books even though the trilogy *Rounders 3* was published. I lost contact with friends and foes and in-betweens, and with making a living. There were hundreds of little sufferings, such as slipping on a wet walk and falling over a low retaining wall, smashing in several ribs. An elongated swelling about the size of my lower arm formed over these skin and bones. Then I started coughing so that I could feel and hear the joy of ribs and cartilage grinding out a symphony from hell. I went to Dr. Christopher Merchant.

He was amazed that a now sixty-four-year-old man had the child's disease of whooping cough. There wasn't a lot one could do at this age, he said. You either died or it wore out in six months to a year. The coughing and consequent grinding never stopped. I went to bed for two months hoping somehow to live long enough to finish what I was now calling the "damn thing." I couldn't hold back, so I wrote in bed as hard as my old previously busted-up hand would

Here's what five-and-a-half years of work and 30 years of research look like. Max and Pat stand behind the completed manuscript of Bluefeather Fellini *in 1993. Max filled 21 yellow legal pads and Pat typed it into 1150 pages which became Max's masterpieces,* Bluefeather Fellini *and* Bluefeather Fellini in the Sacred Realm.

allow. Yes, that's right, I had decided that the Great Spirit would want me to do this book in longhand. My fingers swelled so that I had to tape them up every morning like a prizefighter before a championship bout. I truly began to believe, with all the pain of body and soul, that I was going for the championship with Ol' Blue, but I also felt the winner would not be announced for maybe fifty years. I haven't changed my mind yet.

—from "Many Deaths,
Many Lives" in *Hi Lo to Hollywood*

For a professional writer, this book (it's really one book) didn't make any sense at all. For decades, Max had driven editors flat nuts by writing novellas, that in-between-length story that is somewhere between a short novel and a long short story. Max has always liked the novella form, as he says it's the perfect length to be translated into film. But editors only see that they will either publish a volume thin enough to see through, or have to combine two or three novellas to make a half-decent-sized book. They pleaded with him to lengthen these into novels, but he refused, saying, "When the story's done, that's it."

Not a smart way to earn a living as a writer, when the basic premise has always been that if you make things easy on an editor, you'll get checks in the mail.

"I turned down lots of book deals and writing deals," Max said. "I didn't feel good about them in my soul, you know?"

He laughs. "I'm a selfish sonofabitch," he said. "I write for myself. I have never written for the money. I've had to hustle every damn dime for myself."

But *Bluefeather* was the best (or worst) idea he'd ever had for a book. It smashed every convention he'd imagined for himself. From its conception to publication it consumed more time than all the rest of his written works combined. It nearly wrecked his health, and he wrote it in constant pain. It took years away from more profitable writing. He was forced to sell some favorite paintings done by friends to buy groceries. And he was convinced it would never be published.

"*Bluefeather* came to me in 1951 or 1952," Max says. "I started making notes. Many of them were notes written on bar napkins. On shopping bags. On scraps of paper. On sheets of mining stationery. Way back in the mining days I was working on this, and I didn't even know what it was.

"When I finally got enough guts to look at the notes. . . . Jesus Christ! There were boxes of them! I realized I had forty short books or twenty normal-sized books with all these notes.

"Scared me flat-ass to death. No way I can live long enough to write all this. So I'd go walking and walking. Thinking about it. Just about decided not to do it. And then this voice came down into my head and told me to write this book in longhand and then I could condense it."

To this point, Max had typed his work, and then Pat had retyped it on their computer for sending off to the publisher. But now he receives a message to write it in longhand. On what will become the longest work of his life, he is determined to do it the slowest possible way.

"You can't realize how much it hurt to do this," he says. "I mean hurt physically."

He holds out his right hand in a fist. "This knuckle is gone completely, and these others hurt like hell. Fist fighting and all that shit . . . digging in old caved-in mines. Now I have a dilemma. This is my life, this is something I feel is massively important. This is something I have to do with my life.

"So all this pours in my damn head and I went in and looked at it and I didn't know if I could do it. So I went for another walk and I prayed this time. Prayed to The Great Mystery. Tell me without fail, I prayed, can I finish this cockeyed monster?

"And it came to me . . . boom . . . make it into one. Telescope it. Telescope it.

"That's just what I did. I took the knowledge and notes of forty books and put it into one sonofabitch. The last two years writing this book—this hand's been broken eleven times—I had to tape this hand every day just like a prizefighter. Those knuckles would swell. I'd untape it at night so it wouldn't swell up on me even more. But I had to finish the book. I had to do about ninety days of it in bed because of that inner-ear thing (from being blown up in France). I couldn't hardly get to the bathroom. I fell on the stairs once. Don't know how it didn't kill me."

Max filled more than a thousand sheets of legal pads and Pat typed them into the computer. "While we were editing it, month after month," he says, "I just took a typewriter eraser and pointed (at what I needed changed). She wouldn't dare let me touch the machine. I told Pat thank you for your priceless help. That was beyond anything. I said we'll probably never sell this."

Sometimes you have to put the truth in fictional form to make it work. To enhance it. When you fictionalize something, you can turn it into art, into literature, into a bigger truth.

—Max Evans

There'll be a period when he's extra tuned in or something, and we had all kinds of supernatural things going on. Especially during the writing of Bluefeather. It isn't all the time.

—Pat Evans

For more than five years, Max shut himself up each day with legal pads and wrote this huge epic of the Southwest, of World War II, of mining, of the Santa Fe art scene, of the spell just being in the Southwest has on a person.

And of caverns and spirits and the metaphysical.

"Under any circumstances—under the best of circumstances—it would've taken me at least three years to write it. I had to take the time to let The Great Mystery tell me what to write. It's not that I actually wrote it," he says, "so much as I was ordained to copy it."

So here Max Evans, the difficult spit-in-your-eye writer from New Mexico, has once again handed the publishing world something they had no idea how to handle. Here was an eleven-hundred-page journey through the eyes of a half-Italian, half-Indian, all New Mexican miner, dreamer, soldier, worker, and mystic, and what are you going to do with it?

New York editor, Marc Jaffe (who had been the paperback editor for *The Rounders*), read *Bluefeather* and called Max on the phone.

"His first words were, 'Max, this is a Homeric epic that will stand for all time. We'll have a deal and get this all settled and we'll be underway.'

"We talked for about forty-five minutes. And then the editorial board turned him down. They said, this is an interesting book, but we don't have any idea how you'd market a thing like this. The publishing world had turned almost completely commercialized in those five and a half years it took me to write this book."

"It had all changed in just that little bit of time. They wanted Stephen King and those series. Give 'em a mystery and keep 'em coming, that kind of thing.

"Well, I tried four or five other places and received the same damn thing. They couldn't see how this thing could make any money. Greg Tobin (then at Bantam) said he'd do the paperback, but he couldn't do the hardcover. So I sent it to Luther (Wilson, editor of University Press of Colorado). He'd built the press to where it was five hundred percent above where it had been. But that was the limit to what he could do. They wouldn't allow any more."

Luther, who had published other works of Max's when he'd been with the University of New Mexico Press and was an old pal, as well, went to bat for *Bluefeather*.

Several big problems with this. For one thing, the University Press of Colorado had never published fiction before. And, when the average novel runs somewhere between three and five hundred pages, here's this *Bluefeather Fellini* manuscript with eleven hundred typed pages. Big trouble.

Max was able to solve the second problem by literally cutting the book in half and making two books out of it. The idea for this came to him in a dream, and he cut it in a place where both books could stand on their own.

After a struggle, Luther Wilson was able to talk the board into taking a chance on what were now these two books.

"I was astounded," Max said. "We sold three editions and Tobin (by this time at Quality Paperback Book Club) published it in paperback and got three editions out of that. We got the front page of the Wall Street Journal and a few things like that.

"A lot of strange things happened out of that. I have had people read that book and to this day cannot say a word about it. They'll start to say something and will stop in mid-sentence. It's a strange thing. One I can't comprehend. Nor does it matter, I suppose.

"I've had people who liked me read that book and after that, they'd look at me and try to get away. I've had people call me and they had gone to all kinds of trouble to get my unlisted number and told me that book had changed their lives. That they saw things in a whole new light. A lot of things had become apparent to them that they'd been blind to. They thanked me and thanked me. I've had people like (critic) Charles Champlin and (novelist and historian) Robert Conley and (writer and editor) Dale Walker tell me that the war part was equal to the best they'd ever read.

"Conley called me and said, 'You could put Homer's name on it and your name on the Odyssey and never tell the difference.'"

Max considers *Bluefeather* to be his master work.

"I'll make a prophecy," Max says. "Some time within fifty years—I think it'll take fifty years—there will be enough people (who understand the different facets of *Bluefeather*) to put together what I actually did. But it'll take fifty years. And what the hell will I care?"

He laughs. "What the hell will my kids care in fifty years?"

"That book caused strange reactions in people," Max says. "Conley read the book and called (Greg) Tobin. He asked if Greg had read it yet. Tobin says, 'I'm sittin' here lookin' at it on top of my desk and I'm scared to death.'

"I know this sounds like ego, and I don't give a shit. There's something about that book. I've had people who have read all my stuff who won't read that book. They're afraid of it, I think. I finally figured it out. This sounds like the biggest egotistical thing in the world, but I can't help it. It's the goddam truth."

He smiles and lowers his voice.

"They're afraid I'm that good. And they can't stand for an old dumb-ass ex-cowboy, miner, smuggler, jailhouse brawler to have done that. They can't handle it."

You Can't Hunt with Your Eyes Closed: Coyote and Raven

∽ **When Raven found Coyote** that day, he was crouched, eyes squinted tight shut. Raven landed and strutted to a nearby hump of dirt where he could watch his friend.

"Taking a nap?"

"Hunting," Coyote said. "Don't bother me, Raven."

Raven chuckled. "Hunting? For what?"

"Rabbits. Juicy, tasty rabbits. Rabbits that run slowly and taste . . . taste . . . oh no! Now you've done it!"

"Done what, Coyote?"

"Ruined the hunt. Destroyed my concentration. Doggone it, I was doing OK there for a while, then you came along. . . ."

Raven looked from the mesa to the east, which was red, to the mesa to the west, which was white.

"No rabbits here," Raven said, puzzled.

"Of course not," said Coyote. "That's why I was hunting."

"You can't hunt with your eyes closed."

Coyote cackled. He liked the sound of it and tried it again. Yes. Cackling is going in the book as a fun thing. A good thing.

"Oh Raven, mighty and sacred bird of the Alaskans, legendary giver of life and fresh water. Vanquisher of savages in days of old. . . ."

"Cut the corn," says Raven.

"Point is," Coyote said, laughing, "you wouldn't know rabbit hunting from toast. What do you hunt? Road kills."

"And insects and frogs and lizards and. . . ."

"And road kills," says Coyote. "And road kills are famous for not moving. Now you take rabbits. Those little boogers can flat fly, leaping sagebrush, cutting through the corn fields, doing a di-do around Grandma's amaryllis. . . ."

"What's your point?"

"You have to know where the rabbits are, my friend, before you can partake of their succulence."

"And by closing your eyes?"

"I see them. I see them that way. I locate them in my mind and then I'll know where to go to find one. I can feel them out there. You think coyotes eat rabbits because they happen across them? What are the chances?"

"That's nuts!"

"Nuts? Nay, I say. That's hunting. That's using the old noodle. That's taking yourself from the everyday and transporting yourself to a higher plane, seeing things that others don't."

Coyote took a deep breath. He didn't like that much, so he cackled again. Better.

"My brother, Ol' Max, he knows this, too. He can live it and write it, too. Makes him a wonderful good writer, but a very eccentric cowboy."

"Things like that don't happen, Coyote. You're just making that up."

"So you're saying, Raven, that the world is just what you see and touch and hear and there is nothing of the strange, the metaphysical, the slightly . . . scary?"

"Exactly."

"Then how is it that a raven and a coyote can have a conversation?"

Coyote cackled again. This could become a fun new habit.

The World of Shadows

If there is one thing that sets Max Evans apart in the minds of those who know him well, it is his many layers. People who have known him for more than forty years quietly say, "You know, there's more to Max than you might think."

And there is.

When someone grows up during the Depression in an area of the country known for its rock-ribbed practicality, the last thing you'd expect to find is a mystic. And while "mystic" might be too strong a term, it really isn't too far off.

Long-time readers of his who have limited their fare to *The Rounders* trilogy and the slapstick humor of *Bobby Jack Smith You Dirty Coward!* were more than a bit flummoxed at reading *Bluefeather Fellini*, because it went beyond the visible and the obvious.

In this most important work of his career, Max looks into the shadowy places of life, peeks into the quiet things that flit through our peripheral vision, embraces ideas and creations and beings that can't be photographed or recorded.

But he didn't have to write any of this from pure imagination. He's been there. He's heard the music and seen the shadow creatures and has known secret things. This isn't always a good thing, either. A part of this almost ruined his writing career.

Some of it he was given by his Cherokee grandmother, Birdy Swafford. Some of it he came upon on his own, and when an old cowboy from *The Hi Lo Country* dares to write of such things, he risks losing readers.

And this has happened, too. But he had to do it, because it's as much a part of his life as the land itself, and the animals, and the people . . . the ones you can see and photograph.

This extra-sensory blessing, or curse, first revealed itself to Max while he was riding across the Staked Plains of eastern New Mexico near his home in Humble City. He was looking for grass for the family cattle on some of the neighbor's ranches. This was, by this time, the Great Depression. Most of the neighbors had accepted the federal government's offer of $10 a head to shoot their cattle. This left empty ranches in the area.

He was seven or eight years old then, and alone except for his mare, Dolly, on a flat sea of tan land and blue sky.

"I saw this old shack out there, standing all by itself," Max says. "And I saw this hand in the doorway, waving me up there. Old Dolly started bowing her neck and throwin' her ears, really gettin' ready to booger, you know. I kept giggin' her and spurrin' her up, and I finally got off her and walked up.

"It was scary. Inside, the earth was just freshly torn out of this one room. The floor ripped up. I walked around and around the house and couldn't see anything. Then I got on the horse again and rode around and around that house some more, looking for a human being. But there wasn't any. Then I was smart enough to ride around in larger and larger circles, looking for tracks. All I saw were the tracks of a whole bunch of horses that were in that pasture.

"So I'm riding off thinking of what happened. I'm trying to blank it out of my mind. It made no sense at all to a little kid.

Max says goodbye to his grandmother, "Birdy" Swafford before he left for war.

That was before I spent that school year with my grandmother and started learning about these things.

"All of a sudden, that whole herd of horses charged. I could hear them just thundering. They ran past me and ran all the way to that fence down there and then they stopped and whirled. They were looking back at that house, just quivering. Scared to death. I was going to ride in and tell my daddy or mama about this.

"I rode almost to the edge of the little town and I looked back and saw this man sitting on a dark horse, looking at me. He was stopped behind me. He had a flat dark hat and he was watching me. Every time I moved, he moved closer. I was really boogered at this point.

"And then all of a sudden I wasn't boogered any more. Without knowing it, I was having my first great metaphysical experience and I was accepting it as something that wasn't going to be explained to me. That I was being told something. Then I looked back and he was gone.

"Something had happened that couldn't be explained, but I accepted this. I didn't tell anyone about it until I told my grandmother, some two years later."

This, as it turned out, was providential not only for Max, but for thousands of readers in the years to come.

In an area of the country where many women tended to worry most about recipes and hairdos and church socials, Birdy Swafford must have been an oddity. Everyone in the tiny town knew she was an Indian medicine woman and mystic, but no one would talk about it. She talked about it with Max, though, and occasionally smoked her pipe. But never, Max says, in public. "She was pure love," Max remembers. "There wasn't a kid, wasn't a single soul that she didn't love. While she was alive, she kept the clan together."

"I got quite a lesson in human nature there (at her home)," Max adds, chuckling. "You know, a lot of those people had Indian blood, but no one would admit it. My grandfather (Swafford) couldn't let anyone know about his Indian blood. I always wondered why none of the people (who came for readings) used the front door. These were church people. I knew them. And I could never understand why these extra-religious people would come and sneak around to her back door for their readings and she'd treat them for all their damn ailments. And they'd hide to do it. I'd watch and listen, and this was giving me one helluva psychological lesson into the human beast here. I was gaining it, and I was seeking it.

"She couldn't always help people, either. Sometimes she could help their minds, though. I wondered if a person could do this on demand, but I don't think so. It's simply a gift. Sometimes she'd have to say come back in a day or two and we'll try this again. And she never charged, but sometimes they'd leave her things. Some food, maybe, things like that.

"That gave me a funny feeling. We'd sit on the porch at night. She had one of those porch swings. They're wonderful in every damn way. We'd sit out there in almost any kind of weather. She'd tell me spiritual stories that happened (to the Cherokee people) in Oklahoma and way back in Georgia.

"It was a wonderful time. I eventually told her of this (experience at the empty house), but she didn't explain it, either. She just smiled and nodded, as if that's what I was supposed to see. It was an opening up for all this stuff I was supposed to see through her."

Nor was Birdy Swafford the only person in the family with "the gift."

Three years after Max and Pat were married, they visited the elder Evanses in Texas. Pat remembers well what happened there.

"Max's mom (Hazel Evans) was totally psychic," Pat says. "But of course, in those days it wasn't really proper to call it that. She'd had visions, too, over the years. Like when her sister was killed. One day she just looked up at a box of Quaker oats and said her sister was dead. And it turned out she was. But she just chalked it up to women's intuition. It wasn't fashionable to be psychic in those days, or to be Indian, either. Even part Indian."

On this trip, Pat remembers the family sitting around after dinner and someone saying "Hazel, why don't you raise the table?"

"She put her hands flat on this small table," Pat says, "and raised it about two inches off the floor. I thought, what is this?

I'd never heard of anything like this, anywhere. We couldn't put it down, either, by pushing on it. She truly did that, in front of several people. It was a parlor game. You didn't have TV, so you played cards and raised tables," she says, laughing.

"My mother was psychic," Max says, "and could see things way ahead, but the church got them so goofed up . . . . My dad had this church thing. Most of them did. They weren't open to these things until much later on in their lives."

W. B. Evans donated the acre of land where the First Baptist Church now stands in Lubbock, and he helped build it, personally. Pat remembers him digging the foundation with a shovel, wearing a white shirt and tie.

But it was his Grandmother Swafford who steered Max toward the metaphysical. Max doesn't like to talk about it much, except to casually say things like, "Back when I could read people's minds. . . ."

But Pat will. Says Pat, "She (Birdy Swafford) fashioned him, I think. Her influence has been there through our whole lives." She recalls, in fact, the gift from Grandmother Swafford that almost ruined Max's career.

"Grandmother Swafford called us into the kitchen the next night," Pat says. "She wanted just the three of us in there. We were drinking tea. It was winter. She said, 'Well, Maxie, I'm not going to be here very long. I won't ever see you again alive.'

"We said, 'Oh, we'll be back soon.' As far as we knew, she was in good health for an old lady, but we knew what she meant.

"And she said, 'I don't have anything to give you. Except my gift. My gift of tea reading (but she didn't call it that). You can't make any money out of it; it's a gift.' And she read our tea leaves and said we'd be in a great blizzard going home, but don't worry about it, because it will be fine."

"Well," Pat says, "we got the blinding blizzard, just outside Taos, but we crept along and made it just fine."

The day after Grandmother Swafford's "gift" in the kitchen, Max and Pat started back to Taos from Morton, Texas. Before they got to Taos (and the blizzard) they stopped in Bronco, Texas, on the New Mexico state line. Max's Uncle Slim was working there for a ranch woman named Anita Field.

"This is a Max (thing), you know," says Pat, laughing. "We had never met this lady, but she invited us to supper. Anita was a prosperous lady and very nice. After supper we were sitting there and we had coffee. And the conversation got kinda . . . you know, it needed help . . . and Max said, 'Anita, I think I'll read your tea leaves.'

"He'd never done this before. He just pulled this. I thought . . . this better be funny. Well, he picked up her coffee cup and said, 'Well, Anita, you're going to buy a bar.'

"She hit the ceiling. She was mad as a hornet. She said, 'Who in the hell told you that? These loudmouths! Nobody is supposed to know that!'

"We didn't know a soul there, we told her. Max said, 'It's in the cup.'

"She says she was definitely making a deal to buy a bar and her family was against it. He told her several different things, too. He said he saw a child. She was going to have a child. She was a single woman then. Later, she adopted this little girl. And got married, too."

"When we finally got off to bed by ourselves, Max said, 'Do you believe it? I actually could read that cup.'"

"He never could tell our future, but he could tell Woody Crumbo's and all our friends'. That became a terrible burden. It could have ruined his life. People found out about it, you know. It was a constant stream of people coming over. He didn't have time to paint. Woody was there every morning (for his reading)."

For about two years, Max had his grandmother's gift. Sometimes it was almost frightening.

"I remember," Pat said, "we'd sit and watch people and Max would know what they were thinking. He'd know what they were going to do. You might see a man come out of the post office carrying a package and he'd walk to his car and get out a key and open the trunk. Then Max would say, 'Oh, he'll change his mind and put that in the car with him.'

"And sure enough, he would."

"It was driving me crazy," says Max. "You'd think it would be fun, reading people's minds, but it's terrible. These people who say you can turn it on and read minds on demand are crazy, too. You can't. Sometimes you can and sometimes you can't.

"I got to where I hated it. People don't think in complete thoughts, either. They think in little spurts. Little here, little there. Jump around all over the place."

The "gift" began taking more and more of Max's time. One day, he and Woody Crumbo went to a medium in Tulsa, Oklahoma. She told him, says Pat, that he sure enough had "it" and that, sooner or later, he would have to decide what to do with his life. He could be an artist, she said, or have the "gift."

> Everybody who reads this is gonna think he's a nut, but it was a gift. He could have kept it, like his grandmother did. But she didn't have anything else, you know. We had other things to do and we couldn't afford to do this.
>
> He just didn't have the time. It was all taken by people. Woody, mainly.
>
> —Pat Evans

Max says it was actually the famous medicine man of Taos Pueblo, Joe Bernal, who told him how to rid himself of it.

"I told him what happened and he sat me down and said, 'Well, you want to be an artist or do you want to be a medicine man? Which do you really want to be?' I said I wanted to be an artist. He said, 'Well, we better get rid of it, then.'"

He gave Max some peyote and told him how to make some medicine prayers and said the next day it would go away.

"I'd taken that damn peyote that night. Two buttons of it," says Max. "I puked for a spell. Then, after I made those prayers, I had these visions. I made use of them in (the novella) *Candles in the Bottom of the Pool.*

> The sounds came to him faintly at first, then stronger. He leaned against the smooth dirt plaster and heard the clanking of armor, the twanging of bows, the screams of falling men and horses. His chest rose as his lungs pumped the excited blood. His powerful hands were grabbing their own flesh at his sides. It was real. Then the

struggles of the olive conquerors and the brown van-quished faded away like a weak wind.

He opened his eyes, relaxing slightly, and stepped back, staring intently at the wall. Where was she? Would she still come to him smiling, waiting, wanting? Maybe. There was silence now. Even the singing of the desert birds outside could not penetrate the mighty walls.

Then he heard the other song. The words were unin-telligible, ancient, from forever back, back, back, but he felt and understood their meaning. She appeared from the unfathomable reaches of the wall, undulating like a black wisp ripped from a tornado cloud. She was whole now. Her black lace dress clung to her body, emphasizing the delicious smoothness of her face and hands. The comb of Spanish silver glistened like a halo in her hair. His blue eyes stared at her dark ones across the centuries. They knew. She smiled with much warmth, and more. One hand beckoned for him to come. He smiled back, whis-pering, "Soon. Very soon."

—from *Candles In The Bottom Of The Pool*

"I had these visions of clear water and sand," Max says. "At one point there were three suns and a man came down by the river. He waved at me three times to come across that river. Somehow I knew that when I refused him, it was over. It was like a dream, but I was wide awake. When I refused him, it was like a curtain came down over the scene. All that magnificent grandeur closed and was gone.

"I hardly slept that night. In the morning, I was anxious to get into the post office. When I did, I found I couldn't hear any-one's secrets. I didn't want to know their damned secrets."

From that time on, Max was free to be an artist, and he was. Friends stopped coming by for readings. He was also free to be a writer, and, later, he was.

So the gift from the kindly healer, the loving grandmother who fashioned so much of his life, had to be set aside . . . but she had given him a gift and a choice.

The spiritual part of Max never really stopped. In fact, it became intertwined with his writing. Pat remembers vividly what went on when Max was writing his novel Faraway Blue, the story of the struggle between the Negro cavalry troops stationed in New Mexico—known as the Buffalo Soldiers—and the Apaches under the brilliant generalship of a chief called Nana.

"It was the strangest thing," she said. "That book had a lot of spiritual help. When I was typing that book . . . well, Max does have a medicine pipe, you know. When he smokes it, it's for somebody else, not for himself. I was up typing, and one day the room filled with this smell of his medicine tobacco.

"I asked Max why he was smoking his medicine pipe, but he said he hadn't smoked it in weeks . . . in months! So I guess that must have been Nana smoking the pipe," Pat says, laughing. "It happened twice during that book, and both times it was when I was working on (parts about) Nana.

"He needed spiritual help with that book. Max said nobody really knew much about Nana. He did a lot of research on him, of course. He said I don't think people really know him (Nana) that well. And I need help from him."

Pat sits quietly a moment.

"This butterfly—oh, I don't want to get into that. . . ."

Why not?

"Well, this butterfly would just hang around Max out in the yard. Now this was winter. And every day that butterfly would be out there in the yard with Max. And then Max'd come in and write all these beautiful things about Nana with such great feeling and compassion. And I think (Nana) helped."

(Max) took me to his back yard on his seventieth birthday. He was writing *Faraway Blue* at the time, and he said, "(Apache chief) Nana visited me. Right here." He's a very spiritual man.

—Dr. Jeb Stuart Rosebrook, historian

"Nana came to me one day," Max says, quietly. "He just came into my head (Max spreads his fingers and lets them float down onto the top of his head) and then I knew. I knew what to write."

Now he saw the General swinging his rifle toward him. He knew he would get his horse first. Nana went into the floating space now. The vacuum of time stopped where everything hesitated for a fulfillment. The Winchester centered on the General's mouth, and Nana saw the lead leave his gun and his old half-blind eyes could see the bullet as it moved toward its target. The hunting spirit left his body and guided the bullet through the General's upper lip, knocking the roots of two teeth to bits and tearing apart the vertebrae that connected his head to his spine. Before the General fell backward, spewing blood on the ground, the hunting spirit had returned to Nana's soul.

—from *Faraway Blue*

Max the Electronic Menace

He came over to stay with us one night. In the morning the battery in my van was drained.

—Robert J. Conley,
novelist and official historian of the Cherokee Nation

Then, of course, there is Max's legendary ability to stop any piece of operating equipment within his view without trying (the computer printer, for one thing, will not work when Max is in the same room).

Many years ago now, actor Brian Keith was a guest on The Tonight Show with Johnny Carson. As Keith walked out onto the set, all the lights went out.

When order was restored, Keith explained to Carson's audience that he sometimes has that effect on machinery. His mere presence could cause circuits to fail and diodes to go ballistic.

"But I have a buddy," he told this national television audience, "who is worse than I am. He once shut down the Super Chief."

True. That buddy was Max Evans, scourge of everything electrical.

According to Pat Evans, she and Max stepped aboard the Super Chief in Los Angeles' Union Station one day and all the lights went out. It caused the train to be extra late leaving Los Angeles.

"Hell," says Max, "I once shut down the telephone system of an entire hotel for three days. The only phone that worked in the whole sonofabitch was in my room. People were calling my room to make reservations. So I got pissed at the loss of writing time and started taking reservations from all over the world. The real chaos started after the phones fixed themselves."

Robert Conley and his wife, Evelyn, were surprised one night while staying with Max and Pat in Albuquerque by the sound of the television set coming on.

"That TV set comes on by itself—over and over—in the middle of the night and it automatically turns to Channel 7," Conley says. Seven, says Max, is the sacred Cherokee number.

And when Pat is typing Max's manuscripts onto the computer, he is only allowed to point with a pencil at the screen. He is not allowed to touch it.

His daughter, Charlotte, says her father can't wear any kind of watch, either. It'll die.

One of the reasons Max takes the train, it turns out, is because he can't seem to get through the airport metal detector . . . or any metal detector . . . without setting if off. He's tried several times, Pat says, without a single blue jean rivet or any other tiny metal part, and still sets it off.

"He's a menace," Pat says, laughing. "He's just a menace, that's all.

"But I finally found him something he can't break. He has a microwave and heats things up in it. That microwave is his best friend now."

Questions That Have No Answers

I'm going to write this metaphysical book, if I can get Pat to type it. She's not comfortable with the metaphysical stuff. I have a lot of this stuff done in a book I call Hexes but I can't get Pat to type it. She just won't do it. She's got it hidden. I tried to get it so I could get someone else to type it for me, but she's hidden the goddam thing. Well, she says 'The time isn't right.' God bless her, I guess that's part of being a good editor.

—Max Evans

But all of these things—the gift of Birdy Swafford, the man in the empty line shack, the visitations of Chief Nana—blended together, combining themselves into the legends of the ancient and mysterious country known as New Mexico and finding a home in the receptive mind of one of its greatest writers.

Some things, Max says, are beyond explanation. There are some questions that have no answers that we're allowed to know. In a literary life, it can become a zesty seasoning for ideas.

Woody Crumbo was just wonderful. He was like a brother and we loved him. We had such good times together. One day, I remember, we climbed the sacred mountain behind the (Taos) Pueblo. The snowdrifts were up to our waists, but we didn't care. We were just kids, really, having fun.

We sat up there on the mountain and we could hear this chanting coming from a cave behind us. But it was . . . nobody. There was nobody there.

It was a very soft little chant, coming and going. At first I didn't know if the others heard it. But we all heard it. And there was nobody else around for many miles.

—Pat Evans

The three were about twenty paces from the face of the tunnel, on their way back out, when Bluefeather halted, hearing the haunting sound of an Indian flute. The others stopped, watching him, eyes wide. At first the sound came so softly that he thought it was emanating out of his head instead of into it. Then the sound swelled rapidly. Bluefeather wondered if he was the only one to hear it. His question was answered when he felt Marsha's hand grasp his upper arm for a fleeting moment.

W.B. Evans, Max's father, mined in the Black Range of New Mexico during 1956 and 1957. Max found his dad's old "Little Dove" mine on a trip in 2002. Photo by Embree (Sonny) Hale.

Bluefeather turned around and shined his light back into the tunnel. Suddenly, the music stopped. There was a silence so profound that it seemed to have a singular existence, with its power being in its non-being. A small pebble fell from the ceiling to bounce on the tunnel floor, making a noise—to the only listeners—far beyond its true size. Then a larger one fell, and another. Then the face of the tunnel bulged out like a huge, stone balloon and shattered, sending large pieces of rock rolling forward. The bluish brown dust puffed forward from the rubble. A rumbling noise came from the tunnel and the bowels of the mountain like the mighty garbled voices of arguing giants. The entire face of the tunnel, the ceiling, and the hang and foot-walls started falling toward them.

—from *Bluefeather Fellini In The Sacred Realm*

Max Makes a Movie....

All Hollywood people lie to you, now and then, but (there was) this one sonofabitch who lied to me all the time. (One time he) cost me four-and-a-half months of work. That is an eternity when you're writing well. Great big young tough sucker. You could tell he ran ten miles a day, one of those bastards. Lifted weights. And, an old man like me—I guess I'd just have to shoot the sonofabitch. I can still shoot pretty good.

—Max Evans

✀ **Max didn't really set out** to become a movie producer. It just kinda happened.

In fact, the whole concept of his film *The Wheel* began out of a concern for others.

"I saw all these kids," Max says, "drinking, raising hell, doing all kinds of fun and frivolous things. Now I'm bad enough myself, but just the same I saw this whole generation going to hell, which we're paying for now."

So he came up with the concept for a film called *The Wheel*. It is a tale of a man, a woman, and a child who find beauty, art, and a living in the Alamogordo, New Mexico, city dump.

"These young people," Max says, "made beautiful art objects out of the stuff they found in the dump. I wanted to

On the set of The Wheel *in the town dump in Alamogordo, David Nelson of* Ozzie and Harriet *is the assistant director looking through the camera while Max' (right) looks on.*

show (young people) that they didn't have to do all these things, that they could literally jerk themselves up by their bootstraps. That was why I wanted to do this.

"I gave it to Robert Altman, and he read three or four pages of it and threw it away," Max says. "I took it to Peckinpah and tried to get him to do it, but he didn't even know what it was. He didn't understand it. Then I realized that, hell yes . . . he's part of the problem!"

So Max decided to take a flyer in film and make the thing himself. And he did it, in his own patented fashion, of course.

"I raised $25,000 at first," Max says, "'cause that's what it took to get a Hollywood crew to Alamogordo."

But raising that initial $25,000 was only the beginning of the challenge. While Max was a well-known novelist by this time, he'd never made a picture before, and Wall Street wasn't clamoring to invest in it. But this is Max Evans, who could sell Tabasco sauce in hell, and wasn't to be daunted.

"I didn't sell stock," Max says, "because I got burned in that ignorance in the mining business. But I'd shoot (the film) all day and stay up all night, calling people and promoting money.

"I raised $229,000," he says. "I found out that was $40,000 short."

The problem was that amateur actors (which he had for this film) didn't always perform perfectly the first time the camera is turned on. And every time you reshoot a scene, it costs money. A great deal of money, it turns out.

"My bookkeeper was a guy named Alex With," Max says. "Great guy. Had a grocery store in the museum section of Albuquerque. Made a fortune a penny at a time. Really knew his stuff."

Even with Max staying up all night on the phone and shooting a movie all day, the money was running short. Alex told Max, finally, that if they were to get the movie finished at all, they would have to limit themselves to a single take for each scene.

"We were about halfway through the movie when this happened," Max says. "The problem was I had all amateur actors and the only way you can have a good show with amateur actors is to have enough money for at least five takes."

So the second half of the movie was shot with the first attempt by camera, crew and actors. And it looked like it.

"It was half great," Max says, "and half very bad. I went ahead and cut it and released it."

It got, he says, "mixed reviews."

It might've set some kind of record, too, because, as Max puts it, "Everybody was screaming at me for money. But every sonofabitch got paid. Everyone in the crew got paid."

Except Max, of course.

"That movie deal was just about as bad as you could do," he says. "I lost it all. Thing is, half of it is absolutely sublime. I don't even know where the negatives are. There's one print of this I've been trying to run down. Oh, I have a single video copy, but it's fourth or fifth generation. I lost the master video long ago. Most of the color is missing, and some TVs will run it and some won't."

But there is that first half, after all

"I'll tell you what," Max says, "if I'd had forty grand more, I'd have had a great picture. I always could—sometimes in very odd ways—gather the green stuff in, but I never bothered to learn how to match the amount with the need."

I'm not that bright. No writer is ever really that bright.
I don't know how they write. It must be another source.
Damn sure ain't from being bright.

—Max Evans

Rex Allen, A Great Guy

Max made a documentary once on rancher Fred Martin, of Magdalena, New Mexico, and another documentary called Every Man's Mountain. For these, he worked with "the voice" of the West, Rex Allen, as narrator.

Allen, former singer, rodeo hand and cowboy movie star with his horse, Koko, had a voice that summoned sunsets, sagebrush and warm friendly feelings around a campfire. His was the voice of nearly all of Disney's nature movies.

"I loved Rex Allen," Max says. "He'd feed you for a month there on his ranch, give you the best food and whisky, take you wherever you wanted to go. But if you needed fifty dollars, hell, he couldn't find it anywhere!

"Ol' Rex was a great guy. He loved Mexican people. He taught himself to speak Spanish fluently, and he'd hire (Mexican nationals) and he'd give them paid vacations. They loved him. They stayed with him forever. And he truly did love them. This wasn't something he did for effect."

Rex was born and raised in southeastern Arizona, and died there, too, after spending many years in semi-rural California.

"Here he was," Max says, "the most conservative old bastard in the world, and some people put him down for it. But he was one of the kindest, most beautiful human beings I ever saw. But he didn't show it off or run around telling people."

Max and Pat were driving around when they heard on the radio that Rex Allen had died.

Cowboy actor and singer Rex Allen was Max's friend for more than 30 years.

"I wanted to go to his memorial so goddam bad," Max says, "but my inner ear was making me so sick I couldn't go. Every damned old movie and rodeo cowboy in the world was there."

In addition to *The Wheel*, Max had an idea for a television series. He would go around and do documentaries on old Western characters—artists, farmers, etc.—while they were still alive and a link to our past in the West.

And while the series was never made, they at least had fun shooting the pilot, a documentary on rancher and cattle rustler emeritus, Fred Martin, of the old cow town of Magdalena, New Mexico.

His story was called *Fred Martin: Out of the West.*

Max's friend, Charlie Ford, worked on this film with Max and on the other films Max made. Charlie became production manager of the Fred Martin film after a high-level staff meeting that lasted less than a minute in the bar in Magdalena.

"The production manager was a guy from Albuquerque named John Summers," Charlie says. "And that night, when everybody was pretty well drunk, Max announced that the crew wouldn't have to be in action until a certain time the next morning. Summers then told them that they would follow the schedule as written and be there earlier.

"Well, Summers' problem," Charlie says, "was that he forgot who was in charge. Max was on him like a tiger and they fought under one of the pool tables. If I remember right, Max bit his ear off.

"It was sudden, it was violent, and it was decisive. The next morning, Summers was on his way back to Albuquerque and I became production manager."

(Max) made a documentary on the Sandia Mountains called *Every Man's Mountain*. And then he did a documentary on the Rio Grande. PBS showed that *Every Man's Mountain* a lot. Rex Allen narrated it.

That was kind of a weird time in our lives. That was in the early 1970s. He was in the bar an awful lot then, and I learned to drink a lot then, too. He wanted someone to drink with.

We always had some people around, and we always had fun. I don't know how he found the time to write, but he'd just blank things out and go write. And when he wrote, he didn't drink, ever. The two do not mix.

—Pat Evans

"When we were in Magdalena," says Charlie Ford, "we knew we had to catch ol' Fred Martin on a Saturday night when he came to town to drink. He stayed out there on the ranch, some sixty miles from town, all week long, then came to the bar and was full of stories, for as long as he lasted. And that wasn't very long.

"He was up in his late eighties then, and got drunk pretty fast, so we were ready for him. We got into the bar in the afternoon and got everything set up: cameras, lights, sound equipment. They had two pool tables in the place, one of them rattier than the other. This drunk was passed out on one of them. We didn't pay any attention to him.

"Finally, here comes Martin in off the range, and we fired everything up. The lights and cameras were on and everybody was doing just fine. We'd forgotten all about the drunk on the pool table. Well, this guy wakes up and finds himself in the middle of all these lights and action, and he gives this terrifying scream and runs out of there."

Max has had some very interesting friends over the years, of course. One time he was down in Arizona with Rex Allen, who lived there, and Slim Pickens.

Well, Rex said, let's have a toast, and he said, "Isn't it great at this time in our lives that we're all millionaires?"

Max told me it was hard to raise his glass to that when he was trying to figure how to pay for his drink.

— Jimmy Bason, rancher and friend

For King and Country . . .

Went in Don Fernando's in Taos one time and saw Max sitting at the bar with his back to me. I walked over and put my hand on his shoulder and he stiffened up. Didn't even look at me. Just stared straight ahead.

He said, 'You take your hand off me or you're in a goddam fight.'

I didn't take my hand away and he spun around, saw me, and said, 'Jesus Christ! It's the governor!'

— David Cargo,
Governor of New Mexico, 1966–1974

It was David Cargo, in fact, who roped Ol' Max into public service. In 1967, Cargo decided to set up the New Mexico Film Commission to entice film makers to use New Mexico as a setting for their films.

"The first person I called was Max Evans," Cargo says. "I'm glad I did, too."

And, as with everything else he has done, Max decided to go into film commissioning in a big way. His own work suffered as he worked to bring more filming to the state.

Finally, Cargo and Max went to Hollywood, rented the ballroom of the Beverly Hills Hotel, and ordered breakfast for sixty.

The result of years of work, The New Mexico Farm and Ranch Museum is centered on forty-seven acres near Las Cruces.

Max told Cargo to leave the inviting to him, and he got on the phone. He spent two weeks enlisting everybody's help.

"Here came all these producers and directors and actors and everyone," Cargo says. "I couldn't believe it. And then I look up, and here comes Ol' Max in with John Wayne. That guy knows everyone."

At the breakfast, Cargo showed a kind of travelogue film that someone had made for the occasion, showing how pretty the state is.

"It was terrible," Max recalls. "I thought nobody would ever come here after seeing that film. But then the governor stood up and began speaking, and what he said and how he said it really saved the day. He was so eloquent and so sincere. The movie makers fell in love within just fifteen minutes."

Later that day, Max and Cargo and other members of the commission went to see the head of Warner Brothers. All in all, the day was a success. In a future trip, Cargo and Max went to Hollywood and simply went to appointments in the film community.

Did it work?

"Dave Cargo told me," Max says, "that he figured it up, and since that time, more than a billion and a half dollars has come to New Mexico through the motion picture industry."

I see Max as a humble world celebrity. He has cracked barriers most people haven't.

—Dr. Roland Sanchez

Nor was that the only way Max was to be involved in public service. In 1988, Max was appointed a founding member of the board of directors for the New Mexico Farm and Ranch Heritage Institute Museum, and served as the museum foundation's first president

Even before there was a board, according to Dr. Roland Sanchez, Max was one of several people, including Felicia Thal and Bill Stephens, who met privately to plan a ranching museum.

The New Mexico Farm and Ranch Museum in Las Cruces was the dream of a number of people, including two members of the original board, Max, left, and his close friend, Dr. Roland Sanchez of Belen, who is both a physician and cattle rancher. Elia Sanchez photo.

One of the benefits of fame in New Mexico is being chosen to judge the chile cookoff. Here, "Judge Max" rests on the University of New Mexico football field during the judging with Pat, Sheryl and Charlotte. Sanchez and Max partnered up to help complete the New Mexico Farm and Ranch Museum. Photo by Dick Skrondahl.

"The ranchers," says Dr. Sanchez, a Belen, New Mexico, physician who also raises registered Santa Gertrudis cattle, "didn't want to be involved with 'sodbusters.' (farmers). But it soon became obvious that neither group could raise enough money on its own to have their own museums. Together, they went to the state for money."

There was a lot of strife on the board at first, and basically it had to do with farmers and ranchers not really liking or trusting each other. Finding a way to get along and work together was crucial. And Max, with the respect he has as a writer and former rancher, was able to keep the peace, according to several people close to the board.

Roland Sanchez was president of the museum board and brought Max onto the board from his former position on the foundation. One board member said Sanchez and Evans made a double team for sanity.

"He had an excellent relationship with Governor Garrey Carruthers," Sanchez says. "We'd talk to the governor, and then Max would say about five key words and the governor would help us right out.

"Max Evans' vision for the museum was that it could not survive as a museum for the local people in Las Cruces, but must be a museum for people of the world. The world, he said, was thirsty for our folklore.

"He's been invited everywhere because his books are almost a bigger hit overseas than they are here."

He was, Sanchez says, the "right man in the right place at the right time. His genius was in helping get the right people in there to do the job to move this along."

Max served sixteen years on that board, far longer than anyone else to date.

Today the 80,000-square-foot museum, which occupies forty-seven acres outside Las Cruces, describes current practices of agriculture and farm and ranch life and preserves the history of that life going back three thousand years.

The Inconvenient Adventure

When you get around seventy, the whole world becomes maintenance. It's not that you're in pain or can't create. Of course you can. But you can't screw like you used to, or do lots of other things, either. All this bullshit comes down to maintenance. Something up here breaks, and before you get it fixed, something down there breaks. So you get that fixed and then you start back up again. That's just the way it's supposed to be.

—Max Evans

❦ **They say you can't reach** the pinnacle of bliss until you've been in the depths, and that's really what happened during what Max calls his "inconvenient adventure." The adventure—a grand adventure—came a little more than two weeks after what he calls . . .

THE INCONVENIENCE

It's a sunny autumn day, one of those crisp days that make New Mexicans glad they live here. It's October 20, 1999, and Max is on his morning walk around his southeast Albuquerque neighborhood.

"I felt this numbness in my left arm," he says, "and I knew right away what it was."

Max quickly returned to the house, took two aspirin, and told Pat he had to go to the doctor's office right then. This doctor shall remain nameless.

"I went down there, but it eased up. His wife was the nurse, and she told me he had a golf game that afternoon in Tucson and they were trying to get out of there. And I thought, what if I'm really having this and he goes off to the golf game? He gave me another exam and he told me to come back Tuesday. The dead giveaway was when I walked out of the office he asked if I had any nitroglycerin. I said no, I didn't have any. I mean, I didn't need to blow a whole ledge down! I wasn't going back into the mining business. But he didn't get the joke. He gave the whole thing away by that. So he let me go home.

"Well, I went upstairs and laid down and it hit me. I jumped up and took two aspirin and I risked killing myself to save myself. I went into the bedroom and got some warm socks, because I knew I was going to be in the hospital for a while.

"I yelled down for Sheryl or Pat to call the ambulance. I went downstairs and laid on the couch so I'd have everything ready for them. I was really hurting. Real bad.

"I figured the odds (on my living) were down to a flip of the coin, so I just started joking. I'd already done everything I could do, so it didn't bother me. Out of my hands. Boy, they got there like that. They put me on nitroglycerin real quick and hit me with that electrocardiogram and he told Pat that two more minutes and I'd have been gone."

In the hospital they "took lots of pictures" and discovered Max had three arteries in his heart ninety-percent closed. The doctors decided to do a triple-bypass operation. They told Max if he got the operation with the doctor they hoped to get, he'd have a good chance. He told them he felt lucky, so they'd wait for the doctor to be free.

"I felt comfortable with the decision," Max says. "But finally the nitroglycerin wasn't doing any good. The pain got worse and worse. I told the nurse and they whipped it right up. And as luck would have it, I drew that wonderful genius, William Deane, M.D. to do the surgery. Isn't that great? It was a miracle, and I told him so. He came and sat down on my bed afterwards and I told him so, and he said it sure was."

Max got home from the hospital feeling pretty good. He thought, "Hey, there's nothing to this. I'll be all right in two weeks. I believe I'll go back and reread Steinbeck. See if he holds up."

The next morning Max was getting ready to read more Steinbeck when World War II again interfered. The inner ear attacked him again and cancelled all plans for reading.

"It usually comes and goes, but this time it wouldn't go," Max says. "So I sat up in bed. Now Pat doesn't believe me about this, because sometimes I'd have my eyes closed, but I didn't sleep for thirty-two days and nights. I couldn't move. I had to sit up, not lie down. If I did (lie down) I had to get up and puke for a couple of hours. I was afraid it was going to tear (the surgery) all loose. So I was kinda in a jam. It was exhausting.

"So after about two or three weeks of this, I looked at the little crack in the curtain across the room and I pinched myself to make sure I was awake. I called Pat and had a little visit with her so she didn't think I was having hallucinations. Visited about the medicine. None of the medicine worked (on the inner ear). So I thought, well, I'm waiting here. I satisfied myself that there were no hallucinations."

Having prepared himself that way, Max was ready to have . . .

THE ADVENTURE

"I made a little prayer to the Great Mystery in the Sky and I said, 'I want to go . . . please take my soul to a place beyond the planets. I want to see where all this comes from. I want the knowledge. I just want to look at it. And . . . like that, I'm there. Beyond the planets.

"The other day I was reading where these scientists have this new telescope that told them the far reaches of the universe were not these brilliant colors they thought it was, but that it was all a tan. They are very badly wrong. It's undulating. It undulates less when you go beyond the planets. But it's bronze. I could see this little red light, a billion or ten billion miles out there. As I got in closer to the light, it changed to blue-white.

"The one massive thing I remember was the music. It was in mathematical figures . . . moving mathematical figures. It was so vast you could hardly see it. It was a wonderful adventure. It was a rare gift. I'm sure other people have seen it, too, but they're not going to tell it because they think they're gonna die, or because people will think they're just idiots."

Max laughs. "Hey, we're all idiots to start with. We prove it over and over. Why be afraid of being an idiot?"

"My desperation was when I came back, trying to get someone to hear me. So it would be some kind of remembrance I could put in a story. That's how chickenshit I am!"

Max has no idea how long he was gone on this trip. Minutes or hours.

"I thanked the Great Mystery. Thank you, thank you, thank you. Oh, what a journey. What can I do? I'll have to write something pretty for you."

Max pauses. "And here's the horror of this. There's much more beauty than horror, but here's the horror. I had all these experiences and I knew they'd go away afterwards. I tried to tell Pat and she thought I was hallucinating. I tried to tell my good friend Doc (Roland) Sanchez, but he'd just pass it off. And I knew . . . this was the horror . . . I knew I was going to lose this.

"I still couldn't move around or lie down after that," he says, "but at least I had this wonderful adventure to think about."

He says he's lost the memory of at least ninety-nine percent of the experience.

It took about three months to get the nausea under control and to get his heart back into the right rhythm. Finally, the heart rate got under control, thanks, he says, to Doc Sanchez trying pill after pill on him until he found one that worked. And the acupuncturist, Ms. Alexica Trujillo, got his inner ear calmed enough to let him sleep some.

"And you know," Max says, "after that cleared up, I felt better than I had in twenty years. Seriously. I was ready to create better than ever because I'd been blessed to see, for a brief flicker of time, the source—the creative battery of everything."

Max On Writing . . .

You have to look at the ridiculous in this life. If you look long enough, you will see how ridiculous most of it is, and how much fun it is. That's what you should write about . . . the ridiculous and the fun.

—Max Evans

✂ **"A real writer is someone** who can't help it," Max says. "Their genes got messed up way back there somewhere. They were chipping pictures on rocks, trying to tell stories. They didn't know why they were doing it. There were still critics standing there, too.

"They'd rather write than run up and down mountains, I guess. The noise of all that damn chipping probably kept the tigers away."

When Gabriel Marquez's novel, *One Hundred Years of Solitude*, emerged into a world thirsty for new writing styles, it led inexorably to the Nobel Prize for writing. Critics called his style of mixing real and imaginary "magical realism." That was in the 1980s.

But Max Evans was writing "magical realism" back in 1950, beginning with his short story "The Call." And he has continued to use magical realism over a half century of writing now, blending reality with the surrealistic. This probably reached its peak in Max's repertoire in *Bluefeather Fellini in the Sacred Realm*.

He laughs. "I was writing magical realism before they had it named."

Such are the problems of shunning big assignments with big publishers and choosing instead to rope calves, have fun, and spend writing time on writing what Max wanted to write.

His literary life, to a critic, sometimes seems to be one long experiment. Just about the time you have Max figured out, he throws you another writing curve and makes you scratch your head again. Let's face it, most readers like to be comfortable in our selection of writers. When we go in a book store and see a book by Agatha Christie or Louis L'Amour or John D. MacDonald, we know exactly what to expect. Oh, we won't know the plot, but we sure know what to expect, and that usually ends up being hours of relaxing fun.

As one wag pointed out once, "Louis L'Amour wrote *Hondo* seventy-five times." And we loved it each time.

But Max hasn't written any two stories the same in sixty years. This makes some readers uncomfortable. Here in New Mexico, you mention Max Evans to ranchers and cowboys and they grin and say, "Yeah. *The Rounders*. Great book." Corner someone in the fancy coffee crowd in Santa Fe, and they might mention "Candles In The Bottom Of The Pool," or "Xavier's Folly." Those are stories that appeal to that crowd.

There may not be another single writer who has flexed as much literary muscle in as many directions as Max Evans. If there's a type of well-written story he missed doing, it's more than likely just because he hasn't gotten around to it yet.

Max once said, over lunch, "One time at a book signing, this guy came up and said, 'My daddy loves your books because you write about people who make a living with their hands, and they are always the underdogs.'

"Well, no super intelligent critics ever caught on to this, and neither did this dumb-ass writer called Ol' Max."

Max liked that and thought it was true. And, to a certain extent it is. But he also writes about artists and dreamers and investors and sponges on society and writers and developers and gamblers.

In other words: people.

"I don't write about gringos, Jews, Hispanics, Indians, Blacks," he said. "I write about everybody in the Southwest exactly as I've encountered them."

Max Evans may be the ultimate in do-it-yourself writers. He began reading, figured he could handle that job, too, and just got started. Self-taught novelists are pretty rare. Most serious literary people come from a university background where people who can't write encourage those who can. But cowboys from eastern New Mexico who just decide one day to be writers don't happen very often. As far as that goes, we can think of only one who succeeded: Ol' Max.

As with many writers, Max is more comfortable writing than discussing writing. After all, it's a pretty personal and private kind of job.

"I don't have any idea what it takes to be a good writer," Max admits. "Just keep writing and writing, I guess. It's like fly fishing. You can take a master of fly fishing, and he really can't tell you much except the angle of fly casting. A great fly fisherman will tell you that.

"A really great fly fisherman has become so by doing it a long time. Some are born better, instinctively better, and it doesn't take them as long a time.

"When a neophyte asks them for the magic. When a neophyte says, 'How do you do that? How do you catch those fish?' invariably the great fisherman will tell them, 'Just do it for a very long time.'

"And that's all there is to writing, too. Oh, there's two or three little ol' tricks to learn, which can be taught in less than five minutes: putting hooks, opening chapters with a paragraph that holds your interest. The best literary writing in the world uses these same little tricks.

"For the rest of it, what kind of soul did you give it? That's going to give it a certain quality even when you get skilled. It'll have a greater quality or lesser quality. The only way you get that real skill, once you learn those little tricks, is just writing and writing and writing and writing. That's all there is to it.

"If you feel good about (a new writer) you can do certain cold-blooded editing that another editor might not do. But that has nothing to do with writing, that's just correcting.

"Among the really top literary-type writers I've met in my life—met a few of them. Met Thornton Wilder once, Aldous Huxley, a few others. Anyway, among them that I know of, at one time in their lives they were really heavy readers . . . every goddam one of them. They were obsessed with reading. They'd read everything. I'm the same way. Can't help myself."

Max has operated a lot by the old cowboy expression used when threatened with being fired: "I was looking for a job when I found this one."

He's made his life and work his own and has done this at great expense.

"I've never been a guy to make editors happy, I'm afraid," he says, smiling. "I'm a selfish sonofabitch. I write for myself. I haven't written for the money. I've had to hustle every damn dime for myself."

> He figures his work out ahead of time. He goes out and walks, and he comes in and we don't talk and he goes right to work. He doesn't scratch anything out or hardly make any changes. He just does it.
>
> —Pat Evans

One man who can put some perspective on writing and Max's place in it is the famous television producer, David Dortort. He brought us Bonanza and High Chapparal for many years. In an interview with the author for a newspaper column, this longtime friend of Max's said, "Almost all of today's (television) programs are geared to New York City and Los Angeles and most are very negative. There's this big vacuum in the middle known as the United States.

"Until we get some different attitudes with network executives from those two cities, it's not going to change.

"You take something like Max Evans' work. That has such beautiful writing, such a feeling for the country. Like *The*

Rounders . . . they're immortal. Nothing will defeat them. And his *Hi Lo Country*. That's the kind of thing that's lacking.

"There are those we call the big buck artists and they put these things on without a sense of responsibility about the public air. They just take advantage of it and manipulate it. What we need is a return to a good, solid strong feeling about yourself as a person and about society. We need to emphasize the things that made this country great. And they're just not doing it."

This appeared in the pages of The Albuquerque Journal in 1990.

But the fact is, those people who turn out screenplays about New York and Los Angeles need wheelbarrows to haul the loot to the bank. Hollywood is a great temptress. She dangles fame and big bucks in front of a writer's eyes, and a good writer looks at the situation and often sees a new car or a rebuilt kitchen rather than a niche in literary history. Max has never made any bones about his not wanting to be a starving artist in a garret. He works better on a full stomach, and has spent too much of his time hustling the things he wants to write rather than writing the things others are hustling.

"I could have been very, very rich," Max says. "I've been offered huge chunks of money and I've turned them down. They would have made me very famous and a lot of money, but I said no.

"I may have been a sonofabitch in this world, and I have and I hope so, in many, many ways. But there ain't a living human being who can show that I even once sold out the gift of my writing."

I think he's one of the greatest writers alive. We got to be friends and I felt like the guys who got to sit around and drink ale with Shakespeare.

—Robert J. Conley,
novelist and official historian of the Cherokee Nation

El Greco could take a truth and stretch it into a greater truth. That's what I've tried to do with writing. I studied El Greco as a kid and I kept wondering why is that so great when it breaks all the rules? It's just like a great piece of writing, you take a truth and then enhance it, rather than deceiving with it. It makes the truth stronger.

—Max Evans

Damn the Academics . . . Full Speed Ahead

So, Max, do you have any advice for writers just starting out?

"Yes I do. Never hit a critic.

Ever since The Fight in Ramon Hernandez's place in Taos, the people Max refers to as "those damned academics" have plagued him. It has been difficult for many people who broke into literature by attending classes for thirty years to take seriously the work of a former cowboy whose sole claim on the world of writing is that he knows what he's talking about and does so with soul, humor and love.

In 2002, reviews began to be released of *Hot Biscuits*, a collection of fiction by actual ranch people, collected and edited by Max Evans and Candy Moulton. Although one of the stories ("The Old Man" by Jimbo Brewer) won the 2002 Spur Award for short fiction, and though Max's contribution ("Once a Cowboy") came in second, and despite the fact that another story ("One Man's Land" by Taylor Fogarty) can easily be considered to be among the best fiction ever written about life in the West, and despite rave reviews by people who know what they are talking about, there are dissenters.

And they are dissenters, Max believes, just because they have to make a political point.

One clear example is a review of *Hot Biscuits* by Hana Norton in *Southwest BookViews*. Here are some excerpts.

[I]n general, the stories by the working folks feel like, well, fiction: mainly nostalgic, oddly sanitized of the actual grind and grime of a ranching life which has not changed much from the previous century—cattle blinded by worms; branding, castrations and de-horning; horse "breaking"; trapping and poisoning of wildlife and the bravura and brutality of rodeo. . . .

At the same time, however, these authors appear oddly unaware that it was their activities which had already irrevocably changed the West and cleared the way to, perhaps, its demise in this century. But that's just my opinion.

For Max, this illustrates part of the fight he's had for nearly fifty years . . . trying to get "the West" taken seriously as a platform for literature. He pinned a note to Ms. Norton's review.

"Ms. Norton did not give a single redeeming statement in a very long review. Quite an accomplishment when the book is full of beauty, pathos, humor, and truth by those who know. This is a totally dishonest review . . . its source easily recognized."

Max's longtime Hollywood agent and close family friend, Bob Goldfarb, has always been aware of this rift.

"We were brought together by Henry Volkening, Max's literary agent in New York," Bob says. "Russell and Volkening only took on the finest literary talent of the day. Henry Volkening really admired Max's work and considered him a real find . . . I hesitate to use the term 'primitive artist,' because his work isn't primitive, but he didn't come out of the academic school of literature.

"I was immediately taken by his work, and I was immediately taken by his personality and Pat's as well. We formed a professional and personal bond that has never weakened."

Max has never drawn a line between business and personal, either. If he likes someone, that's it. When Bob Goldfarb's young son was having some troubles growing up, Max and Pat invited him to stay with them for the summer, and the experience helped him greatly in later life.

As much as Max grinds his teeth over "those damned academics," it is only fair to point out here that some of his greatest admirers and personal friends come from the ranks of teaching in our universities, including the late Dr. C. L. "Doc" Sonnichsen, Dr. John R. Milton, Robert J. Conley, Dr. Jeb Stuart Rosebrook, and Tony Hillerman.

All these men have plenty of initials behind their names.

Max is really above the academic levels. His human experiences are beyond it.

—Dr. Roland Sanchez

With Max's work, you get multiple levels in his work if you take the time to read it again and again. Max just defies categories. It might take a few years, but eventually he'll be recognized.

—Robert J. Conley,
novelist and official historian of the Cherokee Nation

Max never pursued a college education, but he has done what he wanted to in life. He has made his mark, and some people are afraid to do what they are supposed to do and just come through this world and don't leave a track. But old Max Evans has, and I do not think they can plow up his tracks.

—Herman Eubank, Army buddy

Sometimes, at a Signing . . .

I am a damn good novelist, and the dumbest sonofabitch that ever walked . . . and I can prove it!

—Max Evans

In the fall of 2002, Max was winding up a rather whirlwind signing tour for two of his books, *Madam Millie* and *Hot Biscuits*. His final signing was in Santa Fe and, unlike his first signing there earlier in the year, this one hadn't had much publicity. It was, however, well attended by a steady stream of people.

"All of a sudden," Max says, "I look up and here's this great, husky guy. Beard. Standing there with one arm behind him. I thought, 'Jesus Christ! Is this some sonofabitch who's going to knock me in the head?'

"Finally he butted in, as politely as he could. And behind his back he had this long, blue feather. Beautiful damn thing. I thought he'd painted it.

"He said, 'I've waited for years to give you this. *Bluefeather Fellini* is absolutely the greatest book I've ever read, and it changed my whole life. There are things in that book that— I've talked to people who have read it and they just completely missed—and they are so simple. If they'd just open their minds to what's in that book.'

"I could tell he wasn't going to buy any book. He didn't have any money. I was going to give him one, but I had to take that beautiful feather out to Luther's car. That special feather he'd given me. We walked out to the car together, and he told me his name two or three times, but I couldn't understand it. I just couldn't. He didn't ask for my address or phone number, either.

"He said, 'Well, I live in Abiquiu (New Mexico), and I just had to give you that feather.' And he turned and walked away. Didn't have a car, either. He just left."

Max is a fascinating combination of introspection and cheerleading. He treasures having a private life, and yet can read his story about the tomcat and the bishop's balls over statewide radio without blinking an eye. He enjoyed being a shotgun rider in one of Peckinpah's films, but doesn't feel comfortable at a book signing where he is the center of attention. But being a successful writer depends on a guy's fame spreading, so a fellow has to spend a certain amount of time getting famous enough to sell books.

Max has tried to find a way to modify this enough to earn a living and still not be bothered by crowds.

"I never have been really famous, except temporarily . . . twice," Max says, "and I didn't like that at all. It took at least fifteen percent of my writing energy to get over that. It's like a bond, it binds you. I saw it happen to Sam Peckinpah and it drove him completely nuts. I didn't want it to happen to me.

"I'd spend about fifteen percent of my energy getting me far enough along (in fame) to where I could earn a living, and then I'd just cut it off. It's worked. Twice I let it go too far. It wasn't my fault. It was so fast there wasn't anything I could do about it. It just happened."

Poetry?

I went through a period of writing poems. Out in Hollywood. Pat and I had separated, off and on, for ten months or a year and I lived out there. 1970 or 1971.

I'd go around places, and I'd see somebody—waitresses, bus boys, bartenders, some old boy—and I'd write 'em a poem.

If I liked the way they talked, I'd have this big ol' yellow pad and I'd write 'em one or two pages of poems and just give it to 'em.

I used brown ink. I liked that sepia ink, you know. I know I wrote six hundred poems. There was books after books of poems. Just gave 'em away. Never thought about keeping 'em. It was just something to do.

I'd write funny poems, psychological poems. I'd write archaeological poems, any kind of goddam thing. Free verse, you know.

When you're not working, it's a good excuse to make out like you're working. A good excuse.

Three out of four poets use it as an excuse to get out of work. That's the damn truth. Some of them are truly dedicated and can't help themselves.

In Animal's Mind . . .

There were uncountable coyotes, bobcats, skunks, raccoons, badgers, foxes, eagles, owls, hawks, and rattlesnakes who had hunted that night and, if unsuccessful, were still doing so. There were rabbits, quail, doves, field mice, prairie dogs, ground and tree squirrels, sparrows, injured or sick calves and lambs, as well as barnyard chickens and turkeys that had been pursued, killed, and feasted on that night—or were still being hunted for another hour of this early light. There were vultures, ravens, magpies, and double-duty coyotes and innumerable insects and worms moving about to clean up the remains of the nocturnal kills. But to their own naked eyes it was infinite golden-grassed prairies and hills and the dark mesas with tops flat as aircraft carriers.
—from "The Heart of the Matter," by Max Evans,
printed in *American West: Twenty New Stories*
(New York: Forge Publishing, 2001)

There's nobody can get inside the heads of so many animals like Max.
—John Sinor, syndicated columnist,
San Diego Union

✂ **What comes of growing up** on the endless plains of West Texas, and then maturing in the short-grass country of northeastern New Mexico, later to dwell in the high-desert mountains of the Sangre de Cristo country, is that you develop an appreciation of what is around you.

Max did just that. But he went beyond that, also. There are many people who have spent their entire lives in rural areas, looking at what was around them, but without really seeing it. Max saw. Max sought it out and watched it. He saw the differences in the plants and the varying habits of the animals. It might have begun as a Depression-ridden youngster's desire to catch a rabbit to feed the family, but it didn't stay there. It moved on to catching coyotes for a living, hunting larger animals for a hobby

One of Max's greatest pals and admirers was the late John Sinor, who wrote a syndicated newspaper column for Copley News Service which appeared in more than 600 newspapers worldwide.

and for meat, and then to the appreciation of an artist . . . watching it happen with an eye toward how this could best be reproduced for others in art and literature.

Hunters as a group are probably the best-versed in animal ways, as it is necessary to thoroughly understand what an animal is likely to do, and is able to do, and where it is likely to be at any given time, in order to get that one shot. And in the grand tradition of other conservationists, such as Ernest Thompson Seton, George Bird Grinnell, and John James Audubon, Max, too, began as a hunter. He knows a hunter's mind, as well as the animal's.

> Now both men moved at the same gait they had successfully ventured for so many seasons. Each heard his own heart pounding, pounding, pounding the blood that pushed it to their ears and to their brains, enhancing any sound, any movement. Hunter's blood. Even more. Time reversed and then caught up and reversed again. The earth stopped for an unmeasured spell to give the sun and the moon a brief respite. Then the machine-gun beating of their hearts put everything back in motion.
> —from "The Heart of the Matter," by Max Evans,
> printed in *American West: Twenty New Stories*
> (New York: Forge Publishing, 2001)

From his very first published book, a collection of short stories called *Southwest Wind*, Max's ability to look inside the heads of animals was obvious.

> The old prairie dog, a lone figure in the enveloping warmth, sniffed the air for the last time. She beckoned to her young to come forth. Two small heads jerked into sight, beady-eyed, motionless. Suddenly they were on top, scampering about with quick, short jumps. It was their third time above.
> The Old One bellied down, watching them patiently as they chased through the curious world. It was her fifth litter. They had so much to learn in so short a time. They must beware of the enemies. the enemies who rode the

horses and drove cattle before them. A short time back they had thundered over their hole-home. The ground had quivered under the trampling of a thousand hoofs, and part of the den had fallen in. At first she had thought her young were injured, but out of the dust they had crawled, scared but unharmed.

She shifted her weight, grunted. Her eyes still followed them as she lay head to the ground. The young ones were picking up the track of some new bauble in a clump of grass.

She stretched her flattened form, sighing comfortably in the sun. The hay she had stored away the fall before had made her milk rich and nourishing. They were rolling with fat and bursting with energy.

Soon she would begin teaching them what all young prairie dogs must learn in order to survive. They would have to learn how to cut grass with their sharp teeth. There were small holes to be dug and dirt to be carried. The Old One would show them how to weave the blades of bear grass into mounds of dirt that walled their cavelike homes. The grass would act as a binder, keeping the mounds intact so that the summer cloudbursts would have no way of running into the holes. The young would also have to learn to store grass hay for the long winter ahead. All this was important and necessary. With two as bright and healthy as these, she would have no trouble.

—from "The Old One," in *Southwest Wind* (San Antonio: The Naylor Company, 1958)

In one of those deals of his, Max was given a large chunk of money, one alcohol-filtered evening, to write a story about the legendary white deer of San Diego. This was a solitary fallow deer doe who had—through some extraordinary circumstances in the 1960s—become the only deer resident of a one-mile-long stretch of grass and brush in the heart of a bustling city. Max dutifully delivered a short novel called The White Shadow that examines the love lives and drinking habits of several wealthy families who live in homes bordering on the deer's domain, and how each of these people is touched by the presence of this ghostly animal.

The white deer had spent the latter part of the night in a little grassy patio just under the living room window of the Bohannson family. She felt safe there near them. People were her friends. These she felt closer to than any.

Down below them was a little artificial waterfall so well made it would have thrilled the most dedicated conservationist. It was totally obscured from human view. She could drink here in private, and without fear. This is what had first drawn her nearer to the Bohannsons. Gradually their emanations of love and beauty gave her much comfort. Especially now, since she neared the end of her natural life span. However, the perfect and much varied diet of the berries and vegetation of Mission Hills left her still with the smooth, soft coat of a much younger animal. The fact that she was constantly climbing up and down the steep hills kept her heart strong and her limbs agile. The only signs of her true age were the fact that her eyelids drooped down over her eyes a little more when she was tired, and she slept for longer stretches.

She had been here in the hills for over thirteen years now. She had lived in luxury, but she had done it alone, separated from her own kind, totally.

She took her last swallow from the little stream of falling water. Some of it had dripped from her mouth as she walked out to forage in her gorgeous prison. A grey squirrel scampered up a tree and looked around the edge, chattering at her. She bent to take a bite of delicate grass and the trail of red ants moved right by her muzzle, going and coming on their designated trail searching for and packing back the sustenance of life to their den. They had a family of their kind. She did not. The ants had their own freeway millions of years older and more efficient than the one down below her.

Lower she could see the little metal bugs moving back and forth on the concrete freeway. To her, they had become no different than the tiny creatures she had just passed. A great metal bird speared through the sky, up and up. A moment later three more in close formation chopped along much lower, their strange wings whirling above them.

A blue jay flashed in front of her, searching for berries just as she. None of these were more important than the other to her. They were there every day, a part of the movement of her mile-long personal preserve. At first she had occasionally glanced at the waters of Mission Bay, and felt an ancient wondering at the little white-winged water bugs that moved so slowly there. Even now, after a lifetime here, when the weather was right she would stand a moment looking west past the hotels, and all the wood, steel and cement caverns of man, to the blue purple of the Laguna Mountains.

An unfathomable longing would touch her. Somehow she knew she should be there. She didn't think. It was unnecessary, for she was far past the need for that simple process. She was aware that her kind called to her from these mountains and far beyond. She was here, and would never be there. But there was an unclear image that occasionally, yet persistently, tried to solidify itself. It was something from the past, intangible in her mind—at the same time, definite. It remained behind her eyes, always. She would strain, yearning for it to focus out in front. It would not come. The feeling would vanish and her immediate needs and world would come back into focus.

She moved now, reaching up into a bush to take a bite that suited her fancy, or down to the grass when a special clump appealed to her. The white deer walked across the grounds of Mission Hills that had, and would continue to affect the entire world.

—from *The White Shadow* by Max Evans

"There's been a million places in this world where I've known exactly how (a) coyote felt," Max says. "No one had to tell me. And I survived, just like they did."

Every single time, for the entirety of my life that I've heard a coyote howl and another answer farther on, then another all the way out of sound I've felt an unexplainable sadness for all the blood shed and smeared—some justified, some certainly not—to inhabit this West.

At the sounds of the little prairie wolf's lament I feel all the lust for beauty, all the lost and found loves, all the terrible blizzards and dust storms howling in unison, all the countless books and paintings of the West leap from the covers and frames into living reality.

And that reality sways and moves to the chants of thousands of shamans. It's a song of the land, the sky, the water, and all creatures that move upon and in it. It is a song of the soul—the West. The West in all its high and low, mythical and real bigness is a singular place, a place of the heart, of the spirit. A special place of being. Home.

I do not know when there will be more fishermen than fish, more concrete poured than there is land to hold it. I do not know when the air will finally become unbreathable by the great forests and they will turn to brown and moldy wormwood. Maybe never. Maybe in 2050. Maybe tomorrow. Who can stop it? Who can change the current pincered movement west? I don't know. The grand canyons of our minds must somehow work the magic.

I was born here, but part of my ancestors were drawn to it long, long ago and they came just as people come now looking for the same beauty, bounty and freedom, I suppose. I make a prayer for the remaining wondrous wide spaces of the land.

The spirit of the West makes a music of eternal hope. While it's still here I shall love, appreciate and try to feel it all, just one more time.

—from "Song of the West" in *Hi Lo to Hollywood*

Sometimes You Win . . .

Nothing makes sense about these weird things in this
world. It's just fun, that's all. You just go, and something's
gonna happen.

—Max Evans

  Max Evans and his work have received a lot of awards over the
years, and some are listed here. But in 1990, when Max was
named the first recipient of *The Rounders* Award at a ceremony at the Governor's mansion in Santa Fe, new ground
was plowed. Not only did Max win for "living, promoting,
and articulating the Western way of life," but New Mexico
Secretary of Agriculture, Frank DuBois, and Governor
Garrey Carruthers named the new award after Max's famous
novel. *The Rounders* Award is given annually, and recipients
include people like Marc Simmons, Baxter Black, Michael
Martin Murphey, Pablito Velarde, and Elmer Kelton.

A "Max Evans Day" has been held in Albuquerque (1985),
in Hobbs (1968), and once in the entire state in 1999.

Here are some of Max's other awards:

the 1998 Golden Chile Award for Lifetime Achievement in
Cinema, given by the Taos Talking Pictures Festival;

the National Cowboy Symposium's Cowboy Culture Award (for lifetime achievement) in 1993 and The Founder Award in 1998;

the Governor's Lifetime Achievement Award for Excellence in the Arts (New Mexico's highest arts award) in 1993;

a 1975 City of Los Angeles Commendation Award for *My Pardner*;

Two Spur Awards, in 1983 and again in 1988, for his nonfiction story "Super Bull" and his novella, *The Orange County Cowboys*, respectively;

The 1984 National Cowboy Hall of Fame Wrangler Award for best magazine article, "Showdown at Hollywood Park"; the 1995 National Cowboy Hall of Fame Wrangler Award for *Bluefeather Fellini in the Sacred Realm*; and

When famed television producer David Dortort (Bonanza, Big Valley) visited New Mexico with an eye to filming there in 1969, he was welcomed by Jack Schaeffer (Shane, Monte Walsh), Max Evans, and Lou Gasparini, chairman of the New Mexico Film Commission. "He was greatly impressed by New Mexico for filming," Max says, "and loaned us his art director for setting up the Spanish town at Eaves (movie) Ranch. This led to movies like Cheyenne Social Club. *The film commission attracted enough movie makers to the state to improve the local economy by more than $1.5 billion. Photo by Dick Skrondahl.*

An unknown photographer caught this shot of Max at the world premiere of Hi Lo Country *at a theater in Woodland Hills, Cal. In 1998.*

Los Angeles Mayor Sam Yorty gives Max the City of Los Angeles Commendation Award in 1975 for My Pardner.

It isn't every day an award gets named for a book you wrote, and it's even rarer when you get to be the first recipient, but here's Max receiving the very first Rounders Award, given by the governor of New Mexico and the secretary of agriculture to someone whose work keeps the spirit of the west alive. From left, Pat Evans, Max, Governor Garrey Carruthers, and Secretary of Agriculture Frank DuBois in 1991. Lana Dickson photo.

the Western Writers of America 1990 Levi Strauss Saddleman Award for Lifetime Achievement (now known as "the Wister").

In addition, Max is an honorary lifetime member of the Board of Chancellors of the University of Texas; a board member of the National Cowboy Culture Institute at Texas Tech University, Lubbock, Texas; and the subject of a six-hour miniseries, The Man From Hi Lo Country, created for PBS by the University of South Dakota.

And then there was that little flyer down at the feed store in Albuquerque. Someone had brought it in to advertise a sale of ranch horses up in northeastern New Mexico, an annual event that is now called *"The Hi Lo Country* Horse Sale."

It doesn't get much better than that.

The Legend Continues . . .

I can't ever remember being bored in my life. I can go sit for five hours in a train station or an airport, but I'll never get bored. I can study people. I can get a magazine. I can go in the bar if I have the money. There's a thousand things you can do. There's all kinds of stories people can tell you. Many, many adventures to hear about.

—Max Evans

✂ **The first time I met Max** was at lunch at Baca's in Albuquerque. Fellow *Albuquerque Journal* columnist Jim Belshaw arranged it. He said, "What are you doing for lunch Friday? Well, we'll meet Max at noon. Don't plan to do anything the rest of the day."

I thought he was kidding. At nine o'clock that night, my wife called the restaurant to see if I was still alive. I was. Very much. And laughing.

Max's lunches are notorious and deserve space of their own. For one special lunch, where Belshaw and Albuquerque Journal writer and editor Tom Harmon were to be, I had some souvenir gimme caps made up with "I Survived Lunch With Max Evans" printed on them. We gave one to Max, too. It was the only time I can remember when Max was speechless.

"I never was a drunk. I just drank for fun," Max says. Between writing projects, Max became a chain smoker and heavy drinker, but he would quit both the minute he began the next project. And there was never any sign of withdrawal from either the alcohol or the nicotine.

"I wouldn't allow it," he says, simply.

In keeping with the spirit of life being ridiculous and fun, here are a few of the better stories.

We were living in Seattle when our son was born, and we named him after my best friend, Max. Well, I sent Max a telegram saying your namesake is here, and gave the birthday and the weight. In those days, Western Union used to call you and read the message over the phone and then put it in the mail to you.

That's what happened in this case. Problem was, Pat answered the phone, and the guy from Western Union read it wrong. He said, "Your mistake is here," instead of namesake. Ol' Max got an earful there until this got straightened out.

—Chuck Miller, one of Max's closest friends

Sometimes it just takes longer to get someone whipped than at other times, and Max once ran into this particular problem.

"Well, this was in Des Moines and this big sonofabitch was whipping my friends pretty good. I wasn't at all sure I could whip him when it was my turn," Max says.

"See, most of these big bastards you just need to wear them out a little until they lose their wind, and then whip their ass. Problem was, this ol' boy wasn't tiring at all. I thought he might be able to whip me, too, since he had both the size and the wind.

"So I told him, 'Look, you're pretty tough all right, so we need to make this worth my time. I'll bet you $10,000 you can't whip me this week.'

"He talked it over with his friends," Max says, "and then left. They were pretty sure he could kick my butt, but not $10,000 sure."

The Great Mountain Lion Hunt

"Max and I once bagged a mountain lion in Baca's," says Luther Wilson, Max's longtime drinking buddy, pal, editor and publisher. Baca's, for many years, was a fine Mexican restaurant on Central in Albuquerque's Nob Hill area. Its decor was dark wood, red carpet, and about as much lighting as Carlsbad Caverns at night. It was supervised by a dark wooden bar the size of city hall and a monstrous mural of an Aztec warrior holding a swooning Indian princess. Back in the cavernous bar were a number of tables and one in particular was Max's favorite.

Luther and Max once sat down with a calculator and began figuring, and came up with the following statistics; during the first five years of their friendship, beginning in 1980, the two of them met for drinks and talking three times a week and spent around $100,000 on booze. Of course, it was a very productive time, as the discussions eventually led to the first-time publishing of *Bluefeather Fellini*, *Bluefeather Fellini in the Sacred*

When Max's editor and publisher, Luther Wilson, decides to opt for a reduction in royalties, he has a unique way of negotiating with his authors. It is one method Max understands well, too. This was in 1986.

Realm, *This Chosen Place*, and *Super Bull and Other True Escapades* (a collection of non-fiction). It also led to the reprinting of *The Hi Lo Country*, *Xavier's Folly and Other Stories*, *My Pardner*, *The Mountain of Gold*, and *The One-Eyed Sky*.

And it also led to a very close lifelong friendship. When they met, Luther was editor at the University of New Mexico Press and had already been in publishing—especially university press publishing—for many years. When he later moved to Colorado to run the University Press of Colorado, he took Max's friendship . . . and his loyalty . . . along with him. Both *Bluefeather* novels were published there, as was This Chosen Place, the non-fiction history of Colorado's 4UR Ranch and its owner, Charles Leavell.

After some years in Colorado, Luther Wilson came back down to the University of New Mexico Press. Ironically, both he and Max are nearly teetotalers now.

But sometime during the early drinking years at Baca's, with Hoppy pouring drinks at the huge ornate bar and Sally and Catherine waiting on tables, the Great Mountain Lion Hunt was hatched.

It all began because a friend of Luther's wanted a mountain lion hide to make into a quiver for an authentic-looking Indian archery set to be placed in a museum.

"I thought I could just buy this guy a hide," Luther said. "So I called three taxidermists and discovered it was illegal to sell a lion hide. The only way you could get one is if you were a rancher and they were killing your cattle or sheep, or you could buy a license and go get one. So I decided to tell Max about it."

Max suggested they meet at Baca's and talk it over, so they met at the usual time, 11:30 A.M.

"After seven or eight drinks," Luther said, "Max says that what we'll do is go down to Jimmy Bason's ranch (near Hillsboro, New Mexico) and get us one. He said we'll get us some horses and some dogs and go chase the sonofabitch until we get him.

"We had a few more drinks and that began to sound like a better and better plan, so we called Jimmy Bason and told him the whole story."

*Miner Sonny Hale, right, and rancher Jimmy Bason,
sharing stories of the Black Range in Hillsboro, New Mexico—
one of Max's adventurous hangouts. Photo by Max Evans.*

Hunting a mountain lion is, under the best of circumstances, an ordeal. In the first place, cougars enjoy living in or near the steepest, rockiest mountain ranges they can find. This means not only making certain the horses stay shod at all times to protect their hooves (and shoeing a horse is a miserable, back-breaking job), but also realizing that there will be many times when the horses have to be left behind and the mountains scaled on foot. Most lions prowl an area about twenty miles in diameter, too, so they aren't always easy to find. The weather has to cooperate, as well. There should be a little moisture in the air to hold the scent for the hounds, and no strong winds to blow the scent away. This makes London, England, just about perfect for lion hunting, but New Mexico is famous for its dry air and heavy winds. If a hunter takes a mountain lion in New Mexico, he earns it.

Both Luther and Max were aware of these things, too.

"Next day or two after our call to Jimmy," said Luther, "we sobered up and realized what we'd done. So we went back to Baca's and revised our plans.

"Max said he was getting too old for this shit, as we might have to ride around those mountains down there for five or six days to get that lion. So we said why don't we just drive on down to Jimmy's place and sit around and drink with Jimmy and let those young cowpunchers go get that lion?

"So after a few more drinks we called Jimmy and said this is the plan now."

A couple of sobering days later, the two cougar catchers met once again at Baca's to put a little fine tuning on those puma plans.

"You know," said Max that day, "Jimmy's really awful busy. He's trying to keep the ranch together and he's in the real estate business. Maybe we ought to just go down and drink at the bar there and have Jimmy come down and join us and give us a report on how those cowboys are doing with that lion."

"This planning went on," said Luther, laughing, "from July to December. We'd keep changing our plans, and every time we did, we'd call Jimmy Bason and tell him what the new plan was.

"So one day we were having some drinks down at Baca's. It was about four in the afternoon, nobody else in the place but Hoppy and Catherine and Sally. This is December now. In walks Jimmy Bason. He throws a lion hide on the table, says, 'Here's your goddam lion,' and walks out.

"We bagged a lion and never left Baca's."

This lion-hide quiver, by the way, is now in the museum at the University of Illinois.

Risking Life and Limb . . .

Jim Belshaw has, for many years now, been a popular columnist for *The Albuquerque Journal*. One time during the Iran-Contra scandal, when the press was referring to Oliver North as a "cowboy," Jim called his favorite real cowboy, Max, to get his opinion of this description of North.

Ollie North, Max told him, was no cowboy at all. "Hell," Max said, "no real cowboy could ever *lose* ten million dollars."

But Jim's favorite Max story was about their first meeting. Here's Jim telling it:

"It was at lunch at Baca's Mexican Restaurant. Luther Wilson was publishing a collection of my columns, and in the course of conversation he mentioned he was having lunch with Max and would I like to go. Of course, I said yes.

"After the introductions and handshaking, Max went on at length about how sick he'd been and, in fact, he had been seriously ill in the previous weeks. When the waitress came by— naturally Max knew all of them by name—Max launched into a soliloquy that went something like this: 'Well, darlin', I've been awful sick, terrible sick, and that ol' doctor said 'No drinkin',' so that's the end of that. I can't drink, I can't touch the stuff, there'll be no drinkin' for Ol' Max. . . . So about all you can do is bring me a Coors Light.'

"This lunch began around 11:45 A.M. At around 3 P.M., two things dawned on me: (1) I'd never nursed two beers for so long in my life; and (2) I still had to get back to The Journal to write a column for the next day.

"Max, however, had not been nursing his Coors Lights. He'd been sucking them down like lemonades and by three o'clock was a very happy camper.

"I said, 'Fellas, I hate to bail out on you guys, but I have to get back to *The Journal* and write a column for tomorrow.'

"'Why, you sonofabitch!' Max said.

"'Now why are you calling me a name like that?' I said.

"Max dragged on a cigarette and said with great indignation, 'Hell, I've been sittin' here drinkin' beer and smokin' cigarettes all damn day. I'm riskin' my life! All you're riskin' is your job.'"

Max smoked non-stop until about twenty years ago. He suddenly decided to quit and did it immediately. Without any fanfare it was over, much to everyone's relief.

—Pat Evans

The Ballad of Robert Conley's Poem

"First time I met Max," says novelist and historian Robert J. Conley, "was at a Western Writers (of America) conference.

I was in this panel discussion, and at one point someone asked me a question and I said I didn't know the answer."

After the panel, Conley was leaving the room when Max jumped up and introduced himself, saying, "I just want to meet the sonofabitch who isn't afraid to tell people he doesn't know the answer to everything."

Later on, they headed for the bar to cement their newfound friendship. It worked out just fine.

Robert J. Conley, for many years an English professor, has now written more than thirty books, including a few slapstick Westerns. But he is best known for his historical novels on his own Cherokee people. He has been authorized to write the official history of the Cherokee Nation by the tribe.

Conley, his wife, Evelyn, and Max and Pat, are close friends.

Max lived everything he writes about, so he knows what he's talking about.

—Robert J. Conley,
novelist and official historian of the Cherokee Nation

About the only real time they get to spend together is at the annual conference of Western Writers of America, held in a different town each year.

The most memorable of these conferences for Conley took place in Springdale, Arkansas, a few years into his friendship with Max.

"For some reason or other, " says Conley, "this old poem of mine surfaced and was passed around. One of the participants there (we'll call him James, to protect the guilty) started praising this poem of mine. He kept on and on about it. It was real embarrassing."

Later that same evening, Max suggested they repair to the hotel's bar, and Conley agreed that it was a good idea. Then, as Conley puts it: "When Max starts for the bar, he doesn't look back."

As it happened, there was, in this same bar, James, Conley's new but adamant fan, along with a very large, strong man who didn't care for Conley's poem. Conley and Max sat at the bar and tried to ignore the boorish abuse heaped upon Conley's

A fellow writer who became a close friend, Robert J. Conley of Oklahoma, and his wife, Evelyn, are here with Max and Pat at the National Cowboy Hall of Fame in Oklahoma City in 1996. The occasion was Max winning the Wrangler Award for Bluefeather Fellini in the Sacred Realm.

poetry. But Max kept moving closer to the loudmouth, barstool by barstool. It didn't look good.

"All of a sudden," Conley says, "(James) jumped into the middle of this guy. He pounded his face. Blood was flying. The bartender was on the phone, and very shortly thereafter, the police came and broke it up."

Max and Conley still sat at the bar, supposedly minding their own business.

Later, as Conley and Max walked across the parking lot, Max said, "Robert, (James) doesn't know what a favor he did me. I couldn't of fought that old boy, but I was fixing to kill him."

"That's not the best part, though," says Conley. "This next is the highlight of my literary career. Max then said, 'Robert, (James) beat the shit out of that sonofabitch over your poetry. Isn't that beautiful?'"

Max tried to avoid a fight in a bar once, but was forced into it. He knocked the guy down, kicked him in the belly, and then said, "Now, goddammit, get up and live a better life!"

—James Hamilton,
author of *Cross of Iron*, essayist, screenwriter.

People who know Max Evans always make much ado about his often wild escapades and legendary whisky-induced temper. Max, however, also has a heart of gold and will gladly offer the shirt off his back to someone he likes.

Max and I had been friends for a while, and I had even attended a couple of his famous "lunches," (Got home at 6 P.M., drunk as an Irishman from trying to out-drink Max . . . something that one just doesn't do!)

As a writer, I've had several Western novels published by a company in London, England. These books were one-run, limited editions that paid little or nothing in the way of royalties. As a fledgling author, I felt obligated to do some book signings. I was happily signing a copy of one of my novels, *Blood Hunt*, for the small crowd of six curious folks that attended this gala event, when in walked Max Evans. It was no coincidence. He walked straight to where I was signing, picked up one of my books, grinned at me and said, "Can you sign this for me, Bob?"

Needless to say, I felt quite honored and warmed. Max, a well-known author who is probably one of the best writers of our times, had driven across town in horrendous traffic (and not feeling well at the time) just to get me to sign a book. No one had to tell me why he did it.

Book signings are, for insignificant authors such as me, depressing affairs . . . at best. People usually walk right on by and just stare at you . . . showing no interest at all in your creation. But I will always remember this particular book signing as a great moment when I learned something about the true meaning of friendship and about the depth of Max Evans' loyalties.

—Robert Dyer, Western writer and friend of Max's

Max Evans is the easiest person to start a party with, and the hardest to stop. He and Pat came down to Hillsboro to stay with us once, and we were down to the S Bar X for a few drinks.

We came home about two in the morning and everyone was ready to get some sleep except for Max. He couldn't talk anyone into staying up and partying with him, so the rest of us went to bed.

About two hours later, I saw a light in the kitchen. Max was sitting there with our three-year-old son, Brent, and he was letting him sip a drink and telling him stories.

And all these years later, they're still good friends.

—Jimmy Bason, rancher and friend

First Annual Max Evans Fist Fight, Tin Cup, and Skunk Races

It was back around '55, I think. I was in the Sagebrush Inn in Taos, just standing at the bar. I'd had a couple of drinks, but there was nothing going on, so I was about to get a room for the night.

All of a sudden the batwing doors slammed open and here came Ol' Max and three or four of his buddies. They had a gallon jug of wine with 'em, too.

I thought, here's some old boys who have set out to have some fun, and I think I'll just watch 'em.

As the festivities livened up, Max got one of the guys to leap up in the air, click his heels twice, and rip off his shirt. Well, By God, he did it. Problem was, he could only do it once because his shirt was ripped.

I got to laughing so hard, and Max said "Come over and join us, Pardner."

And I did. We had a helluva time.

So every time I was in Taos, I tried to look him up. He wasn't hard to find. We made all the bars. We were welcome in them in those days.

—Chuck Miller, one of Max's closest friends

One of Max's closest pals over the years was Chuck Miller. They had many fatalities together, as well as fun. And they went hunting together, too. Here's Chuck telling about one of those occasions.

"Max ever tell you about the skunks? No? Well, it all happened when we were going quail hunting and we were out in the middle of nowhere going down to Roswell. You know that stretch? Nothing but grass and wind and three antelope.

"Something caught our eye and we turned around and went back, and there were thirty-two skunks all lined up alongside the highway. All dead, of course, but someone had brought them out there and set them up so they looked like they were alive and looking at you.

"Max jumped out of the truck and ran up there, and I grabbed my camera. The last skunk in line was facing off to one side, so Max grabbed a big branch and looked like he was going to whack him with that stick, and I got his picture. Came out beautiful.

"Later on we were in the Four Seasons, talking to Rusty Rutledge, and Max pulls out this picture of him and the skunks and lays it on the bar. Never says a word. After a while, Rusty couldn't stand it any more and asks him what the hell it is. Ol' Max he just grins and says, 'Why, that's from the First Annual Max Evans Fist Fight, Tin Cup, and Skunk Races down in Corona. As you can see, we were only able to get thirty-two skunks this year, but next year we'll have more. Most of 'em behaved themselves, but I had to straighten that one ornery sonofabitch out.'

"Max had him believing it, too, and later on, he pulled the same thing on Sam Peckinpah."

Fernando's de Taos was another one of our watering holes. It was a good place for Max to promote, because a lot of Texans with money would drink there.

One time we were in there and met these ladies from Denver who looked like they had money, and Max was promoting them. We sat at this booth with them and we'd get up and dance from time to time.

Along comes this great big guy named Jim Hill, who was an acquaintance of mine. He just came over and sat down and kinda scrunched us all in there together. Now that wouldn't have bothered us, normally, but Max was working, you know. He was promoting these ol' gals.

Max didn't say anything to Jim, but when Jim asked one of them to dance, that was too much. Max reached across the table with a right cross and laid ol' Jim out cold on the floor.

Then we got up and danced some more. Jim came to about five or ten minutes later and just left.

—Chuck Miller, one of Max's closest friends

MAK EVANS TAKING FIRST PLACE AT FIRST ANNUAL SKUNK WHIPPING CONTEST —

"Now what are the chances," Max asks, "that we'd be driving through the middle of nowhere and find 32 skunks all lined up, and that Chuck would have his camera on the seat next to him and it would be full of film? And what are the chances that I'd find a yucca just the right size for whopping skunks?"

Max claims that if a skunk is whopped between the squirter and the base of the tail, and with just the appropriate amount of pressure, that said skunk won't pollute the atmosphere. This will be tested at the Second Annual Max Evans Fistfight, Tin Cup and Skunk Races in Corona, N.M., if they can find anyone brave enough to finally hold the first one. Kids, this is on a closed course by a professional skunk whopper. Don't try this at home. Photo by Chuck Miller.

One time, out in front of the Taos Inn, Max and some ol' boy got into it. Now Max was pretty fast on his feet, normally, but there were times when he'd had so much to drink he couldn't move very quickly. This was one of those times. When that was the case, he'd just lower his head and charge.

Well, he lowered his head and charged this guy, but the guy just stepped out of the way and Ol' Max crashed his head right through that guy's car window.

But when he could hit, he could really hit.

—Chuck Miller, one of Max's closest friends

Max and I went to jail once, in Taos. See, he was dancing on the table and I was doing something else. There were some damages. Funny thing was, I wasn't arrested until

One of Max's closest pals, and the subject of the story "Super Bull," former Air Force B-52 navigator Jimmy Bason rides on his F Cross Ranch outside Hillsboro, New Mexico in 1986. Photo by Pat Evans.

the next night. I was sitting in the drive-in movie with my wife and watching Victor Mature on the screen. Then the manager said, "Will James Hamilton please come to the snack bar?" but it looked at first like Victor Mature said it. I got up there and they said I had to go to the police station. At the police station, there was Ol' Max, grinning.

I believe Max slipped the judge something under the table, because right in the middle of reading all these charges, (the judge) got a brand new attitude and everything was fine.

—James Hamilton,
author of *Cross of Iron*, essayist, screenwriter.

One time we were down at the Four Seasons in Albuquerque having a few drinks with old Elmer Rigone, a kinda famous cow trader. While we were visiting, this obnoxious guy came to our table and was egging Elmer on. Elmer ignored him. Finally, Elmer said he had to go home and walked out. This guy followed him out to the parking lot.

Well, Max said this guy was going to beat Elmer up, so I ran out and I talked to the guy for a while. I looked around and Max wasn't there.

He was back inside. I asked him why he didn't come out to help. He said he had to take care of his hands, because he's a writer and can't get them injured.

—Jimmy Bason, rancher and friend

One night we were in the Taos Inn, drinking and having fun, and Max kept getting up to go to the restroom. Well, each time he went, it was tied up. After about three times, he walked over to the fireplace, told this lady "Let me show you how Indians put out a fire," and pissed in it.

She went over and tried to cover him with her skirt.
—Chuck Miller, one of Max's closest friends

We did cut a swath through northern New Mexico.
—James Hamilton,
author of *Cross of Iron*, essayist, screenwriter.

Sometimes cowboys go on to do other things. Here Max Evans wields a branding iron for his friend, Sam Hightower, on the horse, at the Mariposa Ranch outside of Taos around 1958. Beneath Max's knee is screenwriter Jim Hamilton, and Hightower went on from ranch work to make millions in Texas real estate.

And, of course, I've got a few stories of my own.

When the time came for Max to be involved in making a promotional videotape to convince the Western Writers of America to hold their next annual convention in Albuquerque, even those of us who had known him for a while had our eyes opened.

This was to happen at a riding stables just north of town, with the spectacular Sandia Crest behind us. One at a time, we each had our say. There were writers Norm Zollinger, Bob Dyer, yours truly, and Ol' Max.

We each tried to come up with some jewel that Albuquerque could offer to writers. Good food, friendly people, red chile, the Sandia tramway, our world-class zoo, things like that.

The videotaping crew kept shooting as, one by one, we pitched this beautiful city.

Max was saved for the finale, but none of us knew what to expect. We knew he couldn't stand public appearances, hated book signings, and wasn't a fan of crowds.

But this was also Max Evans, who could sell snowshoes in Panama, and we learned why.

When it was his turn, Max leaped up on a picnic table and began to laugh and dance like Walter Huston in *The Treasure of the Sierra Madre*.

"Come to Albuquerque!" he yelled with evangelistic fervor. "We've got it all! We've got great food! We have the prettiest girls in the world! We have great weather! We have Indians! We have mountains! Just look at those mountains! We have everything you need! Come now! Come right now! Don't even wait for the convention! Hey . . . this is THE PLACE!"

This went on for five minutes, with Max dancing a picnic table jig the entire time.

Finally it was over and Max handed the microphone back to the crew while the rest of us stood there with our mouths hanging open.

"Well," Max said with a quiet smile, "that oughta get 'em."

It did.

Another time, I was having lunch at Baca's with Ol' Max, and he began talking of his days in Taos.

"You ever been in the Taos Inn, Slim?" he asked.

"Yeah," I said. "Nice place."

"Sure is. I used to love going in there until I cut that guy's throat."

"What?"

"Yep. Had to. Big ol' weight lifter. Had me and Pat cornered there in the bar. Pulled a knife on me. So I had no choice. My aim was off when I broke a beer bottle and cut his throat. I was shooting for his ear, because he'd heard things wrong.

"Ever see what happens when you cut a guy's throat? The blood kinda shoots straight up, like a squirt gun, and gets all over the ceiling tiles. I think that's what pissed off the manager. He told me I couldn't come in there any more. Sure miss that place."

"But Max," I said, "what happened to the guy?"

"Him? Now that's a kinda funny thing. Ran into him on the street there in Taos after he got out of the hospital. Had his neck and head all bandaged up, you know. He walked up to me, shook my hand and thanked me. He said, because of me, he'd found Jesus.

With all the drinking, Max says, he's never had liver trouble.

"Which surprises me," he says. "Hell, I thought the sonofabitch had turned to quartz thirty years ago!"

A Song of Evening: Coyote and Raven

✂ **"So you see, Raven,"** says Coyote, "My brother Max makes a nice evening song or two, doesn't he?"

Raven nodded, and his beak curved into a small smile. "Makes me wonder. . . ."

Coyote squinched his eyes at the shiny philosopher of the wild. Then he unsquinched them about half way. He could see better. Sometimes a semi-squinch works just as well.

"Makes you wonder what, my friend?"

"Well," said Raven, watching New Mexico start to get dark and hearing the chirping of nighttime meals off in the black of the brush, "it makes me wonder if I should have some more . . . well . . . fun."

"Oh yeah! Now you're talking, bird! Now here's what you do, Raven old chum. Every time you find yourself in a puzzling situation, just ask yourself what you can do to turn this into a life lesson. Into a party. And then, if others laugh at you, bust the feathers off 'em. Or peck 'em, or whatever it is you do."

"Thanks," said Raven, quietly, watching the world slip into sleep. "I might just try that. You know, I envy you having Ol' Max for a brother. He sure is a fine role model for those of us who are slightly stuffy."

"Well," said Coyote, chuckling, "why not make him your brother, too?"

"I don't even know him."

"You know me, and I'm his brother, and if you and I decide to be brothers. . . ."

"I like the way you think, Brother Coyote," Raven said, beginning to walk with a slight swagger into the desert night. "Brothers. Not a bad thing to have."

"Say, Brother Raven, shall we head for the waterhole? I'll buy you a drink."

"Doesn't cost any money to drink at the waterhole, Brother Coyote."

"Yeah," Coyote says, falling in step beside his pal, his dazzling smile lighting the way down the hill. "Life just gets better all the time, don't it?"

He's a straightforward look-you-in-the-eye kind of guy. He's compassionate, and will listen to anyone who has a story to tell. A class act. Everyone in the world should be lucky enough to have a friend like Max Evans.

  —Billy Marchiondo, family attorney and friend

Ol' Max's Book Bin

(Max) is one of the most serious readers I know. He, today, reads more than most serious literary people do. His works seem to be Western tales, but they're deceptively literary. I'd put him into more of a league with Twain in *Huckleberry Finn*. His work is much broader than Western literature.

—James Hamilton,
author of *Cross of Iron*, essayist, screenwriter.

✀ **With each book**, Max seems to become a different writer. Each one appears to have been written by an entirely different, but extremely talented, writer. This is just how Max does things.

"I've been condemned for doing that," he says, "because they don't know what to do with you."

Here is a list of Max's books, with a little fun stuff thrown in.

1958: *Southwest Wind* (San Antonio: The Naylor Company)
This is Max's first book, a collection of twenty-two short stories, nearly all of ranch origin. He personally denigrates the stories in this collection ("of course, they aren't any good"), but there are a couple of notable exceptions. One is "The Wooden Cave," which gives a ranch house a personality of its

own. The other is "The Old One," a very sensitive story that probes the mind of a mother prairie dog.

1959: *Long John Dunn of Taos* (Los Angeles: Westernlore Press)
Long John Dunn was a legend long before Max met him. From outlaw days in Texas to running the wide-open gambling in Taos, Dunn's story was colorful, and at times a bit frightening. He also built a bridge across the Rio Grande and operated a taxi service from the train station in Lamy to Taos.

It was hard for Max to believe the old man wanted him to write his story, as more experienced and better-known writers had tried to get the job. This second book of Max's is the result.

1960: *The Rounders* (New York: Macmillan Company)
Fortunately or unfortunately, this first of his novels is probably the book Max will be most remembered for. It is covered extensively elsewhere in this book, but it struck a chord with ranch people, cowboys, and people who always wanted to be ranch people and cowboys, which means nearly everybody.

Written in Taos, it gave Max a career as a writer, a well-deserved reputation as a rounder himself, a not-deserved label of being a Western writer, an entrée to Hollywood, and a helluva lot of money.

> [O]ur laughter is at cracked ribs, broken teeth, the frustrations of bachelor life in a lonely line camp, wicked horses hoping to kill their riders, wild debauches when the lonely men come to town.
> —C. L. "Doc" Sonnichsen,
> the late historian of the West and former
> Professor at University of Texas, El Paso

He's been stuck with the cowboy writer (label) but he really isn't, you know. He's just written a little about cowboys. He's more of a literary guy.

When he wrote *The Rounders*, he told me this is a history book, really. This is how it really is.
—Pat Evans

1961: *The Hi Lo Country* (New York: Macmillan Company)
When Max's best pal from Des Moines, Wiley "Big Boy" Hittson, was shot to death, Max sat down in Taos and wrote this book. As with most of his work, it's mostly true.

This also became a motion picture that was actually filmed by the Hollywood folks at the location in northeast New Mexico where it happened.

This novel is what drove director Sam Peckinpah to want to meet Max, and is the main property the two of them traded back and forth for twenty-five years until Peckinpah's death.

> Max's home country is full of danger, pain, and violence, and that country, as Max sees it, is a metaphor for the world. . . .
>
> —C. L. "Doc" Sonnichsen

The annual birthday party for The Rounders *director, Burt Kennedy (left), brought many Hollywood characters together, including Max, character actor Jack Elam, and Kennedy's longtime companion, Nancy Pendleton.*

1963: Three short novels: *The Great Wedding, The One-Eyed Sky, My Pardner.* (Boston: Houghton Mifflin)

The Great Wedding

In this novella, an unabashed sequel to *The Rounders*, Dusty and Wrangler and Old Fooler have more adventures and still can't escape the clutches of rancher, Jim Ed Love. There are moments in this story, written in Taos, that presage the literary life Max would later lead.

The One-Eyed Sky

Real fans of Max Evans can't discuss his work without mentioning this novella, because it is one piece in his repertoire that no one else could write. Max tells the story of an old mother cow trying to protect her calf from a mother coyote who is trying to feed her pups and of an old cowboy trying to save the stock. It is a quiet, classic tale of survival and literature set way off in a lonely part of a ranch.

My Pardner

When Max was ten years old, he and an old, salty, one-eyed character named Boggs drove a herd of horses for three months across four states to an auction, and Max learned how to "promote" whatever was needed for dinner.

> He'll be remembered as authentic, as one of the great Western storytellers. He also knows how to doctor up a cow. There's no copies around that I've ever seen.
> —James Gammon, actor.

> Books just took over our lives. He'd write and then I had my work to do, too. I'd type, and then he'd find a lot of little things to slip in there, too
> I typed all those books on an old Underwood upright. I made three carbons because there weren't any copy machines in Taos. I look back on those days and wonder how I ever did it.
> Thank God for computers.
> —Pat Evans

"I call this the new Wild Bunch of the Hi Lo Country," Max says. During the filming of Hi Lo Country *in 1997, Max is with Willie Nelson, Billy Crudup and Woody Harrelson. Sidney Baldwin photo.*

1965: *The Mountain of Gold* (Dunwoody, GA: Norman S. Berg)

A true novella, *The Mountain of Gold* blends Max's love of the Spanish people of New Mexico, his passion for mining, and his devotion to beautiful language.

Chill Wills, the veteran character actor with the Foghorn Leghorn voice, was in love with this story of Max's. He tried for years to get this made into a motion picture. Wills had played the rapacious rich rancher, Jim Ed Love, in the film *The Rounders*. And played him very well. But when the book became a television series, Max says, it was short-lived, and most of that was thanks to the same Chill Wills.

"He took over the series (overshadowed the two stars)," Max says. "And that killed it."

"Now who would have thought he'd be interested in that story?" Max says. "But he really loved it."

The Mountain of Gold has yet to become a movie, but one incident during some Hollywood "negotiations" stands out in Max's mind.

Actor James Gammon, left, Max, and entrepreneur Miles Stowe in 1997. Photo by Barbara Bradley.

"We were in this bar on Sunset," Max says, "and Chill Wills was drunker'n a one-eyed goat. I went to the restroom, and when I came back, he had gone into the bar and was talking with a bunch of guys in there. When he saw me, he pointed to me and told them, 'You see this boy here?' Now I was in my late thirties at this time, of course. 'I cost him two million dollars. I took over his series and ruined it.'

"Wasn't that a wonderful thing," Max says, "to admit that?"

1969: *Shadow of Thunder* (Chicago: The Swallow Press)
One of the most passionate of Max's novellas (which he calls, instead, "little books"), this one came along many years before The Bridges of Madison County made rural love popular, but this story is more down-to-earth and powerful. If Max had written just this one novella in his life, he still would be given a place in the world of literature. The images are unforgettable.

1972: *Sam Peckinpah, Master of Violence; Being the Account of the Making of a Movie and Other Sundry Things* (Vermillion, SD: Dakota Press)

Max may be the only writer in the world who can turn in ninety-two pages (and many photographs) and have someone publish it. This tiny book, however, takes a reader into the bizarre world of making a film, in this case The Ballad of Cable Hogue. Nowhere here is found any Hollywood hype about brilliant directors, gorgeous scenery, and world-famous actors, although the book contains all three components. This is a peek behind the cameras at a crazy genius making a movie, written by his drinking and fighting buddy. Max's excuse for being in a soggy hotel in the Nevada desert for more than a month with the crew was that Sam gave him a part playing Slim Pickens' shotgun rider on the stagecoach. What followed was rain, short tempers, people quitting, rain, short tempers, people being fired, rain, cabin fever, budget problems, fighting, rain, brief interludes of genius, heavy drinking, and rain.

> Max is about the most memorable guy I've ever met. His stories are so bold and interesting. Even the way he opened a pack of cigarettes . . . just ripped the top off and all the cigarettes fell out.
>
> —James Gammon, actor

1973: *Xavier's Folly and Other Stories* (University of New Mexico Press)

When a small-town plumber dreams of bringing a top ballerina to his town to give the place some appreciation of the finer things, another Max Evans novella is in the works. This work is included with other short fiction, but can easily stand alone. It's just that Max once again told his story without using more words than he needed to, and the publisher didn't want to print a book that might slip through a crack in the easy chair.

1974: *Bobby Jack Smith You Dirty Coward!* (Los Angeles: Nash Publishing)

This slapstick comedy about a cowboy who studied Napoleon and plans to take a small cow town by force, is the closest Max has ever come to writing what most of us consider a Western. But of course it begins with the forcible rape of the local school marm, which few Westerns use as a device to hook the reader.

1977: *The White Shadow* (San Diego, CA: Joyce Press)
This is the bizarre story of a fallow deer doe who managed to live for years on about eighty acres of high-rent hillside surrounded by San Diego. In keeping with Max's penchant for writing no two books in the same style, this story would make a marvelous soap opera-ish miniseries on television, by necessity being more about the people who live around the deer's domain than this quiet doe herself.

The most bizarre part of the story is how it came to be written and how knowing the right people can make a book an instant bestseller. Here's Max:

"I was in San Diego this one time, and we were out with these newspapermen, recently become publishers, and we were all having fun. These two guys had published a book about San Diego State, and we were kinda celebrating.

"Well, there was this white deer everybody knew about there. Lived over by the San Diego mission. Here was all this land just full of homes and businesses and this deer lived right in the middle of it, alone.

"They decided they wanted me to write a book about the deer. So naturally I asked if there was any advance money to go with this. Well, I'll be damned if they didn't each write me a check for $4,000! After that, I'd have written the encyclopedia for them, you know. Hell, I didn't even have enough money to get out of town before that.

"So I went home, and then I had to write that book. I did, and they managed to lose a chapter or two and really messed it up, but I didn't know that.

"There was going to be a big book signing in a basement in downtown Albuquerque, and that publisher drove over with all these books in his car. He didn't have any distribution. None. Well, he had me for a day or two.

"I thought, well, we'll have one signing anyway. Now this guy was Italian descent, you know, Sicilian, so I went to my friend Johnny Marchiondo, who ran El Cid (night club), and asked him to show the guy around. And I also told Johnny about the book signing and said I wanted a crowd there.

"Well, here were Tony Hillerman and Rudolfo Anaya and Norm Zollinger and all these hot-shot writers, and I had a crowd that ran plumb out the door!

"These were the strangest people you ever saw in your life, and I guarantee there wasn't a damn one of them ever read a complete novel. I don't know how he did it, but (Marchiondo) rounded up all those people in three days.

"Well, that publisher kept running out to the car and getting more books. He kept shaking his head and saying I've never seen anything like this in my life.

"Here'd come some old guy and he'd buy ten books. He wasn't going to read them, wasn't going to open them. I never had so much fun in my life.

"There were a lot of writers and their books in the downtown basement that day. A big basement. They just stood around and wisely, silently stared at the line of strangers in front of my booth. I'd visited with quite a few of (these book buyers) over the years and Johnny Marchiondo knew them all . . . well. Delivery. That's what a true friend does. Johnny Marchiondo delivered.

"We sold every book (the publisher) had. And that was all there was. In those days, they had the bestseller list in Albuquerque, and it jumped right to the top."

1986: *Super Bull And Other True Escapades* (University of New Mexico Press)

This is a masterful collection of Max's non-fiction. The title story is one of the funniest true stories ever written about a rancher (his pal, Jimmy Bason), whose obsession with catching a wild bull on his place rivals Captain Ahab. The other eleven stories include the first story Max ever wrote for publication—"Killer on the Carrumpah," about a coyote hunt near Des Moines—which appeared in the Denver Post in 1950, and one of the finest non-fiction sports stories ever written, "Showdown at Hollywood Park."

To me, Max's greatest quality is his loyalty. He is intensely loyal to his friends.

When he wrote "Super Bull" about my adventures with that bull, it was a non-fiction story and it won the Spur Award for non-fiction. But Max actually fudged a bit on the dates, because this happened before our son, Brent, was born, and he wanted to mention him. So he did.

—Jimmy Bason, rancher and friend

1987: *The Orange County Cowboys* (*South Dakota Review*)

This novella, written in Albuquerque, wraps up the adventures of Dusty and Wrangler by bringing them into the modern day and showing how technology has changed a cowboy's life. Inspired by the true exploits of two of Max's California buddies, Ed Honeck and Al Johnson, it was first published in *South Dakota Review*, and later became the third jewel in the trilogy published as *Rounders 3* (1990) by Doubleday.

Max's introduction to this trilogy is worth the price of admission alone.

To celebrate both a birthday and the publication of "Super Bull," in 1984, Max threw what was called "The First and Last Cowboy Appreciation Awards." All those pictured were given awards. Seated, from left, is publisher Luther Wilson, film director Burt Kennedy, Dr. John "Frosty" Johnson III, syndicated columnist John Sinor, and bush pilot Joe Greene. Standing, from left, Max Evans, race horse owner Marvin Ake, columnist and historian Howard Bryan, race horse trainer Lyo Lee, and rancher Jimmy Bason.

Ed Honeck, one of the main characters in *Orange County Cowboys*, was also Max's lifelong friend.

"I've literally spent more time with him," says Max, "than anyone except Pat."

Max met Ed on Sunset Boulevard, where Ed was a promoter for a rock band. He later took a job in Orange County with a friend of his, Al Johnson, owner of Tapmatic Corporation. Ed Honeck was the advertising manager for the firm.

"It was kind of a trap for him," Max says, "but it was a beautiful trap. They let him travel all over the world."

During Max's prolonged stays in California while dueling with the film industry, Ed Honeck's Orange County home was Max's hideout.

"He had this wonderful place down there," Max says. "It was full of books and paintings and music. Ed was a student of World War II. When I'd get worn out, and after Sam (Peckinpah) died, and I didn't have a place to escape to, I'd go down there and stay with him.

"I did a lot of writing down there."

Ed was also an avid fan of Max's work, and Max says "He knew just about every line of every one of my books."

Unfortunately, Ed died of cancer while still in his fifties.

"I'm probably the one who killed the poor bastard," Max says, laughing. "But at least he had fun on the way out."

1993: *Bluefeather Fellini* (University Press of Colorado)

Covered extensively elsewhere in the book, *Bluefeather Fellini* is really the first half of Max's masterpiece, the other half being *Bluefeather Fellini In the Sacred Realm*. This novel, instead of being thinly-disguised fact, as with many of Max's books, is a work that parallels Max's life experiences.

> *Bluefeather Fellini* really was my life's work. Hell, it took a whole lifetime to learn all that crap.
>
> —Max Evans

1994: *Bluefeather Fellini In The Sacred Realm* (University Press of Colorado)

Here are the original, actual Orange County Cowboys themselves, Max's good pal Ed Honeck (the tall thin one) and Ed's boss, Al Johnson, president of Tapmatic Corporation.

In this second half of Max's forty-years-in-the-making masterpiece, reality blends into fantasy and then takes a left turn into the metaphysical. It is this book in particular that has left a lot of Max's staunchest fans (salt-of-the-earth country folks) scratching their heads. But it also flexed Max's writing muscles so far that many top writers had their mouths hanging open in awe when they finished scratching their heads.

Dale Walker, a top writer himself, summed it up for many in the pages of the Rocky Mountain News: "The most gloriously strange novel of the West that ever fell into my hands . . . (it) is a strange, utterly compelling masterpiece."

1995: *Spinning Sun, Grinning Moon: Novellas* (Santa Fe: Red Crane Books)

This is a gorgeous collection of Max's best novellas, including *Xavier's Folly*, *The One-Eyed Sky*, *The Mountain of Gold*, *My Pardner*, *Old Bum*, and *Shadow of Thunder*. Of particular note is the inclusion of Max's most reprinted novella, *Candles in the Bottom of the Pool*, a haunting tale that mixes a Santa Fe cocktail party with the metaphysical, mental illness, love, history, and murder.

1997: *This Chosen Place: Finding Shangri-La on the 4UR* (University Press of Colorado)

This non-fiction book chronicles both the beautiful 4UR Ranch near Creede, Colorado, and its owner, empire builder, Charles Leavell. It also spins tales of the many colorful people

Max with two Texas legends, artist and writer Tom Lea (standing), and land developer and construction magnate Charles Leavell (seated), at a meeting in the Museum of Fine Arts in El Paso. Max's book, This Chosen Place, *tells Leavell's story, and the story of his ranch, the 4UR in Colorado. Max calls Lea "The most underrated painter and writer in America." His book* The Brave Bulls *has become something of a classic.*

who have owned the land or gone through the place in more than a century of its existence.

1998: *Hi Lo to Hollywood: A Max Evans Reader* (Lubbock, Texas: Texas Tech University Press)

The most complete collection yet of Max's short works, Hi Lo to Hollywood contains many of Max's own favorites, including gems of short fiction like "Blizzard," "Don't Kill My Dog," "Big Shad's Bridge," and "Third Grade Reunion," and essays that tell more about the life of the writer. Of particular interest are "Riding the Outside Circle in Hollywood," "Dinner with Frank," and the lyrical love paean Max calls "Song of the West."

1999: *Faraway Blue* (New York: Forge Books)

In writing this novel of the Apache wars in New Mexico, Max slips into the minds of both the Apache chief, Nana, and of the central character in the cavalry, Sergeant Moses of the vaunted "Buffalo Soldiers," personalizing a slice of little-known Southwest history as well as anyone has ever done it.

2000: *Albuquerque: Spirit of the New West* (Albuquerque: Starlight Publishing)

Max was commissioned by the Albuquerque Chamber of Commerce to write this book and he concentrated on the flavor of Albuquerque, past and present. In his words, the exotic charm of New Mexico blends with the comfort of an old slipper. This is also (very much) a photo book, a coffee-table book designed to lure businesses into locating in New Mexico's largest city. The book has been sent all over the world.

> (Max) knew more about New Mexico than anyone I'd ever known. I'd never been around anyone like him.
> I didn't know he was a writer for a long time, but I knew right off we were going to be friends. He told things the way they were and people appreciated it.
> —Lucky Boyd,
> former manager of the Albuquerque Hilton Hotel,
> now owner of Lucky's Limousine Service

2002: *Madam Millie: Bordellos from Silver City to Ketchikan* (University of New Mexico Press)

Through two of his friends, Charlie Crowder and Jimmy Bason, Max met Mildred Clark Cusey, "Silver City Millie," when she was an old lady. Both men thought Max should write a book about the life of this famous Southwest prostitute and madam.

He did, although he had to wait many years before it could be published to give some people enough time to die.

Madam Millie became almost an overnight critical success. The book was runner-up in the Western Writers of America's best biography category. But the big award came when a large group of Southwest university professors, librarians, and historians from the Arizona Historical Society named the book "the best reading of the year."

In June 2003, Max was one of several famous New Mexico authors invited to a series of lectures at the University of New Mexico. Each author was given more than two hours to speak to students and the public in a large assembly hall, and each was broadcast statewide on live public radio. Max was asked to read from one of his books, and he chose *Madam Millie*.

It was a fascinating experience, because here was Ol' Max, touted as one of the top writers in the state, reading on live radio the story of the bishop and the whorehouse tom cat. In the story, the cat waits until the bishop is "in the saddle" and then pounces, holding tight to the clergyman's testicles.

"My balls! My balls!" screams the bishop, jumping up from the bed with the cat firmly attached.

The story went out over the radio just as Max had written it and just as he read it.

Bet the listeners don't forget Max any time soon.

2002: *Hot Biscuits: Eighteen Stories by Women and Men of the Ranching West* (University of New Mexico Press)

For more than twenty years, Max had wanted to assemble a literary volume composed of fiction written by actual ranchers and cowboys. After drafting the help of Wyoming rancher and writer, Candy Moulton, he found eighteen stories for this one-of-a-kind book. One story, "The Old Man," by Amarillo's

Jimbo Brewer, won the 2002 Spur Award for short fiction. Max's own contribution, "Once A Cowboy," is alone worth the price of the book.

2003: *Now and Forever: A Novel of Love and Betrayal Reincarnate* (University of New Mexico Press)
The metaphysical blends with love and mining in this novel that transcends the boundaries of death and generations.

> I gave up painting, which I loved more than life itself. I loved it. It made me feel fantastic. I only needed three more years (to be really successful) . . . Crumbo had been such a great mentor and showed me so many great tricks . . . three more years. But I gave it up to write.
>
> And I never, never, ever sold out my writing. It's almost impossible (not) to (sell out), really. I can see where stronger men and women than me would do it. But I, by God, made a vow that I would write what I damn well felt like writing . . . the best I could . . . for my entire life. I knew it would ruin me, over and over, but it didn't make a damn, I done 'er.
>
> *And it's too late to change now.*
>
> —Max Evans

Afterword

For me, the Code of the West is simple. You never let a friend down . . . ever. And you don't go after your enemies if they leave you alone.

You can live a long time on those things.

—Max Evans

❧ **For many years** I was a columnist for large newspapers, and my specialty was writing a thousand words at a time about some interesting person. The first thing I learned was that no one wants to read a résumé unless they plan to hire someone. The second thing I learned was that you can't encapsulate anyone's life in a thousand words—not if you intend to do it justice, anyway. So the job of a writer with limited space is to find one thing about a person and tell that story, giving the reader a taste, a flavor, a slight touch of who this person really is.

Even in writing a biography, where space is not such a limiting factor, this still applies. In writing about Max Evans—who has done everything twice—it applies even more.

It occurred to me one day that my job on this book resembled dealing with one of New Mexico's ranch roads, those hardened tracks that cut through grass, timber, arroyos, and mud holes until they reach a windmill, house, corral, campsite, or some other rural treasure.

After years of use, tiny faults in the dirt cause tires to erode them a little deeper. Tough spots tend to stand tough against the tread. Every time another tire touches them, the softnesses sink deeper until a road through New Mexico hardpan starts to look like moguls on a ski run. It becomes a washboard road.

The driver of a pickup on this kind of hard corduroy road has a choice to make; he can either creep along, letting the tires dip slowly in and out of the washboard recesses, or he can spur that baby up to about fifty-two miles per hour and let the tires skip their ways along the tops of the high spots.

If he chooses the former, it takes forever to get somewhere and the view never seems to change. Between the creeping speed and fifty-two miles per hour is a punishing, back-and-forth and up-and-down action that will tear a pickup to pieces.

But at fifty-two miles per hour, the scenery goes by in changing beauty, the shaking of the vehicle becomes a pleasant vibration, and there comes to the driver almost an exhilaration of knowing he's taking a chance on hitting an arroyo or an oil-pan-killing rock around the next bend.

That is when it is all right to shove the Resistol hat back a bit on the forehead, give a cow-frightening yell out the driver's window, and feel pretty darn good about things.

That's why this book doesn't get bogged down in minutiae about Max's life. There is a lot of minutiae about anyone's life, and Max is no exception. But his writing has always been a cowboy's answer to washboard roads: cut the clutter, hit the high spots, full speed ahead. His life has been lived the same way.

So, I trust, has this book.

Thanks for riding along. And, as Ol' Max always says, have fun.

—Slim Randles
Albuquerque, New Mexico

Acknowledgements

✂ A great many people helped with this book and gave hours of their lives to it, but one man in particular has to be singled out here. Dennis Dutton, also known as Karma Tenzing Wangchuk, of El Rito, New Mexico and the Greek Isles, worked for seven years with an eye toward writing a book someday himself, compiling notes and interviewing Max and his friends (including some who died before I began this book). He gave me eight boxes of notes and more than a hundred hours of taped interviews. Without this massive help, this book would not have been possible. Many thanks, amigo.

I've tried to list as many of the rest of the people who helped as I could, and I trust I didn't omit too many. My hat is off to them:

Jerry Airhart, Catherine Arntzen, Jimmy Bason, Jim Belshaw, Buddy Bevers, Lucky Boyd, Howard Bryan, Governor David Cargo, Charles Champlin, Robert J. Conley, Woody Max Crumbo, Lana Dickson, David Dortort, Robert Dyer, Herman Eubank, Bernard Evans, Charlotte Evans, Corky Evans, David Evans, Max Evans, Pat Evans, Charlie Ford, James Gammon, Bob Goldfarb, James Hamilton, Sam Hightower, Tony Hillerman, L. Q. Jones, Brian Keith, Grem Lee, Buddy Major, Billy Marchiondo, Destiny Marquez, Chuck Miller, Fern Lea Peter, Bridget Randles,

Ollie Reed, Wesley Roberts, Dr. Jeb Stuart Rosebrook, Jeb Rosebrook, Elia Sanchez, Dr. Roland Sanchez, Dave "Red Ryder" Saunders, John Sinor, C. L. "Doc" Sonnichsen, Greg Tobin, Dale Walker, Jon Welch, Luther Wilson, Morgan Woodward, and Kitty Jew and her patient staff at New Chinatown restaurant in Albuquerque.

"Adios, amigo," says Max. "Have fun!" Photo by Pat Evans.

CPSIA information can be obtained
at www.ICGtesting.com
Printed in the USA
LVHW040320180323
741726LV00001B/1

9 780826 365033